Company Culture

by Mike Ganino

for dummies®
A Wiley Brand

Company Culture For Dummies®

Published by: **John Wiley & Sons, Inc.**, 111 River Street, Hoboken, NJ 07030-5774, www.wiley.com

Copyright © 2018 by John Wiley & Sons, Inc., Hoboken, New Jersey

Media and software compilation copyright © 2018 by John Wiley & Sons, Inc. All rights reserved.

Published simultaneously in Canada

For general information on our other products and services, please contact our Customer Care Department within the U.S. at 877-762-2974, outside the U.S. at 317-572-3993, or fax 317-572-4002. For technical support, please visit https://hub.wiley.com/community/support/dummies.

Wiley publishes in a variety of print and electronic formats and by print-on-demand. Some material included with standard print versions of this book may not be included in e-books or in print-on-demand. If this book refers to media such as a CD or DVD that is not included in the version you purchased, you may download this material at http://booksupport.wiley.com. For more information about Wiley products, visit www.wiley.com.

Library of Congress Control Number: 2018938102

ISBN: 978-1-119-45784-8; ISBN 978-1-119-45785-5 (ebk); ISBN 978-1-119-45788-6 (ebk)

Manufactured in the United States of America

10 9 8 7 6 5 4 3 2 1

Contents at a Glance

Table of Contents

Introduction

Welcome! Nice to meet you. I'm Mike Ganino, and I care about company culture. It's the only real way to create a sustainable business. It's the key to crafting a legacy worth celebrating. And it's the answer to most of what ails modern business. Company culture has a positive impact on nearly every business metric from sales to innovation and from customer satisfaction to employee retention. Famed business guru, Peter Drucker, is often quoted saying "Culture eats strategy for breakfast." That's only the partial truth in my book. Culture eats whatever it wants and doesn't stop to politely ask for seconds. It permeates the way your team develops strategy. It defines the way you treat each other, your customers, and your community.

About This Book

This book demystifies company culture and clearly lays out a practical road map that managers and leaders at any level can start using to enjoy some of the benefits of a great company culture. Whether your title says CEO, founder, manager, director, supervisor, leader, or VP, you have the power to start improving your culture.

This is about changing the face of work to create a positive, productive work experience for everybody. It's not about a specific type of culture. I won't be dictating how your culture should be, but I do want to help you create one that's effective, intentional, and sustainable. There's some basic human psychology that can help you achieve those results, and I'll share that with you.

While I think most organizations could benefit from ideas in each chapter, you can jump around, read out of order, and focus on what's most important to you now. Check out the Table of Contents or the Index and pick a few areas that you think need some attention in your business. I've given you simple, practical ideas in every chapter. The ideas don't need to be executed chronologically but can be for maximum impact. No matter where you jump in, you can start making changes today.

Culture at work is a big topic. It's about relationships, norms, and expectations. No book alone could ever completely change your culture or cover everything there is to consider about culture. What I've done is given you inroads to start thinking about how key organizational areas impact culture so you can start to unravel and rebuild.

Here's the deal. It's my book, full of my ideas, and colored by my experiences. It brings together twentysomething years of professional experiences from restaurants, hotels, airlines, retail, tech companies, startups, Fortune 500s, and nonprofits. It's steeped in wisdom from the people I've learned from, read about, and studied. But it's also based on things I've done, ideas I've executed, and models I've put in place — whether in my own companies or those for which I've consulted. It's full of fresh ideas that I share in keynotes and training workshops — ideas that clients and audiences have put into practice to bring their teams together, change performance, and boost culture. There are going to be places where we disagree, where something else may work for you, and where you're unwilling to try something out. That's okay. Culture is complex. Relationships are complex. And there isn't a one-size-fits-all model. I've tried to give you room to test, analyze, and adapt these ideas for what's right for your team.

Foolish Assumptions

Since you picked up a book called *Company Culture For Dummies*, I feel pretty confident in making a few assumptions about you. You're most likely someone who works inside of a company. Maybe your role is management or you may be in the human resources department. Perhaps you're the owner or an executive. How am I doing so far?

Perhaps lately, you've been noticing that your employees aren't as engaged as you'd like and can see that's impacting sales, innovation, and deliverables. You've tried happy hours, ping pong tables, and nap pods (I know, right!?!?). None of it is working. Treating your employees like children who need to be constantly entertained isn't improving business results. You've finally decided there must be more to company culture than weekly massages and movie tickets.

Don't worry, you've come to the right place to find clarity for your culture questions!

Icons Used in This Book

Throughout this book, you find small pictures in the margins. These *icons* highlight paragraphs that contain certain types of information. Here's what each icon means:

REMEMBER

The Remember icon marks ideas and information that is worth keeping top of mind as you start to make plans for your culture. In sections with lots of information, I'll use this to give you simple reminders to help you start taking action.

TIP

Consider these your little fairy godparents — looking out for you, watching your path, and giving you simple ideas for making the most of your efforts.

WARNING

Culture curmudgeons are out there waiting to squash your success. This little symbol marks the times when one of them may try to attack, but don't worry, I give advice to help you power through and find success.

Beyond the Book

This book is packed with ideas, checklists, tools, and resources for you to use to improve your company culture, but it also includes some bonus information on the Internet to help you get started. If you're ready for a quick rundown and easy-to-use overview of the big ideas behind company culture, check out the *Company Culture For Dummies* Cheat Sheet at www.dummies.com by entering "Company Culture For Dummies Cheat Sheet" in the search box.

Where to Go from Here

Hopefully up! At least that's the premise of this book — that you can start applying practical ideas to improve your company culture. Depending on where you're starting, there are lots of good places to begin your company culture improvement journey. If you're trying to really understand everything that goes into company culture and how it all impacts the outcomes, then I'd suggest you start at the beginning. Grab a notebook and start taking notes on ideas you can use in your company.

Looking to better define your mission and values? Then head straight to Chapters 6 and 7.

If you grabbed this book because you really need to improve the quantity and quality of your job applicants, then you need to check out Chapters 8 and 9. But then keep going straight into Chapter 10 to learn more about creating a better onboarding experience.

Wanting to improve the way your managers lead or how you lead managers to successfully contribute to a more successful culture? Then dive right into Chapters 4 and 5.

The possibilities for improving company culture are endless. The investment you make of your time, energy, and intention in making positive shifts to your company culture will pay off in dividends. Let the journey begin!

1

Getting Started with Company Culture

IN THIS CHAPTER

» Determining exactly what company culture is

» Creating the conditions for a culture

» Clarifying what great cultures have in common

» Understanding what company culture is not

» Knowing when your culture might be at risk

Chapter **1**

Understanding Company Culture

C an you really change culture? Does it start from the top? Does it bubble up from the bottom? And, why does it even matter, anyway?

Company culture is one of the hottest topics in the business world today. Leaders, managers, journalists, and employees alike are all talking about it. And here's why: Good company culture sets apart organizations, and places them miles ahead in the fight for talent, the shaping of the external brand, and the bottom line results.

So, how do you get started in turning your company culture into one that is best in class? It all starts here. In this chapter, I give you the basics: defining culture and how it can affect your staff, your customers, and your profit margin. Then, I explore the different levers that contribute to culture and show how it can be used to impact your brand. Throughout the book, culture is discussed in extreme depth, but it all has to start with a basic understanding. Time to begin!

Defining Company Culture

Company culture can be defined as the repeated pattern of behavior of your team based on assumptions learned through experiences and passed down to other people. It's about so much more than perks, benefits, and the feeling around the office. Sure, those things can shape culture. They send signals to people about the relationships of the people in the organization and the tone of the working environment. But there's so much more that culture encompasses.

At the core, company culture is the way an organization expresses itself through values, behaviors, actions, and group norms. The culture of the organization is always evolving and constantly being tested to show what it's really all about. The cultural norms of the organization are the ones that determine what's encouraged, what's rejected, what's in, what's out, and set the environment in which work will be created. When aligned properly, the culture of the organization can create engagement, drive results, define expectations, and help to unleash discretionary effort and energy.

Company culture can be understood by looking at:

>> **Values and beliefs:** Looking beyond the fancy values statement in the employee handbook to see what's really valued in an organization speaks volumes about the culture. The real values of the organization are the ones that are adhered to whether spoken or unspoken. They show signs about what matters most, what's celebrated, and what winning looks like to the organization. All of this is built upon the beliefs of the leaders and the people in the organization. The underlying beliefs about work, each other, customers, and the company drive the values that shape the culture. Check out Chapters 4 and 7 for more on beliefs and values.

>> **Behaviors and communication:** These are the real-world manifestation of the values and beliefs of the organization. The way in which the team behaves, acts, and communicates creates the conditions in which the company operates. Companies can be fun and jovial, or conservative and measured in their actions and communication. Both work depending on the culture you are trying to create — and both create very different cultures. Regardless of what's documented and shared, the reality of the culture shines through in the way people perform and communicate. Head to Chapters 7 and 12 for more on these ideas.

>> **Systems and structures:** The way the organization is — well, organized — speaks volumes about the culture as well. The systems for getting things done, communicating, sharing, and collaborating speak to what matters within the company. The hiring process, the onboarding process, the training programs, and the way that goals are set all shape culture. Even the way

meetings are run, communication occurs, and decisions are made start to reveal the true nature of the organization. Check out Chapters 10, 11, 15, and 16 to gain more insight on establishing systems and structures in a variety of ways.

Approaching Culture as Your Organization's Operating System

In a computer system (or cellphone), the operating system is the layer that lives between the hardware and the software. It's the tissue between the apps on your cellphone and the actual physical cellphone itself. Without the operating system, the apps can't run. If the operating system is ineffective, out-of-date, or otherwise impaired, then the hardware and the apps get buggy and don't function properly.

The same thing is true of your culture. It's the operating system that runs your business — or rather, it's the operating system that mostly significantly impacts how the parts of your business run.

Realizing that culture isn't part of the game — it *is* the game

I have consulted on organizational culture with clients around the world, and the most common misconception at the outset of our engagement is that culture is a linear thing. My clients believe that culture started one day, and that we can together pick it up and make changes. It seems like culture is a component in the game of business right alongside operations, legal, product, marketing, and real estate. It's often relegated to being the job of the human resources department and measured with an annual survey (see Chapter 3 to learn more about how to better measure culture). But culture isn't just a piece of the puzzle to be picked up and added to the overall picture; culture *is* the puzzle. Your product, your communication, your leadership, your market share, and your brand are all outcomes of the culture you create. When you think about some of the most-loved brands in the world with products and experiences that people rave about, you can start to see that the culture within the organization is what helped produce those customer-pleasing results. These are the kinds of cultures that create conditions where employees play to each other's strengths to create even better offerings, the kinds of cultures that rally teams behind being first to market with a new technology, and the kinds of cultures known for positively approaching conflict and crisis to safely navigate change.

Culture is the game you are playing. The things you choose to put into the culture from mission to values, from the way you hire to the way you communicate, and from the way you set goals to the way you review performance are all the tools that help to define culture and create the game your employees play each and every day.

Molding, not creating, company culture

Organizational leaders often say that they're "ready to start creating culture." Wrong again. Culture is created as soon as two people start interacting. As soon as the social contracts are formed around how we treat each other, the messages being sent and received start shaping the culture. The great news is you don't have to worry about creating culture. It already exists.

Getting intentional about the type of culture you'd like involves a lot more than just writing down your mission and values. In fact, you can look across industries and find examples of companies that have expertly crafted mission and values statements but still suffer from a toxic, sluggish culture. The goal is not to start creating culture but to mold it. Culture is a string of relationships all striving to get to a shared goal. You can foster, mold, nudge, and cultivate culture by focusing on those relationships. The bad news is that you can't just go away for a weekend and create a new culture overnight, and your team may have some bad habits that have developed over time which are creating less-than-desirable conditions in your organization. The good news is that you can start exactly where you are today to improve your company culture. You can get clear about what's working and do more of that while also sorting out what's not working and begin to develop new habits and systems around those areas.

The sooner you begin to acknowledge your current state, clarifying your desired state, and map out a path to take you from here to there — the sooner you can start celebrating the culture wins on your team.

Controlling the conditions

You know how certain places make you feel a certain way? Maybe it's a fancy dinner party with new friends, or perhaps a backyard barbecue with family. Or maybe it's a visit to a new city or a return to a favorite one. Each of those experiences is full of messages and communication. You have a relationship with the whole experience — the people in it, the way you feel about the physical space, the energy around you. All of that creates culture.

Culture is the conditions created in your business. The most you can do is control certain inputs for your team — you can choose tools and office perks, hire certain people, celebrate certain values, and codify desired behaviors. All of this ultimately creates the conditions that foster a specific type of culture.

If you think about one of these examples, it becomes clearer. The dinner party with new friends includes certain kinds of music, bringing out the fine china, maybe putting some "icebreaker" questions on the table, curating the guest list just so, and serving specific kinds of food. All these details create a specific condition, which ultimately impacts the way people treat each other and the space. The culture starts to get created. Over time, with repetition and attention, the culture gets stronger. With each passing fancy dinner, the culture is further defined. When someone new is introduced later, he or she can quickly pick up on what's normal, what's celebrated, and how the group functions. All of this is culture. And you didn't even need a handbook to "create" it.

While you can't create culture, you can do a lot to design the experiences so that culture is molded and shaped in a specific direction. Each of the chapters in this book gives you some ideas about using different areas of your business to nudge culture in a specific direction. If you realize that your company is struggling without clarity around where you're headed, then start with Chapter 6. To get focused on hiring better for your culture, dive into Chapter 9. If you want to improve the diversity and inclusivity on your team, start with Chapter 16.

Treating culture as the perfect result

Culture isn't magic. It's not something that even needs to be demystified. It's the perfect result of all the inputs. It's not a sign about what you are or who you are but rather a reflection of what you do. It's the most powerful force in your business. You (and your team and customers and marketplace) can see it, feel it, and experience it.

Whatever culture you have is the perfect result of the things you put into it. If your culture is energetic and lively, it's probably because of the people you choose to bring on the team, the way you organize them, the relationships you curate, and the style in which your leaders communicate. If your culture is focused and ambitious, communicating with intention and sincerity, that's because of specific inputs.

It's not that hard to figure out what's going on with a business — just watch the culture. It will tell you exactly where the pain point lives. It'll lead you — like the little breadcrumb from the *Hansel and Gretel* fable — right to the source. Your culture is the perfect result of all the messages and relationships in your business. This means that whatever is happening in your culture is linked back to some specific action taking place in your business. If your culture has become one where people are disengaged, then you can fix that by being more engaging (see Chapters 4 and 5 for being a more engaging leader; see Chapters 6 and 7 for creating a more engaging mission, vision, and values statement; and see Chapters 12, 13, and 14 for ideas on improving how people work together).

When you look at your culture, feel confident that whatever you see is a result of something in the business, which means that you ultimately have control of the variables that can improve your culture as well.

The Best Company Cultures: Different but Essentially the Same

Companies like Southwest Airlines, Google, In-N-Out Burger, Zappos, Disney, Wegmans, USAA, and Netflix are all celebrated for their company cultures. Other organizations like Apple and Amazon have been in the press for their cultures — both good and bad. Yet working inside one of these organizations feels drastically different. You wouldn't show up to work one day at In-N-Out Burger and confuse it with Google. It's not just the products or physical space that's different. The relationships, decision-making styles, messages, communication, and overall vibe are different. Clearly they have different cultures. In fact, you can even visit different locations of the same brand — like Trader Joe's — and get a slightly different culture.

Each organization (and even the specific teams, departments, and locations within it) can thrive with a drastically different culture. It's okay that Apple's environment can be intense and forward-thinking, focused on rapid innovation and next-level quality. It's also okay that the culture at Wegmans centers on putting employees first and high levels of care. Both can be great. Both can be levers for getting great work done.

REMEMBER

Regardless of whether your aspirational culture is results-driven, service-focused, innovative, or happy, the best cultures all have some of the same DNA. There are components that help make them work no matter how different the end result may feel. Consider this list of things all great teams share as well.

Establishing clear goals

Whether organizing the world's information, being the low-fare airline leader, or delivering happiness, great cultures have a clear target and a shared rally cry. The people in the organization have an absolute understanding of what they're all trying to create together. The tribal part of our social being seems to do best when we're all aligned toward a common cause (look to Chapter 19 for more on setting goals). The more explicit, clear, and honest this target is in your business, the better your culture.

Setting simple rules

The best cultures have simple rules around how people should treat each other, make decisions, and get things done. This doesn't mean there are rule books lying around everywhere, but that through establishing systems for hiring, training, collaborating, serving clients and customers, and working together, the organization has started to be specific and clear about what matters most so that everyone can get on board and contribute. The rules, meaning guidelines and systems, are simple and clear, not only because they are stated but also because you can see them consistently applied across the organization. Leaders role-model the desired behaviors and actions, managers hire for them, people are celebrated for them. If we go back to the concept of the tribe of social beings, you understand what gets you kicked out of the group and what makes you a contributing part of the group.

Delivering useful feedback

Cultures begin to decay when people aren't able to give each other feedback. You can see it in work cultures, home cultures, school cultures, and even national cultures. When people aren't able to give each other feedback, everything seems to stagnate. Great cultures are feedback-rich. They are full of people giving information about each other's performance that leads to improvement, professional growth, and organizational success. The people in feedback-rich organizations look forward to hearing from each other because they know the information is going to be helpful, useful, and thoughtful. In these organizations, two-way communication about performance seems to flow in all directions. The rising tide of performance improvement raises all ships. For more on the value of feedback, see Chapter 14.

Steering Clear of the Perks Pitfalls

Just as important as understanding what culture is, it's vital to get clear on what company culture is not. The media and career websites of lots of popular companies would have you believe that culture is about perks, benefits, and quirky offices. It's not.

The start-up industry has given us lots of great innovations, from mobile apps that can help us find love to medical technology that can boost our quality of life. You may think that a company's perks, be it a ping-pong table or a Wednesday afternoon beer cart, are the reasons for its success and something to emulate.

Those things are nice, but they don't do much to improve the relationships of people at work. And they have very little to do with the things that all great cultures share.

The reality is that these perks that make work feel more like a Caribbean resort and less like a business are just icing on the culture cake (and, in some cases, hiding really toxic cultures underneath). They may help you attract a few new people to the team, but they won't improve your results in the long run. In organizations with strong cultures, the "extracurricular" activities and perks like these can be helpful in creating cross-departmental collaboration and relationships where, in addition to ping-pong tournaments, the team is talking about the next innovation or pitch. In organizations with a weak culture, these activities tend to be the way people escape work for a little bit because they aren't that engaged with it or each other. The good news is that there are many straightforward ways to improve culture to bring about a positive working environment, long-term employees, and measurable successes. The next 21 chapters show you just how.

Recognizing the Symptoms of an At-risk Culture

Throughout this chapter, we've looked at ways to understand what culture is all about. You might have even recognized some of the ways your company is already celebrating and instilling a culture that drives results while creating a great work experience for your team. But maybe you are still worried that your culture is at risk and you want some help framing the signs of a toxic culture.

WARNING

Here are a few telltale signs of toxic cultures:

>> **Lots of gossip:** People talking negatively about each other behind their backs is a sign that culture is in trouble. Check out Part 4 for some tips on improving team communications and collaboration.

>> **Leaders' bad habits:** If your management team misses meetings, loses their tempers, misses deadlines, or communicates poorly (or not at all), you may have a culture problem. Check out Part 2 for ideas on enhancing leadership and management skills.

» **Nothing to aim for:** Do most people in your organization lack any definable goals? If asked, do they struggle to tell you what they're working on, by when, and how success will be measured? All signs point to culture doom! Check out Chapters 6 and 7 to get started with developing your organizational mission, vision, and values. Then head over to Chapter 19 to help create clarity for your team.

» **Lack of candor:** Are people avoiding being honest? Does everything just sound manipulatively insincere? Culture suffers in organizations where people aren't able to be honest, direct, and open in a kind and thoughtful way. If you think your company could use some help in developing a strong feedback culture, then head straight to Chapter 14.

» **Watch your back:** Do people throw each other under the boss? Is the team often in blaming mode because there's a lack of safety and discomfort in failure? Is everyone competitive with each other? Cultures with this kind of vibe need a major overhaul to bring things back to a positive and effective way of working. If improving your team's communication and collaboration is your focus, read Chapters 12 and 13.

Chapter **2**

Reaping the Benefits of a Healthy Culture

I t's a rare manager, leader, or executive who would toss aside organizational culture these days. Too much has been written in the headlines about the impact of culture positively and negatively on a brand, from culture-centric stars like Zappos, Publix, Southwest Airlines, and Google to companies that have had their culture linked to headline-making negative news like Uber, Volkswagen, Wells Fargo, and Forever 21. We intrinsically know that culture matters, but it's easy to think a great culture is just a nice-to-have instead of a core requirement for success. It's easy to dismiss good culture as some kind of magic created by snacks, craft coffee bars, and inter-office slides. But it's possible to link culture to nearly every important benchmark a company measures: sales, profit, market position, employee retention, safety, and customer loyalty. Company culture is the core system that determines whether your team delivers results — or just skims by.

It's trite but true — things are moving faster than ever. You can create infinite amounts of product efficiently and affordably across all industries. Still, innovation and service are the only ways to really produce a sustainable organization. Both of those qualities require talent, and talented people demand a culture in which to thrive. Culture is ultimately about getting the conditions right so that the people in the organization are able to produce the results that drive the business. Nearly every business result is improved with a strong culture, and smart business leaders are using culture to gain market share. Every single investment in company culture can be an indirect (and critical) investment into the customer experience.

Improving Key Business Metrics with Culture

Business is easily defined by metrics, goals, and profits. Every company has specific financial targets it needs to hit in order to continue to operate. Those targets are tied to sales, manufacturing costs, raw ingredient costs, labor spending, marketing expenditures, and other costs. Executives and managers fiercely guard their target numbers and work to achieve desired results. But what makes those things happen? What is the incubator where sales, profits, and spending are nurtured? Culture creates the condition for the best key business metrics.

Some of the interesting industries to look at for extra proof that company culture has a strong impact on standard business metrics are retailers, chain restaurants, and hotels. When all other factors are equal (prime real estate location, identical products, consistent company policies, and national branding), why do some locations or divisions within a bigger brand do better?

Two more segments ripe with fodder for culture champions are the airline and grocery markets. Think about it — airlines mostly fly the same style of planes in different trade dress, use the same air space as each other, often share the same airports and gates, and have flights that are sold on the same marketplace-style websites. Yet some airlines have high brand affinity, better top-line revenue, stronger bottom-line revenue, and enduring legacies. And grocery stores are usually located on the same type of large parcels of land, sell roughly the same products for similar prices, and often have the same standard layout. So why do some grocery stores drastically beat the others when it comes to brand affinity, customer loyalty, and employee engagement? Culture is one of the answers.

Sure, sometimes consumers make decisions based on cost or convenience. But they also make decisions based on the customer experience. The customer experience is impacted greatly by the culture of the company. Does the culture foster an environment where creating customer happiness is the norm? Is the culture one that celebrates together? Are the employees themselves happy and enjoying their work?

TIP

Think about a few specific metrics in your organization that you'd like to see improve — sales, turnover, inbound recruiting (see Chapter 8), or employee review scores (see Chapter 3). As you begin any specific cultural work, benchmark the before and after to see how your business metric changes as the culture improves. Remember that some metrics will take longer to move, so plan accordingly (see Chapter 3).

Increasing sales

The biggest way to show the power of culture is to link it to one of the most common metrics of organizational success: sales. The almighty dollar takes the cake when it comes to key performance indicators. We like to watch sales grow. We like to see sales trend lines increasing and growing. We like to see double-digit percentages on this side of the profits-and-loss statement. Linking culture to sales is the best way to track the long-term benefits of a strong company culture. Here are some of the basic ways you can increase sales and how culture is a driver for each:

» **Frequency:** Your customers, clients, patients, or members are the lifeblood of your organization. You need them to return — and the more frequently they return, the better for your organization. An investment in company culture is really an investment in the customer experience. When your customers (or whatever you call the people who really pay the bills) feel the vibe of a positive and engaging company culture, they come back more frequently. If the experience your customer has with the team is positive and helpful, they return. When the culture in your organization allows your employees to focus on the customer — instead of office politics — this positively impacts your customer. In the tech-heavy, digital world we live in, we're looking for experiences that help us connect. A positive company culture does that in spades.

» **Purchase size:** Another way that company culture can help boost sales is by driving the average purchase size for each customer. Customers today have a lot of choice and a lot of information before they come to see you. The employees in your company have a huge opportunity to engage them from there — to make recommendations for other value-added services or products, to encourage more visits, to inspire a cross-sell. We spend money in places we like. Employees that work in a great culture are much more likely to create great customer experiences because they feel good about themselves and the company they work for. They are eager to spread this feeling to customers. In that way, culture is deeply linked to more customer spending and thus to the top-line revenue of your business. Companies that don't invest in company culture are left to compete on price alone in the court of customer opinion. Customer experience creates the atmosphere that encourages customer spending.

» **Recommendations and referrals: Every dollar spent in an organization needs to produce some type of return-on-investment (or ROI).** In an ROI-obsessed business landscape, the greatest marketing efforts are those that are being curated, positioned, and spread directly from your customers. Word-of-mouth marketing has been around since before the actual profession of marketing began. We've relied on our trusted friends and family members to help us get the best products and experiences. People who have great experiences with your team are more likely to speak about you. Your team is more likely to create a positive, engaging experience if you get the conditions right. Culture wins again.

Sales are a lagging indicator of culture. Your efforts to improve culture will bring great change to your sales if you give them time to take effect. Assume that sales will follow culture by 2 to 4 quarters and compound from there.

Boosting profits

The history books are full of products, companies, campaigns, and rock stars that were really good at making money and just as good at spending it. Once you've leveraged your culture to start making rain, you need to make sure that you keep some of it as well. If culture is all about getting the conditions right for the results you want, then it is prudent to be thoughtful about the stories your company tells about profits. The people you work with — whether you call them employees, associates, crew, staff, or partners — make decisions every single day about the allocation of their time, your resources, and the company profit. As such, how you deal with profits becomes a large part of your company culture, and the metrics around profits can be tracked to the health of that culture. Here are some ways this impacts your company's bottom-line:

>> **Spending:** Making choices about what to do with company resources is a common part of most employees' weeks. While not everyone has an expense budget, most people are making choices every day about how much product to use, how many programs to run, or which resources to invest in. Without a strong culture, your employees are less likely to be diligent in their efforts to protect your brand and think twice about spending, waste, and profits.

>> **Saving:** Employees also have a huge impact on the amount of money a company could be saving. Think about the logistics manager who finds ways to reduce shipping cost, or the front-line employee who takes an extra moment to be more careful with fragile equipment. All of this adds up to big savings that would be more difficult to find in an organization with a less positive employee culture.

>> **Discretionary effort:** This is probably the key benefit to improving profits through company culture. The more of themselves that your employees are willing to share, expend, and give to their work and your clients, the stronger your profit line will be. Think about how often an employee makes a choice to make one more customer call for the day or to go out of his or her way to tackle a small task now so it doesn't spiral out of control later. These are all ways that employees can leverage the same finite resource (themselves) while delivering more value to the company.

Retaining great talent

Ever heard someone say, "If they want the job, they'll shut up and do the work"? How about, "I pay them so that should be enough"? The best response to that old-school style thinking is, "How's that working for ya?" The truth is that — barring a recession-style period where good jobs are hard to come by — the employees are in power. They have choices about where to work, how much energy to expend there (see the last bullet in the preceding section), and how long to stick around. Except for changing industries, positions, or locations, the biggest reason people leave one job to take a similar job elsewhere is company culture. You may be thinking: What about money, what about specific projects, and what about ping-pong tables? You could argue that those are factors of company culture, but really they're just bandage solutions to a larger problem, especially when culture is one of the leading drivers of employee retention.

How does culture keep employees from jumping ship? Check out the following factors:

>> **Professional growth:** Organizations with a positive company culture are full of development opportunities — and not just the cutthroat, get-ahead-at-all-costs type of places. People make decisions to stay in a job because it allows them to keep learning and leveling up their experience. Professional growth is a core component of company culture and a critical factor for employees looking to create sustained engagement with their team.

>> **The "me-too" factor:** Let's face it — a lot of the companies making news about their great company cultures (Google, Wegmans, USAA) have no trouble finding and keeping great people. The expression "what's in it for me" is at play here. You want to work somewhere that casts a positive light on you. It's why people leave organizations after bad press gets leaked about the business. By having a positive company culture, employees correctly believe that it says something about them to have worked at that organization. Don't believe it? Check out Amazon or the public speaking circuit — they're both full of former Disney, Zappos, Apple, and Google people. The "me-too" factor means that your investment in company culture pays off by retaining your best people.

>> **Finding our tribe:** Much has been written about the power of connection and "finding our people." Whether at work, in life, or in community, we want to be around people who share our ideals, our passions, and our energy. We thrive on connection in this way. Given that most people spend a significant amount of time at work giving their energy to serving, creating, or sustaining some organizational product, service, or idea, it makes sense that work is one of the places that creates much of our self-identity. If your company culture is toxic or disengaging, then consider the types of people that are sticking around. Look at your voluntary turnover and consider whether you may be losing some of your best people due to company culture alignment. Now consider what would happen if you created a thriving, engaged company culture. What type of people would be drawn to stick around because they found their "tribe"?

>> **The power of purpose:** Employees today are looking for purpose. It's easy if you are a social-mission-drive organization doing something to save the world, but what about the rest of us? Tapping into purpose isn't always about doing something global, but it is about doing something specific. In organizations with strong cultures, employees feel like they are part of something bigger than themselves. They feel connected to the mission of the company, to the leaders, and to the quest to create something great for the client.

Enhancing recruitment

The work world has shifted, and the organization no longer has the upper hand. Before the Internet and social media came along, if an employee had a bad experience at work or a group of employees were upset about a company's culture, they had limited options: quit, complain to HR, stage a coup. But the tables have turned, and in today's 24-hour news cycle with social media, blogging, and review sites, the employees hold much of the power.

Employees can create an account on an employer review site, such as Glassdoor, and score the CEO, their coworkers, the benefits, the culture, and whether they'd recommend the company as a place to work. They can share stories, images, and feelings on Facebook, Instagram, LinkedIn, or Snapchat. All these platforms can be used in a positive way to boost your recruiting efforts (and your retention efforts). Companies like Netflix, HubSpot, Google, Wegmans, Southwest Airlines, and Edward Jones have been able to leverage the power of their culture to drive recruiting with all the content out there about their work environment.

While you can't force your employees to write something positive about your company, the better your culture is the more likely they are to do so anyway. You can even create campaigns to encourage people to add their voice to review platforms (see Chapter 8).

In addition, if employees are happy with the culture in your company, they are more likely to recommend friends, share your open positions, and actively recruit from their networks to help bring great people to your organization. This not only improves the quality of your candidates but can help reduce cost for your recruiting team.

Delivering exceptional service

Before you skip over this section because you aren't in one of the "service industries," you may want to consider that no matter what you do (nonprofit, healthcare, agency, legal, government), you're exchanging some product/service/offering for money (whether direct or through funding). You are a service-based business — and the better your service offering is for customers, clients, and constituents, the more opportunity you'll have. Nothing drives great service like a positive company culture. Companies like Ritz-Carlton, Zingerman's, USAA, and Centro have become known more for their service and experience than their products in some way. And before you shut the book because you work deep in some non-customer-facing role (like finance or HR or IT), also consider that you have internal customers who have external customers. How you serve them will show up in a real way when they're on the front lines. Customer service is always a reflection of what's happening on the inside of a company. When the culture on the inside is positive, the service on the outside will follow suit.

Improving productivity

Customer service isn't the only thing that gets better with an intentional company culture. The effort and energy your employees put into their tasks, roles, and responsibilities are choices they make. Sure, you can create a checklist or dashboard to keep them on track, but the execution toward those outcomes is still up to them. The best way to ensure you're getting the best from them? You guessed it — company culture. Investing in the employee experience is one of the most effective ways to increase the productivity and output of the team. Whether you're a salon in Salem, a bar in Boise, an agency in Akron, or a hospital in Honolulu, you'll see an increase in productivity, output, and outcomes when you double down on boosting the company culture.

Nurturing brand affinity

Company culture is the new marketing. Take online shoe retailer Zappos, for example. Their "Delivering Happiness" approach extends beyond the customer service team into the entire organization by ensuring core values like "create fun and a little weirdness" and "build a positive team and family spirit" are deeply embedded throughout their teams. They even have entire training programs where outsiders can come experience the famed Zappos culture. Like other culture brands, we know more about their company culture and employee experience than we do about their actual products, supply chain, or business models. Major business publications report on the best places to work. We give awards for the greatest places to work. We buy books to learn the secret sauce of our favorite brands at work. Sometimes, we even go to workshops to see the way they work.

Consumers feel good about spending money with companies that treat their employees well — and add to the fire when they hear about a company with a toxic culture. People believe it says something about them when they make a choice of how to spend their money, how to invest their time, and where to seek their experiences. When people have a positive feeling about a company, it encourages them to be a customer — again and again. It's almost like a little of that positive mojo rubs off on them as a consumer — they get bragging rights for being a customer. Think about all the products you buy and companies you support, at least in part, because the brand affinity gives you a little boost in status. Leveraging your company culture to tell stories about your brand is impactful and effective (see Chapter 8). Once your employees are living your culture, it isn't that hard to bring the public along too.

TIP

If you have a PR agency working on spreading positive buzz about your product, offerings, or the newest app you've launched, start talking to them immediately about telling the stories behind your work environment. If you have a company blog, start using that to tell stories about how you work. For more ideas on this, see Chapter 8.

Tallying the Cost of Bad Culture

Lost productivity, lackluster product launches, mediocre customer service, and dwindling profits are the all-too-common remains of a lousy company culture. When the conditions inside of a company don't inspire employees, create community, and focus energy, the organization is left rudderless. Sometimes this results in a lot of wasted time, energy, and resources — and, in other instances, it leads to something far more insidious and damaging.

A toxic company culture doesn't always end up making front-page news, and levels of toxicity can vary drastically. There are certainly big ways that culture can buckle your business, but there are also lots of slow ways that a toxic, unintentional company culture can chip away at your company.

WHEN THINGS GO WRONG

It's easy to see what happens when a culture takes toxic to the extreme. In 2017, shared-car giant Uber suffered a major backlash after its culture was put on public opinion trial for claims of misogyny, sexual harassment, and discrimination. In 2015, German car manufacturer Volkswagen was embroiled in scandal when it was uncovered that some of its cars had higher emissions than tested due to a manipulative programming decision to evade emission standards. One could easily make the case that the company culture at VW was a "win at all costs" type of place. And one of the classics when it comes to culture gone wrong is the story of the Enron scandal that bankrupted one of the world's largest financial institutions and sent shock waves about the power of company culture.

The big spend

Look at your financial records. How much of the expense side of your ledger is related to employee costs? When you add up salaries, taxes, benefits, office space, parking, perks, and recruiting expenses, where do you land? Thirty percent? Forty? Sixty? For many businesses, the biggest expenditure is the amount spent on employees. For companies with a toxic culture, these costs eat up even more of the cash. From money spent on recruiting to money (and time) spent dealing with personnel issues, from the costs of turnover to legal fees — it ain't easy to make a profit in an organization with a bad culture.

TIP

Do the math for yourself. Add up all the following: salary and bonus costs, employment taxes, benefits, office space and parking, perks, employee tools (HRIS systems, payroll provider, email), recruiting expenses (advertising, application-tracking software), and a rough estimate of the number of hours spent on recruiting, training, and HR-related things. Multiply that total by the average rate of the people doing that work, and then divide that number by the number of employees at your company. Now you have a rough estimate of the true cost of an employee. The cost of replacing any employee is about 20 percent of the employee's annual salary on the low end. If you factor in lost productivity of the staff member, lost productivity from the distraction of the rest of the team (plus their time replacing the person), not to mention losing intellectual capital, plus one of your insiders going to a competitor, you start to see some scary numbers due to a toxic culture.

Losing great talent

The cost of an employee is only part of the equation when it comes to the impact of company culture on human capital. When a culture goes wrong, the best people are the first ones to leave. They no longer feel like part of something great and start to look for greener pastures. Because they are the best and brightest, those pastures are all too happy to offer them positions full of promise. Think about some of your best people — they probably bring to the table great service, great product, great ideas, and tons of discretionary effort. When those people leave, you lose all of that. It's also likely that the vacuum created by the sudden loss of high-performing contributors to your team will drastically change your culture for the worse. Depending on how long a star player has been working with you, you'll also see some wisdom, knowledge, and experience leave your company that can't easily be replaced right away with your next hire. Losing great people hurts — and one of the biggest reasons they abandon ship is the company culture.

Declining innovation and creativity

Look, it takes real staying power to survive in these quickly changing, turbulent times. It seems every industry is ripe for disruption, and no sooner than a second category is created does a third option appear in the marketplace. In the healthcare industry, we've seen the rise of the patient experience. The restaurant and hotel industries are facing radical shifts in the way consumers interact and use their services. The gig economy is rapidly shifting the dynamic between agency and freelancer. Regardless of the industry you are in, it's a safe bet that you, too, are facing an unprecedented call for change as well.

Company cultures that thrive on feedback, can move nimbly and quickly, and can galvanize around a new frontier will keep winning. The toxic and unhealthy cultures struggle to produce new ideas. The energy in the room is not one of "take that mountain" but rather "is it 5 o'clock, yet?" The lack of psychological safety and team dynamic leads people to hold their best ideas, to not speak up and share, and to stay focused on self due to the risk of being treated poorly by coworkers and management. When the culture is toxic, instead of business focus, everyone is worried about simply making it to the next weekend and dreaming of their next vacation. Innovation and creative solutions to the pressing issues of today are the last things employees care to bring to the table. When speaking up in a meeting gets you a look of death from your coworker or is met with apathy from your manager, you quickly decide to expend that energy looking for your next career move instead of the next breakthrough business idea.

Increasing safety risks

Sometimes the cost of culture goes beyond simply the profit and loss statement. From food service workers who feel the pressure to cut corners to achieve targets to airport employees who rush through safety checks to keep things moving — we've seen examples of the life-threatening risks involved when a culture values something other than safety. Companies with the best safety ratings, lowest employee injuries, and highest consumer trust scores are those that have a strong culture. The places that make the 5 o'clock news due to a major safety scare are often those with cultures that lack trust, transparency, feedback, and collaboration. From fast-food chains to regional airline carriers, from manufacturers to medical centers, from construction sites to NASA — a culture that promotes unsafe risk-taking for short-term gains is one ripe for a critical emergency.

When your company deals with potentially dangerous situations, getting company culture right becomes mission-critical. Take a look at your organization: Where might safety concerns occur within your daily operations? Then consider how strongly in place the systems and habits that support safety protocols and feedback loops are. Are the people on the front lines able to quickly, effectively, and without fear of punishment speak up and get something resolved? Or does your company have a command and control environment that may stop someone from raising a hand?

TIP

Values like "safety first" or "integrity" buried deep in the employee handbook or hung on the break room wall mean nothing if those behaviors are not a cornerstone of the cultural norms of your business (see Chapter 7). What if instead of being a passing message, your value around "safety first" was deeply imbedded into the way your organization worked? You can leverage your culture to make sure your values show up in the way your company hires, communicates, promotes, and runs. This is the power of culture. Look at your stated values and see if you can map them to very specific behaviors your employees perform every day.

Damaging customer service

You've probably had a bad experience at a place you normally love, right? It happens sometimes simply because you're a human dealing with other humans. But what happens when that customer service snafu becomes a customer service norm? What about when an account manager consistently under delivers? Or a customer support team consistently responds apathetically?

When company culture no longer inspires great service, word gets out. Think about cellphone providers, health insurance companies, government agencies, and cable service operators. All these are categorically known for giving low-empathy, apathetic, by-the-book customer service. This isn't because of a "bad hire" but because of institutionalized culture issues at the very core of the organization. Such negativity seems to particularly haunt commoditized-type offerings but can also wreak havoc on craft retailers or boutique agencies.

Company culture is the energy that the customer experience runs on. It takes a vibrant and intentional environment to reproduce the type of high-engagement experiences customers are demanding in today's marketplace. The reality is that most owners, managers, and executives aren't the ones on the front lines delivering service, and all the policies in the world won't do anything to shape customer service if the culture doesn't support and promote that type of energy.

IN THIS CHAPTER

» Crafting, launching, and leading a
   culture survey

» Using a culture dashboard and other
   tools to track culture

» Identifying signs of a toxic culture

Chapter **3**

Benchmarking Company Culture

When you ask most leaders if culture matters, they almost always say "yes." In fact, most say culture is one of the most important factors in why their business is better than the competition. If you ask how they measure it, though, most say something along the lines of "it's a feeling" or "you can tell when you walk around the office." While such statements may be true, gauging cultural health by feel provides measurements that are vague at best and totally off the mark at worst. To stay on track, you must get clear on exactly where things stand currently and throughout the course of your organization's cultural development. And to accomplish that, you need tools and methods that reliably measure success. With clear and repeatable ways to measure culture success, you can track progress, which will provide the motivation needed to stick to your culture initiatives.

How healthy is the culture? A healthy culture helps achieve desired results in other areas of the business. It consistently produces great work from a team while making them feel engaged and satisfied. This chapter helps you answer that question by showing you how to measure your culture's health at any point in time. You find out how to create a culture survey to benchmark your baseline and how to use the survey and other tools to measure progress. You discover how to tie culture wins to key performance indicators, even bottom-line results, which is especially important if you're allocating precious organizational resources to culture activities. And you find out how to use your feedback results to improve your organization's culture.

Creating and Conducting Your Culture Survey

People are funny; they can say or do one thing while thinking the exact opposite, a talent that comes in handy when your mom asks what you think of her new hair color. However, this quirky human characteristic can work against you when you're trying to gauge your company culture health. Employees may not complain, fearing the repercussions. They may appear happy and satisfied while they're looking for the nearest exit. It's not always easy to figure out the best way to collect feedback.

REMEMBER

Healthy cultures all share a few of the same attributes while maintaining their own unique "personality": They have a clearly defined vision, they have shared goals, they have easy-to-understand rules, and they share feedback across all levels and all teams.

One way to gather information and insight from your staff is to conduct a simple culture survey. Such a survey uses a numeric scoring system and also contains a few open-ended questions to encourage employees to create more detail about what they truly think and feel about the company. In this section, I explain how to create and distribute a survey that elicits honest feedback, and how to interpret the results in order to make the changes that improve your culture. If trust is low in your organization, it may be best to make surveys anonymous to help people feel safe sharing feedback. You can use this information to establish your starting point, or *baseline metric,* so that you can track progress over time.

Using a survey doesn't guarantee that all employees will speak up about the things they love and things they wish were better about your company. It isn't the most effective way to solve a very specific challenge someone is having, but it is a good way to look at the overall feeling of the team. You can more easily notice themes and patterns when done in aggregate. It's also easier in many cases for your employees to share their honest thoughts when it's not a face-to-face conversation. Having a few minutes in private to give some ideas is less anxiety-ridden than walking into the HR or manager's office.

TIP

I encourage you to use an electronic survey to facilitate gathering and processing results. This will make it easier for most employees to complete while also making it easy to organize data, track over time, and save results for future review. Many affordable tools are available for creating surveys and gathering feedback in an easy-to-read format. Check out Google Forms or SurveyMonkey for cheap (even free!) options to get started. An added bonus is that these tools report the feedback in graphs, charts, and spreadsheets for easy analysis.

Drafting your survey questions

You'll be glad to hear that drafting a culture survey is a snap. All your culture survey needs are the following four questions:

>> How likely are you to recommend ACME Co. as a place to work?

>> What is the primary reason you gave that score?

>> What would make you rate it higher?

>> Why didn't you score it lower?

The first question elicits a response that enables you to gauge overall employee sentiment, but it doesn't tell you why employees feel the way they do, so the second, third, and fourth questions are critical. By asking these open-ended questions and reviewing the responses, you can start to understand the biggest drivers of your culture. Without them, you're likely to just feel frustrated and confused. The first question is called the *employee Net Promoter Score* (eNPS).

TIP

Survey participants like to know why certain questions were selected, so for each survey question, add an explanation below it about why you're asking the question and how the responses will help provide clarity about culture. See Figure 3-1 for a sample survey. Check out the next section, "Scoring the survey," to identify how to tally the results.

How likely are you to recommend ACME Co. as a place to work?	1 2 3 4 5 6 7 8 9 10
This question will help give us a baseline metric to measure our employee Net Promoter Score.	
What is the primary reason you gave that score?	
This question helps us understand the main motivations behind your score and can provide useful information for us to use to help improve your work experience.	
What would make you rate it higher?	
The responses to this question will give us insight into areas that may need attention, improvement, or upgrades.	
Why didn't you score it lower?	
The responses to this question will help us understand what's working well, what to keep, and where we might invest more resources.	

FIGURE 3-1: Sample survey questions with explanations.

REMEMBER

Less is definitely more when it comes to survey length. By asking only a few targeted questions, you decrease respondent fatigue and increase the amount of actionable data you get back. In a world where social media videos disappear in 24 hours and political statements are made in fewer than 140 characters, keeping your survey clear, concise, and to the point is crucial. If you're looking for specific topical feedback, see the later section on employee opinion surveys.

Scoring the survey

Once you've completed the survey, it's important to use the data to get a score. All the comments and suggestions are helpful on a qualitative basis — but you also want to have a quantitative measurement so that you can see how future improvements impact the overall eNPS and thusly company culture. This is a number that all managers in your company should be obsessed with understanding, measuring, and monitoring with their teams as it can really help provide a view into how things are going.

For the first question, use a drop-down menu or radio buttons to enable respondents to rank the organization from 0 to 10, with 0 being "not a chance" and 10 being "absolutely." You'll use these numeric responses to calculate your eNPS. Responses to the first question produce a highly reportable, easily trackable, and consistent metric that you can add to your company dashboard.

Scores from 0 to 6 are considered detractors, 7 and 8 are labeled neutral, and 9 and 10 are considered promoters. To get the eNPS score, the total number of respondents is used to determine the percentage of detractors and the percentage of promoters. Then the detractors are subtracted from the promoters to arrive at the eNPS.

For example, say 100 people responded to your survey as follows:

» 50 people were promoters — they marked a 9 or 10

» 25 people were neutrals — they marked a 7 or 8

» 25 people were detractors — they marked a 0 – 6

First, you would discard the score for the neutrals. You should use their comments and suggestions still from the follow-up questions, but their actual score won't be used to calculate eNPS.

Then you will determine the percentage of promoters and percentage of detractors. In the example, it would be 50 percent of the 100 survey respondents as promoters and 25 percent as detractors. Then you subtract the detractors from the promoters (50 - 25) to get your eNPS of 25. Now don't think of this as a normal grading in school. In this model there is a range from -100 to 100.

For the second, third, and fourth questions, you give respondents an open-form text box to add their thoughts. Avoid the temptation to use drop-downs or multiple choice options here because such options start to skew the information. By asking these questions, you're giving employees a chance to voice their thoughts, and that in itself can give your culture a boost. You will use the 0 to 10 rating as your core metric and then the responses to the open-ended questions will be used as the qualitative data to improve the scores in the future and to understand what is working best for employees who scored your company a 9 or 10.

Getting executive and senior-level buy-in

Before you go forward with sending out your survey, you want to establish executive and senior-level buy-in. If feasible, you should schedule a session with all people who have direct reports so that they understand what's happening and can answer questions from their employees. You can start this with the executive level, move down to directors, and then to front-line managers, or you can just have one global manager session. Whichever way you approach it, you want to make sure that your leadership understands and is committed to the importance of finding ways to measure and track culture. Take a look at Figure 3-2 for a plan to get upper-level buy-in.

Agenda for Management Buy-in of Culture Survey
The CEO, founder, or other most senior leader would partner with someone leading the survey — typically an HR person to meet with the rest of leadership team (executive team, directors, or other core leadership group) to discuss the organizational commitment to improving culture and how the survey is the starting point in creating a measured approach to the work. They will review the overall plan for the process and the desired benefits to the organization, the employees, and each leader. The goal is to gain buy-in and set realistic expectations for time commitment. The team should be able to answer questions about timing, reasoning, and process for their employees.
The CEO, founder, or other most senior leader communicates his/her personal commitment to organizational culture including why it matters for the success of the business, how it impacts long-term success, and why it matters in the short term as well.
The HR person then outlines the culture survey logistics, ensuring that each leader can speak to the process if asked by their team. Providing an outline of the survey questions, the key dates, and the follow-up is a helpful way to get it all in place and provide clarity.
The HR leader defines each person's role including where people should go for support, more information, or technical challenges on submitting feedback.
By the end, everyone should understand the benefits of the culture survey including: * Why eNPS is a simple and impactful way to measure overall culture * Using the feedback to improve organizational opportunities and to further highlight/ enhance organizational wins * Establishing a strong and consistent system of feedback-sharing from the team * How the information will be used by the leadership team to make improvements * When the scores and comments will be shared with the employees

FIGURE 3-2: Sample agenda for leadership communications about survey initiatives.

Launching your culture survey

Ready, set — not quite yet! With your survey designed and ready to distribute and leadership on board, it's time to get your communication plan in check. Many well-intended culture surveys never get much momentum because employees don't understand why it's important and what's going to be done with the information. Before hitting "send" on the surveys, share the following information:

>> What the culture survey is

>> Why your company is doing it now

>> What you're trying to achieve

>> How feedback will be collected and reported

>> Who will be participating

>> What the timeline looks like for completion

>> What to expect next

Draft a message to all employees to communicate the launch of your survey. Figure 3-3 shows a sample email message you can use to get started (with some tweaks).

TIP

In general, you'll get a great response rate with a single launch email and two follow-up email reminders. Space your email messages about three to four days apart to give you a two-week survey window. If your company uses messaging tools like Slack, Yammer, Workplace by Facebook, or Google Hangouts, you can use those to send nudges as well.

Following up on the culture survey

With your survey designed and ready to ship out to your employees, it's important that you think about how you'll share the data with them. The more transparency the better so that employees don't feel like their comments, ideas, and thoughts are landing on deaf ears. If you don't share the details, they will likely think the results were worse than reality anyway. Plan your post-survey follow-up ahead of time to ensure you have a documented path to sharing and executing on the feedback.

FREQUENCY MATTERS

Most organizations see positive results doing the eNPS surveys on a quarterly cycle. Once you get the survey designed and get into your rhythm, repeating it every 13 weeks (once a quarter) is easy. Some organizations have been successful conducting the survey only twice a year; that's the minimum recommendation. Avoid the temptation to conduct your culture survey only once a year because you should have feedback throughout the year to guide you in developing your culture initiatives. Annual surveys also make it harder to earn employee trust and engagement in the process.

Hi {whatever cool name you call your employees},

We will be kicking off our first ever/quarterly {Culture Survey Name} on {launch date} and will need your help to make this a positive and successful experience.

What's the point of the {Culture Survey Name}?

As you know, we work hard to make {Company Name} a great place to work. Just like we measure other important business results, we know that measuring culture is equally important. This survey will generate feedback from employees, which will be collected, aggregated, and analyzed to help us understand what's working and where we can focus our attention for improvements.

We'll then share these results with everyone at {Company Name}. Every team can then play a part in helping us develop our improvement plan. Our goal is to do this {monthly, quarterly or twice a year}.

So, what's next?

We've designed the survey using {Survey Tool Name}, and {people in survey — generally "all employees"} will be receiving a link on {day or date}. Please take a few minutes to answer the questions thoughtfully and leave comments to help add more detail to your score.

A broad overview of this process:

• {date–date} Survey goes out to employees, and feedback collected

• {date} Results will be analyzed and presented to the {leadership team}

• {date} Results will be shared broadly at {all hands/off-site/team meetings}

• {date} Action planning from the results will start. We will share outcomes with you, along with our rationale and next steps, via {communication method — email, video conference, all-hands meeting}

Thank you again for playing a part in our efforts to continually improve the experience of working at {Company Name}.

If you have any questions, please get in touch with {whoever is leading the survey process at your company}.

FIGURE 3-3:
Sample communication to employees.

WARNING

One of the critical mistakes most companies make is that they complete culture surveys and don't take the time to commit to a follow-up plan. Imagine this from the employee's perspective. You've asked my thoughts. I've shared them with you. Then they just go into a big black hole. If you're going to take the time to ask for feedback, then schedule the time to share your findings. Transparency is key, and the more quickly and openly you can share the information, the better.

TRANSPARENCY MATTERS

One of the mistakes companies make is asking for feedback and then not sharing the results with the people involved. Your employees want to learn from the process too, and sharing the results is an important step in creating engagement and community. Obviously, you should remove any personal information or information that would easily call someone out unnecessarily. Typically, I advise to remove any names mentioned in the comments except for the executive team when sharing the results with the employees. By sharing this information, it says to the employees that they are being heard and creates a sense of shared accountability. This matters even if the results are not glowing. The reality is that your employees already know what's going wrong in the culture and with the company — by sharing the results and communicating a commitment to work on those areas together you can take a big step in improving the trust, communication, and shared commitment on your team.

At this point, you should decide who will be responsible for the follow-up and for creating an action plan based on the information. Sometimes this is a few people in HR; other times it's an exec team or group of leaders. It's typically best when it's a cross-functional but small group that's committed to the process. The best ideas for making improvements are going to come from the team, so the more that you can get people involved the better. If the group is too heavily populated with HR staff, the process can sometimes feel more like a requirement coming down from the HR team. When I work with HR executives and managers, I always advise that they take the role of facilitating and shepherding the process while letting the team generate ideas for improvement. After all, the HR folks tend to be great listeners and facilitators — so this process can be successfully lead by them. The follow-up team is responsible for:

» Updating the company on a time frame for results publication

» Meeting to review the results and findings

» Sharing pertinent information with individuals if feedback is more personal or specific in nature (and keeping it confidential)

» Establishing an action plan that will be shared with the company

Connecting right after the survey

Your employees are expecting you to take action. Here are the steps to follow immediately after the eNPS culture survey cycle has closed:

1. **Thank employees for their time, ideas, and candor.**

2. **If you set a goal about a specific response rate and achieved it, send congratulations along with the thank-you.**

3. **At this stage, keep the tone positive and optimistic, with an overall theme of being excited about learning more about the positive things currently going on and the positive ideas to improve in other areas.**

4. **Communicate an approximate date when the results will be shared.**

   This can depend on the feedback. If people are generally really happy and simply recommend a new pizza place for the weekly lunch, then your time frame for sharing may be shorter than if there are significant areas to map out methods for improving. Take a peek at the results before committing to a time to share — but don't wait too long before letting the team know when they should expect to see the results. If you've built a very transparent organization, you can share it all from the beginning by making it possible for people to see survey results for the whole organization as soon as they have submitted their rating.

TIP

As a rule of thumb, two weeks is a good time frame to underscore your commitment to culture, while two months is far too long because too much changes in that amount of time.

Figure 3-4 provides a sample email template you can use to update the company after the survey.

Hi {whatever cool thing you call your employees},

Our Culture Survey ended on Friday with {percent participation}. Thanks for taking the time to provide your candid and valuable feedback. Over the next two weeks, the Culture Survey team will be reviewing the findings and designing action plans for specific areas of feedback.

By {date — typically two weeks or so}, we will share the results and our action plan based on what we have learned. Our goal in this process is to create an honest, open way to improve our culture together.

Thank you,
{Culture Survey leader}

FIGURE 3-4:
Sample culture follow-up email.

Analyzing results and creating an action plan with management

Once all of the results have been collected, it is time to decide how to share them. The first step is getting the executive or senior leadership team together to review the data. This should be done as quick to the end of the survey as possible to keep momentum. The overall goal during this session is to review the findings and to decide what needs attention now, what needs attention later, and which things don't need attention. Similarly, you also want to review what's working.

From that list, you will start to develop an action plan that can be shared with the company with the results. This action plan should include the overall score, the positive notes, the neutral notes, and the ideas for improvement.

The follow-up team is responsible for creating and sharing the action plan. Some organizations decide to involve employees in the planning process in some manner. You may have them review proposed solutions or be in the room to help create the solutions.

REMEMBER

Sometimes, the first time you complete an eNPS culture survey, there may be a lot of items in the action plan. This is totally normal and will reduce over time. If this is the first time you're asking employees about their opinions and ideas, then expect there to be more of them on the first attempt. If you do have many, you may need to extend the action plan a bit to expand beyond the time between now and the next quarterly cycle.

TIP

Whether you approach this as a top-down activity or one where employees will take part, here are some tips to make the most of the action planning:

>> Review the action plan with the senior leadership team and ensure buy-in is created. It's important that the CEO is in support of the action plan and expects a united front. This part of the process can take the most amount of time, but it's worth sticking it out to get right.

>> If not all managers are included in the senior leadership team, then share the results and action plan with them before sharing with their employees. You want to have prepared and informed managers available to answer questions and support the efforts.

>> The action plan will be made up of small quick wins that can be accomplished relatively easily and others that may take a while to really implement. Make sure to build in timelines and milestones so you can track (and share) progress being made along the way.

>> Once the action planning is done, share the results and your new plan at the same time. If you have any areas that don't have plans or need further development, call that out rather than just omitting them. Better to let people know you heard them and will work on something soon than to make them feel that the feedback was wasted.

Sharing the results and the action plan with employees

Once you have a chance to review and process the survey results, it's time to share the results. It's generally best to share as much as possible — even the negative stuff. The only areas that you may want to edit or omit are those with content that only applies to specific people. If some feedback is critical of the CEO or senior leadership, leave it in and be prepared to discuss. Again, transparency is a big way to improve culture and drive engagement. When people feel like they're making a difference and their opinions are helping to create positive change, it boosts your culture in positive ways.

WARNING

Be careful about being too selective about what you share, as omitting too much can cause distrust, fear, and apathy about providing feedback next time around.

Here are some more of the best practices for sharing the results and findings:

>> Be honest, open, and fair about sharing. Share the good, the bad, and the ugly. After all, your employees already know what's going on at the company. They're the ones who provided the feedback. By openly acknowledging the challenges, you send a signal about your willingness to work through them and gain credibility in the process.

>> If the results are mostly negative, it may be helpful to simply acknowledge the seriousness of the problems. You probably won't make the issues worse by airing them publicly, but you can go a little way toward accepting responsibility for making them better. Feeling heard by leadership has a way of making people feel optimistic about a better future.

>> If there are comments or feedback about specific people or teams, share that information privately and empathetically. Make sure to provide context as well — how many people reported an issue, what they said exactly, and how things can improve. Don't use this as a chance to be punitive but rather as a chance to be candid and focused on improvements.

>> This information can be shared in the form of a written document that is distributed via email. It can also be shared via a video or live event where the leadership team communicates the results, the findings, and the action plan to improve.

Tracking Culture in Other Ways

The eNPS method will take you a long way toward measuring your culture by establishing a baseline and providing frequent feedback in a measurable way. In some cases, it may be all you need to begin tracking and making progress in improving your culture. Sometimes the process of doing it consistently and with intention has remarkable impact on the people involved. In that way, doing the eNPS culture survey in and of itself is often enough to start boosting culture in your organization.

Once you get started, you'll probably start to look around for other places where culture can be observed, measured, and tracked. This section will help you think about other ways to put a focus on culture and track it over time. You can start to organize all your culture measurements by creating a culture dashboard.

Designing a culture dashboard

It would be silly to try to run a business without looking at metrics. Imagine a finance team that never reviewed the numbers, or a sales organization that didn't use sales data to track success and forecast business. Any lead in those areas of the organization would be laughed at if their attempt at measuring success was simply "things are feeling good around here lately, so we must be on the right track," or "no one is quitting so we must be doing something right." You've already got the master metric in your eNPS culture survey, so what do you do with those scores over time?

Organizing some of your key cultural information in one place is a great way to consistently keep tabs on things related to culture. A dashboard can be as simple as a spreadsheet that is used to track specific culture metrics on an on-going basis. You can also make this into a physical tool hanging in your office by creating a simple chart like the one in Figure 3-5. It is critical to track these important numbers just like you would other critical business metrics like costs, growth, sales, and productivity. Creating a culture dashboard is a simple way to start organizing all of your culture metrics into once place. As you roll out new initiatives and programs, you can see how they impact your eNPS score and the other key areas discussed in the following sections.

To get started with your culture dashboard, begin with a simple spreadsheet using your eNPS culture survey as a starting point. Then add a few of the following options that you'll be measuring. (See Figure 3-5 and the following sections for details on filling in the spreadsheet.) Schedule time once per quarter (typically after the eNPS culture survey) to update the numbers and share them with the leadership team. To add real transparency and accountability to this, share the dashboard with the entire company. This is another example of using one of your processes to improve culture. The very act of sharing more will increase engagement and make people feel like they're part of helping to track and improve these important numbers.

Area	Q1 2018	Q2 2018	Q3 2018	Q4 2018
eNPS culture survey	8	9		
Glassdoor overall score	4.3	4.6		
Glassdoor CEO rating	98%	100%		
Glassdoor recommendation rating	94%	98%		
Exit interview eNPS rating	6	8		
Referral program hires	3	6		
% of job requisitions with referrals made	45%	68%		

FIGURE 3-5: Sample culture dashboard.

Learning from exit interviews

In the world of HR management, exit interviews are a tool that can be used to provide more information into why someone is leaving. During an exit interview, departing employees are asked questions about their employment experience, why they're leaving, and what could be improved, and are typically given a final run-through of any relevant policies (non-compete, non-disclosure, and so on) and benefits (COBRA, unemployment, and so on). Over time, you can start to recognize patterns that might exist about why your team is leaving. If you notice lots of top performers jumping ship, then this information can provide some intel that can help you start working with your remaining team to make improvements and drive positive culture change. When done poorly, they are a waste of time and resource that do little to improve the conditions.

Similarly, these exit interviews are also beneficial to people who are not leaving your company. Your employees talk to each other — and your exiting employees will likely remain friends with people who are staying behind. By extending some energy in the form of an exit interview, you can help create a better narrative around that person's departure with your current team. The way you treat exiting staff can have a deep cultural impact on the people who remain and see the company as caring, thoughtful, and committed to improvement.

TRACKING eNPS FOR DEPARTING EMPLOYEES

Using eNPS for departing employees can be a great culture measurement because it can give you insight into what your departing team is thinking as they leave. You can do this by creating a simple form for the exiting employee to complete at the time of the exit interview. Use the same format as other eNPS areas by asking:

> "How likely are you to recommend {your company} to a friend on a scale from 0 to 10, with 1 being not a chance and 10 being absolutely?"

The results you uncover will impact possible future hiring as departing employees talk about your company out in the world. This process is also another chance to get a glimpse into how things are working. If every exiting employee rates your company very low, then there may be something wrong. If your exiting employees are still huge fans and willing to recommend others to your organization, then chances are you have some good culture mojo working for you. This can be a good metric to track on your culture dashboard as well. Keep in mind that if you have relatively low turnover, then the scores will move slowly as well. In that case, use it more as directional information to look into and less like something that needs immediate resolution. If your turnover is higher and you are hearing consistent reasons for leaving from top performers, then you should definitely use that information to seek out ways to improve.

EXPLORING OTHER CULTURE TOPICS

In addition to the eNPS for exiting staff, you can also use this time as a chance to ask any of the employee survey questions in the earlier section "Designing the employee survey questions." If you ask the same questions consistently, over time you can uncover ways to improve your culture that could have helped to avoid losing a valuable team member. Not everyone that leaves your company leaves because of culture, but it's useful feedback to track to see if you are losing people due to culture issues.

Here are some other questions that are slightly less measureable but helpful for qualitative culture intel:

- ❯❯ If you had to give an exact reason, why are you leaving?
- ❯❯ Why did you give the eNPS score that you did? Why not higher? Why not lower?
- ❯❯ If you could do one thing that would drastically improve the culture and working conditions, what would you do?
- ❯❯ Is there a way to improve the situation that has caused you to leave us?
- ❯❯ When you think about your coworkers, how would you describe the morale and how they feel about working here?
- ❯❯ What are three things you enjoyed most about working here? Least?
- ❯❯ If you could instantly improve/change three things, what would they be?
- ❯❯ What advice do you have for the new person in your role?
- ❯❯ What do you think it takes to be successful here?

Using online review systems

The days of company culture being a secret known only in a small circle of employees, former employees, and their friends are long gone. Information about what it's like to work at your company is easy to find. Employer review sites like Glassdoor and Comparably have changed the landscape and shifted the dynamic of power when it comes to employer brand.

You have a remarkable tool at your hands in using these review sites to learn about your culture from your employees' perspectives and being able to share the positive things going on in your organization in an effective and low-cost way. By leveraging these resources, you can assess, improve, and promote your company culture.

TIP

When you set up your culture dashboard, take the pulse of your company on these employer review sites. The most common and powerful is Glassdoor, so you can simply choose that one for efficiency. Create a line item for Glassdoor and then record your current overall rating, the CEO approval rating, the recommend to a friend rating, and the total number of reviews. You should update these numbers at least quarterly during your culture dashboard update cycle (see Chapter 8 for more ideas on powering and leveraging these reviews to help with recruiting great people to your team).

You'll likely notice shifts and changes in the scoring. This is a good sign that you need to dig into the comments and messages. What are people saying? What has changed? What's improved? Remember these are lagging indicators — meaning they're only reporting on something that has already happened. So be thoughtful about making any fast, rash changes to things based on these scores alone. You should always use them as a sign to do a deeper dive into things to see what's going on behind the scenes.

Learning from turnover

The best organizations with the strongest cultures do a great job at retaining their employees and reducing turnover of staff. It's expensive to replace employees with training, knowledge transfer, productivity loss, and recruiting costs — let alone the negative cultural impact of people leaving your organization. Tracking turnover should be one of the key metrics in your culture dashboard. Again, this is a lagging indicator and doesn't always tell you why something is happening; however, it's a good way to stay connected.

REMEMBER

When tracking turnover, keep a few things in mind. During hard economic times or holiday seasons, people are more likely to stay in jobs. So this can give you a false read on your turnover success. Some turnover is positive, with people leaving to pursue degrees or moving across the country. Keep in mind that not all turnover is equal, so it's helpful if you have a general idea about why people left as well.

If you see a sudden spike in turnover in a specific department, work location, or after a big change, you can almost certainly assume there's a cultural impact as well.

Measuring the employee referral program

Many organizations use employee referral programs to help recruit new people to the team. After all, who knows better what it takes to succeed in your organization than the people who are already working within it? While it can drastically improve your recruiting, a recommendation or referral program can be another measurement in your culture dashboard.

Think about it — your current employees are not going to encourage their friends to come and work for your team if the culture isn't right. Unless there's a very large payday on the other end of that hire, the desire to maintain status with their friends and former colleagues is going to win every time.

If you have a clearly communicated program (see Chapter 8 for more details on creating a powerful recommendation/referral program), then you should be able to establish a baseline for a percentage of hires or candidates that originated from a recommendation from a current employee. If your current ratio is that 1 in 10 hires originated from a referral, can you set a goal to change that to 1 in 8 in the coming quarters? A positive shift in this area is almost always linked to a positive culture in your organization. Make your referral program metric one that you use to keep an eye on culture as well.

Creating an employee opinion survey

Sometimes, you may want to get more specific in a survey than the eNPS culture survey. You may be looking for specific ideas and areas with strong employee opinions. In that case, look to the employee opinion survey to help you take a deeper dive into what is happening with your employees. While the eNPS score is still the best overall measurement of how your employees feel about their work, this employee opinion survey can help you start to understand what might be working at a deeper level. This might help you uncover some of the specific areas that can use attention.

Designing the employee survey questions

When designing an employee survey, the goal is to be specific and actionable. The issue with most employee surveys is that they don't help you figure out what to improve. In general, you should find ways to measure that are quantitative and qualitative. The model in the eNPS culture survey is an easy one to adopt here as well. Simply score each survey question from 1 to 10 and then provide a space to add more detail with a prompt like "Why did you give that score?"

Figure 3-6 offers some sample survey questions you can use to learn more about what your employees are thinking and wanting.

- Leadership
  - Our leaders have communicated a vision that is exciting and clear.
  - Our leaders consistently demonstrate that people matter and focus on employee success.
  - Our leaders keep us informed about what is happening and how that impacts us.
  - My manager gives me useful feedback in a timely way so that I can use it to improve and grow.
  - My manager makes time for me and is available when I have questions or need advice.

- Work Environment
  - I have the tools I need to do my work at my best level.
  - Our physical workspace is inviting and positive.
  - We have the spaces and rooms needed to do my best work.
  - I am able to arrange time away from work to take care of important things in my life when needed.
  - My workload is reasonable.

- Professional Growth
  - I have access to resources and tools to help me learn more about my role, career, and possible learning areas.
  - The company is invested in my growth and helping me continue to learn.
  - I am progressing toward my personal and professional goals here.

- Social Connection
  - My coworkers are positive, inviting, and inclusive.
  - I feel that I have support from my colleagues.
  - My team is committed to doing great work.
  - Other teams are committed to doing great work.

FIGURE 3-6: Sample employee opinion survey questions.

To garner information regarding other areas, you may want to consider the following:

» Ask specifically about benefits and perks to determine what areas should be included in future budgets.

» Ask about specific learning opportunities to determine training and development programming.

» Ask about specific projects or programs to learn about their effectiveness.

TIP

Try to avoid doing this just once a year in a long formal survey. You'll see better results doing shorter, more frequent pulse checks on specific areas than doing longer surveys less frequently. Remember, culture is happening every day.

Launching the employee opinion survey

Sending out an employee opinion survey is as simple as following the same steps you used for the eNPS culture survey. You may be using the employee opinion survey in just a few departments or a specific office location because you're looking for feedback in those immediate areas. No matter how you're executing the survey, by following the same outlines and process as with the culture survey, you'll have all your bases covered.

It's also important to get leadership buy-in here as well. So make sure to work through the process even if on a smaller scale. Once you have buy-in and are ready to send out the survey, don't forget to share:

>> Why this survey is happening and what the goals are

>> Why these specific questions were chosen

>> The dates for submitting information

>> Whether this is anonymous

>> Who is included in this survey

Following up on the survey

The same rules apply as with the culture survey, so you can simply follow the same steps. It's important to

>> Update participants that the survey is closed

>> Give them a time frame for sharing the feedback

>> Put together an action planning committee

Leading a culture survey workshop

Sometimes when reviewing the feedback from an employee opinion survey, you may find it useful to get information directly from the employees affected. Leading an employee opinion survey workshop is a quick and impactful way to gather ideas, test solutions, and develop an action plan directly with the employees. If the issue stemmed around managers or leaders, then you might organize a group of managers or leaders to create solutions for addressing the employee concerns. In most cases, these will be simple two-hour sessions aimed at solving a few specific issues that were discovered in the survey process.

1. **Get specific.**

   Identify the issues you're trying to solve. What did the survey results say? Why does this need to be addressed?

2. **Form working groups.**

   Schedule four to six people and tell them that you're requesting their help in coming up with some solutions to some challenges presented in the employee opinion survey. Tell them you'll be sharing some results, scheduling a workshop, and asking them to do some pre-work to prepare.

3. **Share results and identify ideas.**

   Share the survey results ahead of time with the workshop group. Ask each person to bring three ideas for solving the challenges presented in the survey results. They should write these down ahead of time and print them to bring to the meeting. Better yet, have them submit them ahead of time to you for printing.

4. **Identify goals.**

   Kick off the session by explaining the goals: to find two or three ideas aimed at solving the issue to present to the leadership team.

5. **Conduct an open discussion.**

   Allow the group to freely discuss the issues at hand. Ask for their thoughts on where each issue may have stemmed from, the impact it may be having on the organization and culture, and why it's a concern for employees.

6. **Define a clear vision of what the company would feel like if these issues were resolved.**

   How would people be relating to each other? What would they say to each other and about the company? Get really clear on a desired future state to help ensure everyone is working toward the same goal.

7. **Post solutions.**

   Have everyone exchange the three solutions they prepared in advance. Go around the table and read them. Once each person shares, have them post them on the wall using tape.

8. **Star favorite ideas.**

   Ask each person to draw a star on their favorite idea. Repeat this three times until you have whittled down the list to the best three ideas.

9. **Review the proposed solutions as a team.**

   Explore how those ideas would look in action and how they would solve the initial issue. Identify any concerns these new solutions present.

10. **Thank them for their time.**

Now you have three great employee-sourced ideas to take back to the leadership team for consideration.

2

Starting with Yourself

IN THIS CHAPTER

» **Understanding why *you* are the first step in a great culture**

» **Assessing your mindfulness and using exercises to enhance it**

» **Using techniques to manage yourself**

» **Exploring your belief system**

» **Muscling up your time management approach**

Chapter **4**

Managing Yourself

To create the kinds of teams and companies that can sustainably deliver for customers and clients for the long haul, you need to have a healthy dose of self-awareness, self-control, and self-regulation. You won't find those characteristics in an MBA program or on the front page of the financial news. Managing yourself is the most important skill you need to develop if you want to build something great. It's also the characteristic that makes you a magnetic and engaging person, which is also pretty helpful as you try to mold company culture. The reality is that we can never really change the world, the people around us, or the circumstances we're in — we can simply change ourselves. We can contribute to the world, the company culture, the conversation, and the circumstances in a new way. This chapter is all about better managing yourself so you can begin shaping the environment and conditions around you to drive company culture to where you want it to be.

Getting Yourself on Board

You may notice that you're often unaware of your thought processes, your beliefs, your perspective, your perceptions, and your default response to things. A lot of people find themselves even unaware of the stories they tell themselves about themselves and others. The typical trajectory of a manager, business leader, department head, or executive usually looks something like this: do individual contributor work really well, make some connections, get promoted to higher-level individual contributor work, make the people and organization around you look good, get promoted to manage other people who do the work you used to do, and so on and so on. But often along the way, there isn't a lot of work that goes into thinking about you. Sure, you take a leadership course here and there. You attend a conference and bring back a new idea. But it's pretty rare to find someone who has had specific training and development on himself. We're often the masters of our craft. We're the gurus of our guild. We can tap into the motivational grit to organize others. But we don't know how to lead ourselves or that we should be doing so in the first place.

When you read the blogs, watch the videos, and dive into the books about companies and teams with positive cultures, it becomes very clear that it takes a different kind of manager to foster the type of intentional, focused environment that shapes great company cultures. From Steve Jobs (Apple) to Tony Hsieh (Zappos), from Ari Weinzweig (Zingerman's) to Herb Kelleher (Southwest), these are all leaders who have made the decision to build a specific type of company culture. They're all different from each other, but each of their organizations is celebrated for having a unique kind of culture that consistently allows employees to thrive and consumers to delight. Each of the cultures and leaders attracts different people, and in that way it's hard to separate leader from culture, culture from company.

The good news is, you can teach yourself to do it too. Being the kind of manager or leader who can shape a positive culture and create something great doesn't require a specific degree, a level of "natural born leader" skills, or even a weekend-long certification course. It happens when you make the decision to get yourself on board. When you make that call that you're going to take responsibility for your space in the world and get intentional about your approach to creating a healthy company culture, you begin to shape the space around you in an impactful and enduring way.

You have to make an intentional choice to start getting to know yourself at a deep level. What do you really value? What do you really want? How do you respond to different things in your environment? Why do you respond that way? Is that the best way to respond? What other responses may be helpful? How do you make decisions? How does what you believe shape the way you manage and lead? Where do you spend your time and what does that communicate about you, your values, and your culture?

WARNING

Change is uncomfortable. Asking yourself to take responsibility for shifting the way you show up in the world and at work is not for the faint of heart. But it is required if you are to become the kind of leader who creates company cultures that thrive. You'll be tempted to skip this chapter if the ideas of emotional intelligence, empathy, and mindfulness are foreign to you. Stick with it — try some of the exercises explained in this chapter for a couple of weeks. See what happens when you take control of your own energy.

People Do Better When You Do Better

Think about the boss you had that had the most positive impact on your work and professional career. The one who really helped you grow, learn, and develop. Someone probably came to mind right away, right? What made that person a great boss? It probably wasn't her degree. It likely wasn't her status or title. You are probably remembering how she made you want to work harder and better, how she handled conflict and success, and how aware of herself she was, which allowed for her to help inspire the best in everyone else on the team.

Similarly, the people around you at work do better when you do better — when you're aware of your thoughts, your motivations, and your sense of self. The ability to lead yourself is deeply intertwined with your ability to positively impact others. Imagine working with someone who is really good at bringing issues into the light — this sounds like a great skill set for a coworker or manager. But now also imagine that person really lacks self-awareness and isn't connected to her own mindfulness. These "issues" meetings probably end up being a lot more destructive than impactful. Think of a human resources professional whose role it is to help create engagement and positive culture but is unaware of the feeling that she is aloof and doesn't listen. She's probably going to struggle at that whole culture and engagement thing, right?

REMEMBER

Your organization is a reflection of you. If you look around your department, team, or organization and don't like what you see, have you considered that they are taking cues from you? If you look around and see some things really working and deeply coded into the fabric of your company, have you considered how those may be reflections of your energy, commitments, and actions? The culture of your team, department, or company relies on each person in it to contribute. The more you can bring the best, most authentic version of yourself to the table, the better the culture is, and the better the culture is, the better the people in it are. When you do better, the people around you do better.

TIP

Think about that boss. You were better because she was better, and you owe that same intentionality to your team. I would argue that the people are better because you are better. You are better because they are better. And the very organization is a reflection of you. So, let's break that down. What did she do? How did she handle people? What kinds of things did she say? How did she lead meetings? Start to get a really clear picture about what it was that made a difference for you. This list is a practical way to start to develop your own list of values.

TIP

If you have never had a great boss, then think about the worst boss you've ever had. Consider the same questions in this section, but from the opposite perspective of what did she do ineffectively in each of those areas. Then add to each thing on the list by thinking about what could have made her more effective.

Becoming Mindful

When you see "becoming mindful," is the first image that comes to mind a peaceful, deep-breathing, vegan yogi sitting under a tree? For many, the idea of becoming mindful is somewhat scary because of the beliefs we have around what it takes to actually reach some state of mindfulness. For example: "But I don't have 60 minutes a day to sit and breathe!" "I don't live near an ashram." "I'm not ready to give up coffee and bacon." Now, hopefully, this doesn't frighten you, but mindfulness is the critical missing link to you becoming the kind of person who can positively impact the culture around you. The good news is, you don't have to do an *Eat, Pray, Love* style tour to become more mindful at work.

Here's a quick "mindfulness assessment" to check yourself against:

» Do you often find yourself apologizing for something you said and didn't mean to someone at work?

» Do you frequently hear surprising critical feedback about your performance or communication?

» When something upsets you at work, do you struggle to stop thinking about it even though it is no longer directly impacting you?

» Do you often miss what someone is saying when the person is speaking with you because you weren't paying attention?

» Do you feel stress by the time you hit the shower in the morning when you think of the day ahead of you?

» Do you frequently find yourself struggling to complete things because you're responding to emails, messages, and phone calls?

If you found yourself answering yes to several of these, then exploring mindfulness as a leadership skill set can provide huge benefits in a short amount of time.

TIP

While some of the language in this chapter is aimed at people in a leadership role, the company culture gets better when everyone learns to manage themselves — when everyone on your team takes responsibility for themselves and how they impact others around them. After doing workshops for all types of organizations, I know that teaching others to manage themselves is one of the quickest culture improvements in which you can invest. Pick a few of the activities in this chapter and begin to teach them to your employees. You can even start off meetings and other events with a few of the mindfulness exercises as a standard practice.

Benefiting from becoming more aware of yourself

Want to make better decisions, retain your best performers, earn more profit, and boost your culture? Then you need to become aware of yourself and be mindful. Here's what mindfulness does for you that manifests itself in you as your best leader:

» **Stronger focus:** When you're able to get your mind to wander less, your focus and intention become clearer. Your ability to concentrate on the issues at hand is better — while working on projects, while attending meetings, and while solving complex problems with your team.

» **Better relationships:** Mindfulness helps you be more accepting, humble, and curious about the people around you, which helps you connect with them in ways that strengthen and deepen your relationships at work.

» **Improved conflict management:** You can't manage conflict well if you're simply responding with the intention to win and without self-awareness. Conflict becomes a loop of unresolved issues without mindfulness. With mindfulness, you'll find yourself better able to understand the root issues of conflict and more willing to work together with others to find resolution rather than simply proving your point.

» **Positive response to change:** You'll be able to embrace and accept the ambiguity, uncertainty, and volatility of the fast-moving modern environment. Your ability to understand your immediate fear response to change becomes more evolved, which enables you to find opportunity in change.

» **Staying calm under stress:** Meditation specifically is really impactful in helping to slow down your fast-thinking, quick-to-action brain. It helps to create some distance between stimulus and response

» **Better memory:** You'll be able to better recognize and remember the connections and conversations you have with colleagues and employees. Mindfulness allows you to be more in the moment with them so that you can recall better in future interactions.

» **Good corporate citizenship:** With stronger communication skills and a knack for positive conversations through mindfulness, you'll be able to quickly establish rapport with people around you.

» **Innovative thinking:** Mindful leaders are more curious and open to exploring new territories and ideas; you'll be better able to handle the ambiguity that comes with experimenting with new solutions.

Take a look at the preceding list and think about which areas you could use the most help with at work. Write down which ones you choose and why. Think about what is currently not working. Then make a note after you practice some of the exercises I give in the next sections to look back in a few weeks to see if things have changed. Compare the current status to what you wrote down to track your progress.

Investigating ways to boost your mindfulness

Choosing to become more mindful doesn't have to be difficult. At its core, it's really about making the decision to stop and be more aware for a few minutes. Check out the following sections for exercises you can do to boost your mindfulness throughout the day.

Breathing exercise

If you pay attention to the way you breathe throughout the day, it can tell you a lot about how you are feeling. If your breathing is shallow and rapid, it can mean that you are stressed or feeling anxious. If you take a few minutes to connect to your breath and control your breathing, you can often help calm those feelings as well by becoming more connected to what's going on in your body and mind. Try following these next steps to gain control of your breathing:

1. **Sit in a comfortable position with a straight back.**

   This is typically best achieved in a non-reclining dining room chair.

2. **Slowly exhale and release all the oxygen in your lungs.**

   Really focus on your breath exiting your lungs.

3. **Inhale slowly through the nose while slowly counting to four in your head.**

   You should feel your lungs fill with air and your abdomen expand slightly.

4. **Hold your breath while slowly counting to four in your head.**

5. **Exhale through your mouth while slowly counting to four in your head.**

   Become aware of your lungs emptying as you exhale.

6. **Hold your breath again while slowly counting to four in your head.**

7. **Repeat this four times in a row.**

Focusing exercise

You can see great benefits from practicing focusing just 5–10 minutes a day. It can also be a good exercise to do before a big meeting, a difficult conversation, or a high stakes event to help you focus and calm your mind a little for high performance. The following exercise is a simple way to help focus your busy mind:

1. Sit in a comfortable chair and set a timer for your desired length of time.

If you are just starting out, try three minutes and then increase the time 10 seconds at a time in future sessions.

2. Place a candle about two to three feet in front of you and light it.

3. Stare at the flame with a soft gaze.

4. Just observe the flame moving around.

Notice whether It's moving slowly, quickly, repetitively.

5. Check in with your breath.

Are you breathing naturally or are you holding your breath at all? Is your breath shallow and fast? Or deep and measured? Your goal is to let your breath rise and fall on its own in a deep and measured way.

6. If your mind begins to wander, simply refocus on the flame again.

No judgment. No need to think "I'm bad at this." Simply just return your focus on the candle.

Eating intentionally

Finding simple ways to bring mindfulness into your daily activities and rituals is the key to making it work for you. Since we eat and drink every day, practicing mindfulness during meals is an easy way to get started and something everyone can do. Think about how often you shove down breakfast, slam your morning coffee, or work through lunch. Mealtimes are a good opportunity to slow down and practice bringing more awareness to your day. Oddly, this is also the method I learned when completing wine certifications during my hospitality days. Try this:

1. Sit down with your food or drink.

Take a deep breath in through the nose.

2. Look at your food or drink.

Pretend you have never seen it before. What is the color? What is the texture? What is the shape? Think about where it came from. Is it farmed? Manufactured? Produced? How did it arrive to your table?

3. **Touch your food.**

   How does it feel? What is the temperature? Is it firm? Soft? Crunchy? Smooth? Sharp? What does it sound like as you drop it back on the plate or set it down on a table?

4. **Smell your food.**

   Is it sweet? Pungent? Savory? Odorless?

5. **Taste it.**

   Observe the taste before you bite into it or swish it around your mouth. Name that taste. After biting into it or swishing it around your mouth, what does it taste like now? How about after swallowing and taking a breath?

Listening actively

One of the simplest ways to improve your culture while also boosting your own mindfulness is through active listening. Most of the time when others are speaking, your brain is probably thinking about how to respond and what you'll say next. Sometimes you may be thinking of something else entirely, which diminishes your relationship with the other person and reduces the chances that you truly understand what's actually happening. Here's a simple way to retrain your brain to listen more actively that you can do anytime without the other person even knowing you're doing it:

1. **When someone begins speaking, take an inaudible deep breath to help focus yourself.**

   Breathe in deeply and slowly and then exhale.

2. **Maintain eye contact with a soft gaze.**

   This is somewhere between "I like your eye color" and "Get a restraining order."

3. **Focus on the words and intention of the other person.**

4. **Become aware of the energy behind the speaker's words.**

   This doesn't mean you need to add extra meaning: "She is clearly angry about Bill denying her expense report." But rather that you're sensing the emotion: "This is important to her and seems to be causing worry." This is typically the hardest part for most people since we constantly want to assign meaning to what we hear versus just letting it be heard.

5. **Nod and make sounds that show you're listening, like "yeah" or "mmhmmm."**

6. **Before you share your thoughts, repeat what she said without judgment or additional commentary.**

   This creates a shared sense of understanding and shows her that you were really listening. We often listen to respond without really understanding what the other person has said — taking this extra step shows her that you are interested in her perspective.

Putting technology to use

In some ways, technology can be a distracting, mindfulness-zapping trap with all the notifications, messages, and addictive social media hooks. But given the prevalence of tech tools in our lives, there are some ways to benefit from technology to help hack your way to a more mindful experience.

TIP

Here are some tech tips for mindfulness:

>> **There's an app for that:** You no longer have to travel or spend much money to tap into mindfulness training. Low-cost application options are available that can guide you through breathing exercises and daily meditations, and can even gamify the process by allowing you to earn "badges" and create challenges for yourself. Some favorites include: Headspace, Calm, 10% Happier, and Insight Timer. Download one of them and commit to trying it out for 30 days. Many of them can even send you a notification each day at a specific time to complete your mindfulness training.

>> **Reminders:** Your cellphone can act as a great tool to help remind you to check in with yourself. You can use the Reminder app that comes loaded with Apple IOS to set reminders at specific times of day or locations so you can consistently do the breathing exercise each morning when you arrive to your office parking garage.

>> **Alarms:** You can use the alarm functions on your cellphone to remind you to complete a focusing exercise each day at a specific time.

Getting Started with Self-Management

Self-management is being able to regulate and monitor your own behaviors, emotions, and actions. It takes into account how self-aware you are, how much you can control your behavior, and how well you can cope with the world around you. Mindfulness and self-awareness are the primers from which to build — the foundation to build your self-management habits upon. The following sections offer a handful of exercises and ideas that can help you learn even more about yourself so you can set your intentions and build a better culture.

Caring for yourself

Above all else, self-management begins with caring for yourself in a way that allows you to care for others even more. The saying "You can't love someone else until you first love yourself" is true at work too. You can't care for the team, the company, and the culture unless you care for yourself first. One of the frequent challenges that comes up for leaders, managers, and culture creators is this soundtrack playing in the background of your mind. It may be saying that you don't deserve to be in the place you're in, it may be shouting that you're an impostor in your space, it may be saying you aren't the leader people need, or it may just be stuck in a loop replaying mistakes you've made. It's no wonder so many managers face such intense burnout, which ultimately shows up in your interactions with others and slowly eats away at the positive equity in your culture.

It happens so frequently: A good-intentioned manager is constantly giving of herself. She works late, she comes in early to create more time for coaching, she does project work on the weekends, and she's focused on putting positivity into her department's culture. As time wears on, she gets less sleep, starts blaming herself for mistakes and fails, spends less time with loved ones, and skips important personal appointments. Eventually, this starts wearing on her at work, and her energy starts dipping. Her team notices and thinks the change is due to something at work, so they start getting worried about their own careers, goals, and projects. The culture starts turning toxic, and everyone starts watching out for themselves instead of the team. High performers start looking for more effective places to work, and our manager starts stressing even more. The cycle continues — and in many cases never gets back to good.

REMEMBER

Respecting yourself, your energy, and your needs is a critical part of being able to powerfully build company culture.

Here are some ideas for improving your self-care:

>> **Nourishment matters.** Fuel yourself with nutritious food by making better choices throughout the day. Does caffeine make you jittery? Then cut back one cup at a time. Are you crashing after lunch and impacting your afternoon meetings/conversations? Then have a healthy snack or add a short walk at lunchtime. Are you numbing yourself to sleep at night with a glass of wine and pint of ice cream? Instead, try the calming effects of chamomile tea or fiber-rich foods like blueberries to help with more restorative sleep.

>> **Sleep matters.** In the last few years, the amount of press, books, and research about the power of sleep has grown tremendously. If you find yourself frequently getting by on less than 7–8 hours of sleep, you're putting your body and energy at a major deficit. Running low is affecting your performance at work, your impact on your team, and the way you communicate — all things that will

negatively impact your culture. Find ways to improve your evening routine — no TV/laptop/phone screens before bed, turn down the lights or put them on dimmers and timers to help trigger circadian rhythms, avoid stimulating activities and foods in the evening to create a bedtime routine that encourages healthy sleep habits.

» **Movement matters.** One of the best ways to get your body awake and energy flowing in the morning is to get moving right away. Create a morning routine that includes some light stretching and movement. You don't have to be queen kickboxer; just go on a brisk walk for 20 minutes to get your blood pumping, clear your mind, and get you ready for the day.

» **Thoughts count.** This final recommendation is a powerful one that has the ability to really shift your thinking. Begin journaling each morning and evening: Grab a pen and some paper, set a timer, and commit to free-flowing thoughts for 5–10 minutes each day. There's so much in your head each day — thoughts, ideas, frustrations, excitements, wishes, dreams, fears. Most people don't ever get that out of their head and then go rushing into the day without priming their thinking or energy. Journaling helps with that by getting it out on paper so you can recognize what's there. There are no hard and fast rules here — just sit down, set a timer, and keep moving the pen across the page. If you get stuck, just write that. Your mind is always doing something — become aware of that and write it down. This type of reflection is an important part of self-care by helping you become more aware of yourself. It's also a critical part of building a great culture because it forces you to get your stuff out of your head, allowing you to connect with others without any roadblocks.

Recognizing your emotions

Often when people think about self-management, they assume that it's about finding ways to ignore your emotions and become a blissed-out surfer without a care in the world. But it's unnatural to ignore your emotions. I mean, we're in the real world. People are jerks. Projects get delayed. Sales fall through.

Real self-management is not about denying yourself your emotions or numbing yourself to the realities at work. It's about increasing your awareness of your emotional response. It's about popping the hood in your default thinking and making sure everything is running smoothly. It's about recognizing what's actually happening in the moment and being aware of how it impacts you so that you can make thoughtful choices about what's next.

It's important to pay attention to the patterns in your behavior and thoughts. Doing so allows you to learn more about yourself. But it's not useful or helpful to judge yourself. In those times where you find yourself beating yourself up over something you've just done, it's better to simply honor the emotion you felt and seek to understand where it came from so you can either avoid it altogether or at least stop it from negatively impacting your actions next time it occurs. Here's a simple plan to get more thoughtful about honoring your emotions:

1. **Acknowledge them:** It's almost like recognizing an old friend. Simply say to yourself "oh yeah — it's that feeling again." You are not your emotions, but you can acknowledge them so you can decide what to do about them.

2. **Name them:** It's helpful to figure out exactly what you're feeling before you let it redirect your actions and create an issue for you. Recognizing the difference between disappointment and contempt is an important part of managing yourself. Being able to tell the difference between excitement because this is an important talk you can't wait to share and anxiety because you didn't rehearse at all is important to clarify before you step on stage to give a presentation to the whole company.

3. **Decide:** Make a decision about whether the emotion is helpful and useful. Does it help you communicate more clearly? Can it be used to enhance your performance? Does it tell you something about what really matters to you?

4. **Let it go:** This doesn't mean you need to be a super Zen person who can just simply allow things to pass, but it does mean you can make a decision about what happens next without responding out of anger or fear or disappointment. If the emotion isn't useful, then let it go.

5. **Take action:** Based on the first four steps, make a decision about your actions from here. You are not emotions. You can use your emotions to help shape your experience and make decisions about your actions without letting your emotions dictate your experience.

Getting to know your intentions

You're here to have a very specific impact, to create a specific kind of life, and that deserves to be explored. Think about the reason you picked up this book in the first place. Lots of companies need culture improvements, and lots of leaders do nothing about it but complain about how employees these days aren't engaged. But not you — you picked up this book. You had some curiosity about how to have an impact, how to change the trajectory of your company's culture, or how to shape it correctly from the very beginning if you're a start-up brand.

Why?

What is it about that that matters to you? What's the focus of your intention as you flip the pages of the book? What's the thing driving you to leave things better than you found them?

One of the most impactful ways leaders can get themselves organized around a project (whether it be a company culture initiative or otherwise) is to draft a personal manifesto. The personal manifesto is a short piece that helps to clarify intentions and focus on what matters. Here are a few goals to keep in mind when drafting your manifesto:

>> Reflect and focus on yourself, your ideas, and why you are leading.

>> Distill, clarify, and sharpen your focus on the project at hand.

>> Get in touch with your beliefs headed into a new endeavor.

>> Give yourself a place to check back in with for accountability's sake.

Writing a manifesto to improve culture

You can use personal manifestos anytime you're taking on something new, find yourself in a rut, or need help getting clear on something. For this purpose, let's write one about your specific needs for company culture work at your organization. Aim for about 1,000 words or so and share it with someone else involved in the project when you're done

Here are some good questions to help you get started on this company culture manifesto:

>> What is to gain? If your company culture initiatives are a big success, how do things improve? What's being said about your organization? Why is that important? How does it change things? What's in it for you?

>> What has led you to pick up this book and do some work on the company culture? Is this an organization-wide concern or more focused on a specific team?

>> What are your main goals and expectations of the work?

>> What do you think about culture in general? About leadership? About groups of people coming together at work?

>> Who are your company culture role models? Why them? What do you think is the same about their style or organization? What is different? Why are those two things important?

>> What happens if you do nothing? How will that play out with your team, the marketplace, your brand? What about your own career? What happens for you if nothing changes?

If the blinking cursor of your word processor is causing you to have writer's block, then simply record and transcribe your responses to these questions, but make sure to get them into a printable, shareable format to review. The more conversational the better.

Sharing the manifesto

Once you're done with that exercise, share it with a few other people. You can create a group session if you're tackling company culture improvements with others. Schedule a "table read" with each other. Have each person on your culture committee complete a personal manifesto by a specific date. Schedule a meeting to review them. Print them out. Exchange them with each other at the top of the meeting (this is an important step because sometimes people "edit" their own writing while sharing, and having others read it will make sure lots of truths get on the table). Tell everyone that the goal of the "table read" is simply to exchange ideas, get some intentions on the table, recognize any shared desires, and explore any key differences before moving forward.

Writing a personal manifesto

Another effective approach for getting clear on your intentions is to complete a personal manifesto without the focus on a specific project or company culture initiative. In this manifesto, you're really going personal by just exploring yourself. All the same rules apply but with different questions. Find 30 to 45 minutes this weekend, find a comfortable spot, and respond to the following questions:

>> What do you want to be known for? When people talk about you and your presence at work, what do you want them to say? When they introduce you to others, how do you want them to highlight you?

>> If the people closest to you at work were to describe the impact you have, what would they say? How would they say you change the environment? What would they write about their experience with you?

>> What do you want? What is it that you really desire and crave? What's a big thing that you want to happen in the world?

When you're done, sleep on it overnight and then revisit it the next morning. Add more, clarify anything that needs more detail, and get more descriptive. Then share it with someone — maybe your spouse or best friend. If you're feeling daring, then maybe a colleague, your manager, or a direct report. This can be a helpful way to start putting your goals, ideas, and plans out there for others to see. It could lead to accountability that helps you get the important things done in your life.

Living your values

Every time you turn on the TV (or scroll your Facebook feed), there seems to be some ideological challenge around values: gun control, federal spending, global warming, vaccinations, the latest red rose recipient on *The Bachelor*. With these endless disagreements comes a lot of talk about values. But in most of these cases, we really are talking about a moral compass and how someone should live his life, not our own personal values. If you think gun control is an important issue but you don't really consider it daily, then it's a moral judgment but not a value. Values are the code of deeply held beliefs that drive your daily interactions, decisions, and behaviors. When asked, most people struggle to be able to list what they value.

Knowing the values that drive our behavior and then being able to use those to make future decisions is a huge part of being able to manage ourselves. It's really at the core of knowing why we do things and how we might shape what we do in the future. It's critical for being able to shape culture, as the company culture becomes an extension of those values within teams (for more on organizational values, check out Chapter 7).

Identifying where values come from

So where exactly do your values come from in the first place? There are many things that can influence values:

>> **Family:** The debate over nature or nurture will likely rage on into the future, but you can't ignore the impact that family has on what you think is right, wrong, important, rude, exciting, and so on. This doesn't mean you don't have slightly different views than Uncle Tom or more progressive leanings than Grandma Linda. It just means that much of what we value and how we view the world is shaped by our family.

>> **Big life events:** The experiences we've been through mold our values. Someone who moved a lot as a child may be more flexible to change than someone who lived in the same house growing up. These events leave indelible marks on the way we view the world, so it can be helpful to take stock of them.

>> **Decision and subsequent positive and negative consequences:** The choices we've made in the past and the consequences of those can shape our values as well. If you once made the decision to steal your grandma's calligraphy pens and then had to return them and apologize publicly, you may have reservations about borrowing someone's office supplies (I will neither confirm nor deny that this incident happened to the author). Sometimes it's just one decision made one time with strong consequences that creates a future lifetime of actions. Some of these are healthy — like not stealing a colleague's stapler — and others may be holding you back unnecessarily.

- » **Religion:** This one is pretty strongly linked to family as well. Many people take on the values that are underlined according to their religious affiliations. Some of these may be useful values with strongly linked positive behaviors, and others could be more damaging. Important to evaluate either way.

- » **Teachers, mentors, and other important figures:** Our ideas about the world have been shaped by the people we look up to in life. Sometimes the reason we look up to them is because they've helped shape our view of the world and how things should be. Think about some of these people in your life. What did they teach you? What mattered to them? How did they express that and why did it stick out to you? How has it shaped how you approach the world?

- » **Media and exposure to events in the world:** The way we see people interact and experiences unfold on TV, in the news, in print publications, and on social media has some impact on our views and values. It can be useful to take stock of those and make decisions about what really matters and what really may be true.

REMEMBER

Getting clear on your values can sometimes cause an existential mini-crisis as you try to understand yourself. It's pretty hard to observe yourself without your own perceptions. We're not used to having to view ourselves from the outside in and just generally accept ourselves as "who we are," so this exercise is likely to cause a little frustration and some deep thinking.

Translating your values to company culture

What do your values mean to company culture? If you have a strong value toward recognition, you may view people with a huge Instagram following as better than you and people with few followers (or no account at all — gasp!) as not really "getting it." If you're someone who values connection, you may like long, deep conversations with coworkers and find people who are extroverted and move quickly through conversations as rude. Understanding all this about yourself is key to understanding your relationships with others, which is an important part of leadership and company culture crafting.

Here's an exercise that can help you better understand the values that matter most to you.

1. Examine the list of values and possible definitions in Table 4-1.

2. Set a timer for 10 minutes and choose the five values that most resonate with you — not the ones that make you sound like a wonderful being, but the ones that really hit home for you, even if you don't always live them at this point.

TABLE 4-1

Values and Possible Definitions

Value	Possible Definition
Achievement	Accomplishing goals and succeeding at projects
Growth	Making progress, gaining promotion, and improvement
Adventure	Taking risks, exploring, new experiences
Balance	Seeking calmness and moderation
Reliability	Dedicated to a cause, meets obligations, follows through
Fun	Finding enjoyment, playfulness in activities
Teaching	Sharing information and helping others learn
Service	Supportive of others in their activities
Relationships	Making connections with others and maintaining them
Power	Influence over others and decision-making
Involvement	Being included, present, and participatory
Creativity	Finding new ways of seeing, doing, and producing
Curiosity	Questioning, exploration, and sense of wonder
Fairness/Equality	Equal consideration, protecting everyone, greater good
Freedom	Seeks independence and options with free will
Impact	Changing the world, seeks a legacy
Generosity	Actively seeking ways to give to others
Loyalty	Staying faithful to the team, the leader, or the cause
Stability/Security	Steadiness, predictability, low-risk activities
Learning	Consistent education, experiences, and growth

3. **Look back at the influences listed in the earlier section "Identifying where values come from" and see if you can find links to your top five values.**

   Are there events that shaped that? Are there specific people who molded them?

4. **Explore the behaviors attached to your values.**

   For each of the values you selected, think about how those shape specific, observable behaviors in your daily life. For example, if someone valued "growth," you may see behaviors like "I read three books a month" or "I attend one industry conference per quarter." Both of those activities are linked to growth and are observable behaviors. Get a blank piece of paper and re-create the items in Figure 4-1 for each value you identified.

Value	
Your Definition	
Behaviors	

FIGURE 4-1: Value activity.

Taking time to learn more about your values won't change your company culture overnight, but it will help you start to identify the things that matter most to you. Completing the activity in Figure 4-1 can be the first step in understanding how you see the world around you, which impacts the way you lead, organize, and guide your team. These values are reflected in the way you treat others and in that way have tremendous impact on the people you work with and the culture you help to create.

Crafting your future story

Do you have a clear idea of where you're headed personally? Do you know what it looks like if you've done well as a manager or leader? Do you have an image of what a great life looks like to you at some specific point in the future? What do you want to create? How do you want to be known?

Most people can't answer these questions, and that's a shame. After all, you spend every day working toward something, headed toward something, and aimed at some specific target in the future. Have you taken time to consider what that future looks like? If you're successful at creating the life you want, what life is that exactly? Everyone (manager or not) should have a personal future story which defines what the world looks like for them at some specific place at a specific time in the future.

Think of your future story as the destination on a GPS. It's not the only place you'll ever go. You'll certainly have other stories beyond this one. It's simply defining where you want to go in a clear way so that you know where you're headed and can recognize when you get there. In our quest for "more," it's important to have some celebratory milestones along the way. Heck, it's pretty helpful to even know what "more" means in the first place (more on that in Chapter 19). Creating a future story allows you to aim your intentions, organize your efforts, and ensure that the life you're creating is the one you want. We explore the importance of an organizational future story in Chapter 6, so for now, this is all about you and the story of you at some point in the future.

To get started with crafting your future story:

1. **Pick a specific time frame.**

   For most people, a good place to start is two to three years into the future because it gives you enough time to dream a little but not so much time that it's easy to put off. You can do future iterations longer once you get the hang of it. For now, pick a spot on the calendar two to three years ahead and write down that date.

2. **Pick a few areas of your life.**

   It can help provide some clarity and guidance if you focus on a few areas to describe in your future story. You may decide family, home, personal growth, career, and health are the ones for you. Whatever they are, write them down and then go into more details on those areas specifically. This can help to guide your efforts so that you don't feel like you are all over the place. Simply pick a few areas that matter most to you and then use the following steps to get more specific.

3. **Add some success measures**.

   With your areas outlined, underneath of each make a few bullet points that highlight how you'd measure success in those areas. Is it that you see Mom once a month? Or that you call Granny every week? Do you measure it by owning a condo at the beach? Or is it a cottage in the mountains? Have you written a book? Or gained a professional designation? Can you run a 5k in under 20 minutes? Or take yoga retreats twice a year?

4. **Now craft a story**.

   With all those story points drafted, it's time to put pen to paper and create the future story of you. Along the top of your page in big letters write "DRAFT" and then add the future date you selected. You're going to pretend that you're writing a journal entry on that date in the future. Almost like you're watching a movie about your future self and describing what you see. Add in all the details that matter and leave out the ones that don't. Not sure if you want a condo in the city or the house in the burbs but know that homeownership matters to you? Then just say, "I love my home and am so thrilled to have a space to entertain friends." Just put in what matters. Set a timer for 20 minutes and don't stop writing.

5. **Make some edits.**

   Give yourself a little space — maybe a week. Then come back to your draft and make revisions — where should you provide more detail and clarity? What did you leave out that now seems important to your future story?

6. Share.

Have a few people that you trust and that care about you read your future story. What resonated with them? What ideas do they have? Once you have had a chance to incorporate anything that matters to you, then you're ready to make that final edit and start living your story.

Here are two ideas to help you make your future story a reality:

>> **Read it.** Give your future story a read once a week for continued inspiration and to help remind you of what you're working toward anyway.

>> **Review it.** Schedule time twice a year (say June and December, but whenever works for you). Print your future story and underline/highlight the areas that you've made progress toward. Sometimes this will remind you how much progress you've been making. Other times it may be the kick in the butt to help you put a little effort toward living into your future story. Are there any actions you can take in the next few weeks to move something forward? Do you need to reach out to anyone to get help? Where do you want to be in six months when you read it again?

Managing your energy

You've probably been around those people who just know how to make you feel good, right? Their outlook, perspective, and approach just seem to change the room. When they show up for a meeting, everyone is happy they're at the table. When they're out on vacation, it feels like something positive and critical is missing from the office. They don't take themselves too seriously (even if they do take the work seriously).

In the same way, there are probably those people who seem to drag everyone down when they walk into a room. Or you go to meetings where everybody is on their cellphone until the meeting starts — no banter, no warmup, no group energy. Imagine the space around you as the area around a boat moving in the water. As the boat moves slowly, the ripples are smooth and cautious, almost calming. As the boat moves quicker, the wake moves faster and with more energy. If the boat starts spinning circles in the water, then the wake gets choppy and dangerous to those around it. Your energy is the same way.

Your energy is contagious, and you can control it. Getting intentional about the energy around you and the way you impact people can really start to change the way other people experience you. Here are a few exercises to help you manage your energy:

WARNING

>> **Inner monologue journal:** It's pretty common to have an inner monologue playing in your head as you interact with yourself, others, and the world. The outer monologue is all the stuff you say out loud, and the inner monologue is that track in the background of your mind — the one that says, "Hurry up, this story is boring them," or, "They probably don't want to hear what I have to say on this, so I'll just stay quiet in this meeting."

Access to and awareness of your inner monologue can be a telling experience. If that track in your head is one full of negative stories or self-doubt, then that's going to negatively impact your outer monologue and persona, which will slowly chip away at your culture. If enough people on your team aren't aware of their inner monologue, you could have a real toxic mess on your hands.

Pick a week and commit to completing this exercise. Carry a small, easily portable journal and, throughout the day, write down the stuff going through your head. It can be helpful to set a reminder for yourself on your calendar or via your smartphone alarm to help nudge you every few hours. Commit to free-flowing writing for 60–90 seconds each time. Don't judge yourself, just write. Once you've got a week's worth of inner monologues, read them back to yourself. Do you notice any repeating patterns? Are there specific situations or times that have consistent thoughts? What trends do you see? Did these thoughts end up being useful or coming true?

>> **Label it:** When you walk into a meeting, get ready for an important call, or prep for a crucial conversation with someone else, take a minute to think about your current energy. What's going on for you? Are you tired? Are you frustrated? Label it. Give it a name. Give it a level from 1 to 10 based on how strongly you're feeling that energy. Sometimes just becoming more thoughtful about your energy is enough to shift it.

>> **Future story it:** Once you're aware of your current energy, take a minute to think about how you want to contribute to the upcoming interaction. What do you want the other person or people to say about your energy? How would you most positively contribute to the culture? Take stock of what the future story of your performance is. You'll have a much better chance of achieving it once you're aware you want to in the first place.

Checking Your Beliefs

What we believe is really just the angle with which we choose to see the world. It's based on our histories, our dispositions, our focus, our attention, our drives. What we believe impacts how we show up in the world. Beliefs are a critical part of managing ourselves and creating a thriving company culture. The beliefs we hold are the foundation for building anything — the real base of what's possible.

If you believe that you have great ideas, that other people are open and willing to listen, and that sharing ideas makes them better, then you'll be more innovative, collaborative, and forthcoming with sharing your ideas. Your relationships, department, or organization is going to be full of people who openly bring their best ideas to the table to be enhanced, upgraded, and executed by their colleagues (and do the same for them in return).

REMEMBER

Your beliefs are unconscious until you start thinking about them. They're the unspoken filters that direct your attention, your energy, and your intention. It makes sense then to check in on them from time to time to make sure they're accurate and serving you well. Imagine your beliefs as little sets of agreements that your mind has made with itself. It can take some investigative work to start to unravel them and understand where they come from and how they shape your worldview. Becoming aware of your beliefs is a critical part of being able to manage yourself and of creating a company culture worth raving about. If it's true that what you believe led you here, then what you choose to believe next will get you there.

Becoming aware of your beliefs

Because your beliefs have such an impactful presence in the way you show up at work, it's helpful to try to explore what you believe. This can be a bit tricky because sometimes as we start to explore a belief, it starts to evolve and shift a little. It seems natural that as we try to define something, we learn more about it — which is why this exercise can be so useful in the first place.

Beliefs can really be about anything: why things happen or don't happen, what something means or doesn't mean, where success comes from, what causes failure, how certain groups behave, what matters and what doesn't matter, what people want and don't want.

Try the following exercise to start to explore what you believe about work. Put 30 minutes on the clock. Grab your favorite writing, typing, or recording device and write "What I Believe About Work" along the top of your page. Then answer the following questions:

>> What do you believe about yourself? Do you believe you are smart? Do you believe people "get you"? Do you believe you're a leader, confident, a strong communicator, an engaging speaker? Do you believe you deserve good things? Do you believe you're creative, funny, likable?

>> What do you believe about your ability to connect with others? How do you see yourself when you meet new people? How do you feel about connecting with employees? Peers? Your manager? Executives? Partners? Customers? Do you believe you connect well? Do you believe you have a high level of empathy? Do you think people like listening to you?

>> What do you believe about employees? What do you believe about the work they do, the reason they come to work, or what they want from you?

>> What do you believe about your customers/clients/patients/donors? What do they really want? What do they expect? How do they make decisions?

>> What do you believe about the future of your organization? Do you believe it has a strong future? Do you believe you will be part of it?

>> What do you believe most people get wrong?

This exercise can be used in any type of organization by any level of employee. It can lead to a really engaging conversation when done in a group. This can be a great way to start an off-site or retreat weekend. The goal is to get writing and share only once the writing is done.

Investigating your beliefs

Becoming aware of your beliefs is just the first piece of the puzzle. Once you realize you have a belief, you need to investigate further to really understand more about yourself. In investigating your belief, you want to explore where it originally came from, how it was strengthened, and what the impact has been on you. If you believe that your beliefs are the foundation of your behavior, then it isn't a far stretch to see how deeply ingrained some of them can be. The quickest way to start to understand your beliefs is to create a "beliefs box."

Grab a blank piece of paper and re-create the "beliefs boxes" in Figure 4-2. Then think about a specific belief you have: about employees, about customers, about coworkers, about the organization, about your boss. Don't pick something that is verifiably true (like that the accountant's name is Alice or Bill lives in a condo). Write that in box A and then complete the remaining boxes.

A. I believe that . . .	B. When was this belief originally created? How was it created? What happened? How long has it been there?
C. What's the impact of this belief on your actions? How does this shape the way you approach things?	D. If you were to change this belief, what other options do you have? Could you believe the opposite? Could you believe something worse? What would change?

FIGURE 4-2: Beliefs box activity.

Repeat this exercise several times with different beliefs. It can be really powerful to do it around a specific challenge you're having in business or in a relationship at work. This exercise works really well in teams as well, with each person exploring his or her beliefs about specific topics. For example, you could kick off a management workshop with the participants exploring their beliefs about hiring, engagement, employees, and so on. You may find that if you focus on a problem that you're facing, this exercise can help you uncover information that will help you work your way out of the challenge.

TIP

Here are some ideas to get you started:

>> I believe customer service is best when . . .

>> I believe great managers always . . .

>> I believe the most inspirational leaders . . .

>> I believe employees deliver their best work when . . .

>> I believe people should be terminated when . . .

>> I believe people like me best when . . .

>> I believe my strongest contribution to the team is . . .

>> I believe I should stop . . .

>> I believe work is . . .

>> I believe success is . . .

Changing your beliefs

You wouldn't know it by picking up a paper or scrolling through someone's Facebook wall, but you can alter, update, and entirely change the beliefs that guide your actions. This is one of the key principles in managing yourself and can have a profound impact on the culture you help to create at work. As you've completed the exercises in the previous sections, you may have found some places where your beliefs are derailing your efforts. You may even be surprised at a core belief that was impacting you negatively. Either way, it's useful to explore some ways to change limiting beliefs so you can move forward with positively impacting the space around you. Eventually, the new way of thinking becomes the new default.

Here are some steps to follow to change your beliefs about yourself, your work, and your organization:

1. Distill it down.

It's hard to change something in general. Get specific. Focus on a core business issue so that as you think about the steps that follow, you can explore your real thoughts about it. Maybe you are struggling with employee engagement and believe that employees today don't have a strong work ethic. Whatever it is, make sure it's something you have an opinion about and then get ready to dive deeper into exploring the beliefs that guide you.

2. Mine for the beliefs.

Once you have a problem to work on, you need to start digging in to see what beliefs may be at the root of your issue. This is where you start mining for beliefs that may be related. Use the beliefs box exercise (see Figure 4-2) to help you explore it more. You may find that the core belief driving your actions is that you believe "there is no good talent these days." Let's keep exploring this example.

3. Dig deeper.

It's pretty clear that you weren't born believing that the good talent pool has hit a drought. Somewhere along the way, that belief was formed, fed, and allowed to spread. Once you've uncovered that you fundamentally believe that there's no good talent out there, it's time to dig into that and explore where that originated. The easiest way to get started is to fill out a belief box on this specific belief. In our "no good talent" scenario, it may look like Figure 4-3.

A. My belief is . . .	B. When was this belief originally created? How was it created? What happened? How long has it been there?
There is no good talent available in the marketplace today. They all expect fast promotions, quick money, and easy work.	**When I first became a hiring manager, it seemed like we would have the pick of top candidates. We would have hundreds of applicants for just one open position. For the last five years, it seems like it has gotten progressively harder to even get people to show up to an interview.**
C. What's the impact of this belief on your actions? How does this shape the way you approach things?	D. If you were to change this belief, what other options do you have? Could you believe the opposite? Could you believe something worse? What would change?
Since we struggle to find people, it doesn't really matter where we post. So we just keep posting on job boards and classified pages. Our interviews have gotten much shorter because so many of them are awful. Most of the time I don't look forward to interviewing and find it draining on my energy.	**If I believed that there were some great people just waiting to hear from me, I could spend some time making engaging videos about our work culture and posting short articles, images, and infographics on social media about what it's like to work here. I could leverage some of my great talent to help me recruit other people like them. My interviews would start on time, be candidate-focused instead of company-focused, and feel more like a comfortable conversation than an interrogation.**

FIGURE 4-3:
Beliefs box based on a specific belief activity.

4. **Evaluate the value.**

What we believe is not all bad; some beliefs are positive and lead to great things happening. For example, when you believe that your employees have great ideas, or your business partner has your back, or your customers are looking for high-quality offerings, all these lead to positive actions. However, some beliefs don't have positive value. So this step is about exploring whether this belief is adding value. Is it helpful? Useful? Does it contribute to a positive culture? In Figure 4-3, you can see how the belief is not adding value in a positive way. In fact, there's no inherent value in the belief at all. If you believe that there is no good talent for your business, what should you do? Shutter the windows? Cancel the contracts?

5. Draft something new.

If you establish that the belief you hold isn't helpful, it's time to create a new belief to take its place. What would be a beneficial belief? What could lead you toward something positive for yourself and your culture? In the example of finding good talent is difficult (which is a very common and yet inaccurate belief held by business leaders), what would happen if you switched the belief to: "There are some great people out there who are perfect for our team, and we need to find creative ways to reach them as if sending out a Batman signal." This new belief is much more positive, probably more truthful, and provides some insight into what actions would be useful to help solve your leadership issue.

6. Identify core behaviors.

Once you've established a couple of new beliefs to consider, the next step is to start to identify the core behaviors associated with them. If you adopted these new beliefs, what actions support them? How would people who believed those things act? How would they spend their time? Explore the answers to see if there are helpful and useful new behaviors for you to adopt.

Exploring the beliefs behind this book

Throughout this chapter, I explain how what you want, what you value, and what you envision can shape your culture. And that beliefs are at the core from which you create everything. Company cultures vary from organization to organization but in my years of consulting, advising, and developing cultures, I know there are a few things that leaders of the most productive cultures all believe. Over the years, these have become not only my personal beliefs about work, but also the ones I help to develop in managers and leaders at companies around the globe. If you are looking to do something great with your culture, company, and career, I invite you to begin exploring what adopting these beliefs could do for you.

TIP

A few beliefs are embedded into the foundation of this book. Check out the points of the "Company Culture Code" given in Figure 4-4 to guide you through examining your beliefs. Also, keep these core ideas in mind as you read through the other chapters of this book — they serve as an important baseline to changing and improving culture.

Company Culture Code

- Work can be a positive, fulfilling place where every person on the team can contribute in ways beyond his or her job description.
- Culture is mostly about our relationships with each other and work, not perks.
- A culture full of diverse opinions, experiences, strengths, and backgrounds, with psychological safety to share and explore, leads to the best products, offerings, and conditions for engagement.
- Our relationships at work are fundamental to shaping company culture.
- Most leaders and organizations approach culture the wrong way (but not you!).
- We can work our way toward a better work life and future together.
- People are mostly good and want to do good work together (oddly, it's our beliefs that usually get in the way of that happening in most cases).
- Reading, learning, teaching, and reflecting are core components of responsible leadership, robust cultures, and meaningful lives.
- We are responsible for the energy we bring to our interactions, work, and culture, and that energy has a remarkable stronghold on how things play out around us.
- Positive beliefs create better cultures, better teams, stronger engagement, better customer service, better client offerings, more innovative products, and ultimately better financial results.
- Culture is really just a series of beliefs about business, service, quality, relationships, leadership, and community.

FIGURE 4-4:
Exploring beliefs through the Company Culture Code.

Managing Your Time

Everything is moving so fast. Technology has increased the speed at which we communicate. Video has improved the efficacy of our interpersonal communications. Social media has changed the way we make dinner plans. Digital advertising has changed how we make purchasing decisions. With all these improvements comes an obsession with being busy. Listen to people around you greet each other — you'll likely hear a barrage of "so busy" or "I've got so much going on" or "catching up on emails all day." No one talks about the exciting work they're completing or the relationships they're building. We applaud ourselves for getting to inbox zero as if the inbox is the work. We leave our days open to reactive type work that doesn't help us do the important things that drive our work forward.

To create the kind of company cultures and teams that thrive and remain sustainable, you must focus on taking back your time. Where you put your attention is important and impacts the kind of culture you're creating. Are you just running on reactivity and tackling whatever project, meeting, or emergency gets thrown on your schedule? Or are you a master of your own energy? Are you creating space to manage yourself, others, and your culture?

TIP

Think about your relationship with time. Are you constantly too busy? Do you frequently curse time because there isn't enough of it? Do other people own and control your time? Do you feel in control of your schedule? Are you able to effectively get things down in the time frame you want? All of these things speak directly to what you value and have a clear impact on the culture you help to create. Adjust how you spend your time so that it more accurately reflects your values. This is the key to making the most of your time for culture.

Understanding the critical commitments of great managers

Do you ever feel like you're pacing through the day from one emergency to the next? Simply crossing things off your list without any real connection to the work? This is a place that so many managers find themselves in each day. The focus becomes the metrics, the projects, and the status updates. It's easy to forget the people behind all of those things. The relationships you have with the people on your team are the bedrock of your company culture. From those relationships come all things that drive culture: trust, loyalty, communication, collaboration, and values.

Here are some of the most important moments that managers should ensure they carve out space for in a busy schedule:

>> Taking time to train and develop your team

>> Making time to practice active listening when an employee needs to talk, even when you're busy and even when you have a project timeline

>> Taking time to interview job applicants and to follow up (see Chapter 9 for more on hiring)

>> Planning and prepping for weekly staff meetings so that you're focused, engaged, and aware of what's happening on your team

>> Carving out time to prep for one-on-ones with your staff so that you can take a look at the last meeting and recent happenings before you're sitting face-to-face

>> Committing to spending a little time learning and reflecting through reading, attending workshops, or self-reflection

TIP

Most people create lengthy and cumbersome to-do lists that just get transferred from page to page each week. Instead you can create three separate lists to help you stay focused and achieve the most important things. Keep a short-term list for things that will take place this week. Keep a long-term project list with the tasks broken up into smaller chunks that can eventually be added to the short-term list. Keep a third list for things you need to follow up on so you can remember to check in. Then set a calendar reminder to update your lists daily or weekly.

Blocking your time

A popular model for time management is called *time blocking.* In this model, you schedule specific blocks of time to tackle specific types of tasks. Instead of scheduling your day in hour-long meeting blocks, you create specific "zones" throughout your day. For example, you may block 30 minutes each morning for "industry updates" and to read important news and media about your business. You may carve out two hours in the afternoon for one-on-ones. If you're responsible for blogging or creating content, you might carve out a three-hour block once a week for that.

In this model, you would also carve out time for reactive work. Give yourself a few 30-minute blocks each day to check email and voicemail. Schedule time each day to respond to emails and requests. As you learn more about when you're most effective, you can move your reactive work to a less effective time in the day, since you won't need to be at your most creative to respond to emails.

Here are a few ideas for you to think about when blocking out time on your calendar:

>> **Front-line time:** Schedule time to be on the front lines with your team or to visit work locations. Depending on your type of business, this could be daily, weekly, or monthly, but you should dedicate specific time to be where the action happens.

>> **Listening time:** Schedule time to get out into your business to see what is happening, to listen to your team, and to bring culture ideas to the surface. This can be in the form of casual coffee catch-ups or lunches.

>> **Meetings:** Can you dedicate specific blocks of time as "open for meetings" and then force-fit meetings into those time frames each day? Far too many people spend a lot of wasted time in meetings, and this is one way to take back control.

>> **Coaching time:** If you're in a manager role, you should set aside specific one-on-one time each week. Don't leave it up to your employees to hunt you down and put time on your calendar. Block specific chunks of time and make them available for one-on-ones (see Chapter 18 for tips on leading better one-on-ones).

>> **Learning time:** Put in blocks of time daily to learn and grow. Can you block out just 30 minutes a day to focus on upgrading your skills and knowledge? Read industry news. Take an online course. Read a book on a topic you'd like to improve.

>> **Reactive time:** Slot specific times each day to check emails, respond to messages, and answer phone calls. If you're like most managers, this may cause you some anxiety at first, but that's probably just because you have a belief that you need to be available at all times. You'll be amazed at how impactful scheduling reactive time can be in helping you gain control over your time and commitments.

IN THIS CHAPTER

» **Getting hip to the new school of leadership**

» **Becoming a servant leader**

» **Getting the most out of your team**

» **Using coaching as a model to lead your team**

» **Steering clear of toxic leadership behaviors**

Chapter **5**

Honing Your Leadership Skills

More than any other factor, managers influence how people feel about their workplace. The way managers act, build relationships, and organize the team is one of the strongest measurements of your culture. The relationship between employee and manager drives so much of our discretionary effort at work and determines whether we engage or stand back.

Clarity breeds confidence and commitment from your team and is an important step in building a company culture that drives positive results. Your employees, customers, colleagues, and stakeholders are always watching you and judging your actions. When it comes to culture at work, your team is taking their cues from you. So before you work on defining the type of culture you want to shape into existence, it's critical to develop your approach to leadership.

In this chapter, you find out what great managers do to create committed and engaged employees. You'll understand the behaviors, focuses, and intentions of great managers and be able to use that information to assess your own abilities.

Reinventing Leadership for the Modern Workplace

There's this idea that certain people have "natural leadership skills." It's as if in the DNA of great managers, there's something that says "yep, this one is going to be a leader someday." While that thought is ego-boosting to some folks who view themselves as having it, I think it prematurely lets a lot of people off the hook for not being better leaders, supervisors, and managers.

REMEMBER

While we're on the subject of manager and leaders, let's just agree that those terms are interchangeable in the context of this book and in the context of building company culture. Too much is written about the difference between leading and managing. They are the same. We are talking about getting a group of people to deliver some product or service in a specific time frame and at a specific cost in the highest quality way possible. Whether you manage them, lead them, or supervise them — they all mean the same thing and strive to get to a successful result.

The old school model of leadership is crashing and burning, and yet so few organizations are rewriting the game plan. The command-and-control style leadership that was born out of the Industrial Revolution is ineffective in the modern workplace. Despite the trainings, the readings, the podcasts, and the books, too many managers still operate by telling people what to do, monitoring activities, bullying people into compliance, and standing over people's shoulders. It's not working. This method breeds distrust, disengagement, disloyalty, and frankly, a ton of stress and unease.

Let's clarify:

>> It's not your job to have all the answers.

>> It's not your job to tell people what do to.

>> It's not your job to babysit adults at work (and if you have to, then keep reading this book for the solutions you need).

>> It's not your job to make all the choices.

>> It's not your job to remind people who's in charge.

We get promoted to take care of people, to help people find ways to get things done, to help them develop their skills, and to nudge people toward achieving the purpose and mission of the company — not to be authoritarian jerks who use fear, control, and title to force people into submission.

WARNING

Here are some of the behaviors that aren't working anymore:

>> Telling employees what to do and exactly how to do it

>> Believing that people have to respect you because of your title

>> Using words like subordinate and minion

>> Focusing on rules, directives, and policies to control people

>> Making decisions in a vacuum without employee input

>> Communicating poorly and expecting people to still meet expectations

REMEMBER

You are in charge of the way you choose to lead the team. You have options in the way you respond, the way you organize, and the way you support your team. You might have had bad examples of management yourself in the past — but you can change that now. You can choose to be the kind of leader you always wish you had — and, in the process, create a culture worth talking about for your team.

Knowing What Great Leaders Do

You're in. Ready to change the way you manage. Ready to embark on leading for the modern organization. You've turned in your command-and-control police badge and are ready to take the oath to be a better leader. Before we dive in, you have a couple of activities to perform to get clear on what great leaders do.

Remembering your best boss

Make a list of your favorite three bosses (or the most impactful ones). Think about the ones who really made you inspired to come to work every day, the ones who showed they cared, the ones who created a strong culture, and the ones who you most looked up to. Use the following list to journal for a few minutes. Once you are done, you can review the list to start to consider the type of leader you most want to be for your team. Use these questions to get you started:

>> How did they communicate?

>> What did they stand for? What was their focus with you?

>> Where do you see those same behaviors in your own work?

>> What is different?

>> How could you be closer to them?

>> In order for your employees to say the same about you, what do you most need to start, stop, and keep doing?

Testing your management preferences

Keep your best managers in mind. Think about the times when you did your best work on the best teams. Then consider the following questions.

Did you perform best when:

>> You were told each day what to do with little understanding of where things were headed OR you had a really clear vision of what success looked like and then could work collaboratively to achieve those goals?

>> You were given project timelines and guidelines and told to execute OR you had some organizational goals to work toward and initiated projects to help move your company close to them?

>> Your manager was nice and provided feedback only when asked or during scheduled feedback sessions/reviews OR your manager provided frequent real-time feedback closely after things happened?

>> Your manager was positive, friendly, and held his critical feedback back OR your manager was direct, clear, and delivered constructive feedback frequently to help you improve?

>> Your manager was worried about her goals, her bonus, and her career OR your manager was focused on the team succeeding and what each individual needed to help achieve goals?

>> Your manager wasn't focused on your professional development OR your manager actively found opportunities to provide training, development, and learning opportunities as a core part of your work?

>> Your manager was inconsistent, unreliable, and chaotic OR your manager was steady, reliable, and consistent?

>> Your manager rarely dished out positive feedback, public praise, and appreciation OR your manager built positive feedback, public praise, and appreciation into regular meetings and created an environment that celebrated wins?

I'm guessing that you mostly picked the statements that come after the "OR," which is what usually happens in this exercise. Some of the examples are clear winners, like giving praise and feedback. Others, like being direct and clear with constructive feedback, create more dissonance. Many people like when their manager does that for them but then don't think their employees want the same from them as a manager. Why wouldn't they? While we're all different and need different things from our managers, the characteristics we admire and thrive under in our managers tend to be pretty similar.

TIP

Once you have made the list of characteristics you most admire, try asking your employees how you rate in those areas and which ones are most important to them. You can do this one-on-one if you've built up trust or through a quick anonymous survey. You can use the results as a way to focus your efforts in becoming a better manager on the areas they most want more from you.

Serving Your People First

In author Robert Greenleaf's work around leadership he coined the term "servant leadership." It's the idea that the job of the manager is to serve the organization and the people within it and has been evangelized by companies like Zingerman's in Ann Arbor, Michigan. Instead of thinking it is the people in the organization's job to serve the goals, needs, and deadlines of the manager, servant leadership takes the approach that the opposite is true. As a manager, you get paid to help deliver a result, achieve big things, and accomplish key projects. Your ability to do that through people is why you were chosen for your role. If you've decided to leave behind the command-and-control method of leadership, then you know there must be a new belief at the core of the new way to lead. There is. It's that the job of managers is to serve the people that report to them.

When managers approach employee concerns like they would those of a customer, client, or patient, the positive shock waves to your culture are impactful. When the team knows that the manager has their back, it makes it easier for them to use discretionary effort in their work. It improves service. But in most organizations it works the other way around. Managers sit at the top and demand that employees bend to their needs. They act is if the employee is there to serve their wishes, make them happy, and get them what's required.

Making your employees your core customer

To become a service-oriented manager, consider two types of customers: employee customers and company customers. What I mean by that is, as a manager, your main customer is your employee. Your employee's customer is the outside company customer. A manager's goal should be to serve the employee customer first because employees will respond positively to that behavior and will in turn apply that same attention to the company customer, making it a win-win.

When I consult with companies on creating a better customer culture, the first place to look for clues about what's going wrong is with how managers treat employees. How can you expect employees to treat customers better than they're being treated?

In organizations with a strong service culture, you can see the manager doing things daily to care for the employees the same as they would expect of a customer. The manager goes out of his way to solve the concerns of his team. He asks how the employee is doing, how he can help, and checks in on their experiences at work.

Bringing the energy to serve

It's a tough job to treat your employees like customers every day, but then, so is actually taking care of paying customers every day. As a manager, your job is to supply the energy it takes to keep the organization buzzing. You don't get to have bad days that leave the team in a slump and then expect them to turn around and deliver for customers. For more about managing your energy, see Chapter 4.

REMEMBER

Managers that know how to manage their energy well are constantly surveying themselves to monitor themselves. Before walking into meetings, they take note of their own energy and mood in order to more positively impact the people around them. When arriving at work in the morning, they take a few minutes to check in on their attitude and energy before interacting with the team in order to create a ripple of great energy.

Solving employee complaints

If you treat your employees as if they're the main customer of your management team, then you have to have a system in place to address their complaints and concerns. Too many organizations leave this to chance without a clear model, but you should adopt the same process you use for customers. Teach your managers to listen more fully to the needs of their employees. To do this, they should let the employee finish speaking and then repeat what they've just heard to ensure understanding and show that they were listening completely without judgment. Similarly, managers should focus on finding ways to say "yes" to employee requests or at least negotiate some level of a win–win situation. This is basic customer service and should be part of your approach to company culture too.

Managing for Success

Being a great manager also means getting a few basics in place to help you define success, reframe your efforts to help your team achieve success, and then appreciate the successes along the way. It starts with a clear vision for your team, projects, and department so that people know what they are aiming for. This extends into finding ways to help your team achieve that success before finally being the kind of manager who appreciates the effort that goes into achieving success.

Creating a clear vision

The first job of any manager is to have a clear vision, one that defines exactly what success looks like. Whether you are leading a department, a shift, a division, a whole country, or just a project, starting with a clear vision is the best way to create expectations around the behavior and norms that become your culture. It's one of the most important parts of being a great leader and one of the most commonly overlooked areas for managers, yet creates a profound impact when done well.

REMEMBER

Your employees are much more likely to help you get to where you want to be if they know where that is in the first place. For all the talk about purpose that exists in the world, writing and sharing a clear vision is the first step in giving your organization, department, and team an inspiring purpose to work toward. For more on creating a vision, see Chapter 6.

Helping your team get A's

You can remember it, right? The feeling of having your paper graded and returned with simply an overall score. No feedback. No ideas for improvement. No idea what to do next time. But you may also remember those teachers who focused on helping you get the "A." You know the difference between someone judging your abilities and someone actively working at helping you succeed.

Great managers are the same as great teachers — they help their team get the "A." Mediocre managers focus on grading the paper. If your employees succeed, then so does your organization, department, and project. Why wouldn't you change your approach to helping them win instead of simply giving them a score?

Here are some simple ways to help your team:

>> Spend time with them at the start and end of projects to make sure they have a plan that will enable them to succeed in the goal.

>> Ask questions about how they plan to get something done, what their next steps are, how they'll communicate it, and where you can help.

>> When critical communications or milestones are due, make time to check in with them and help where needed.

Appreciating even the basics

The best managers are appreciative and say thanks — a lot. They create an environment where people feel like their work is valued, where their effort makes a difference, and where contributions are praised and rewarded. This isn't about creating a Pollyanna-esque vibe either. It's about recognizing the fact that we do our best work when people are watching and when people appreciate those efforts. Find ways to publicly praise the great work the people on your team are doing. Take time during your regular team meetings to highlight achievements on the team. In one-on-one meetings, express your appreciation for the successes of the employee.

Happiness at work matters. People get stuck on engagement, but it seems ignorant to ignore that happy people like to do all kinds of things better — and if you do the rest of the things recommended in this book, you'll have set up the systems you need to ensure that productivity and service and operations keep rocking as well. For more ideas on creating an appreciative culture, see Chapter 12.

Coaching for Performance

Serving the team takes many forms. One of them is being a really good performance coach. Employees in strong cultures want to grow, succeed, and develop their skills. If you look back at the managers you most loved working with, I'd imagine that they helped you with those things as well. Developing the mindset of a performance coach is critical to being the kind of manager who guides your team positively while boosting company culture.

Thinking like a coach

Coaches don't focus on giving nice or even negative feedback; they focus on telling people what they need to hear in a way that they can hear it so that employees can improve. Sports coaches are a good place to look for a comparison. They don't sugarcoat their feedback or give feedback in generalities. They are specific, clear, and performance-focused.

Providing useful feedback

REMEMBER

The number one job of a performance coach is to give useful feedback. If a coach gives a player unclear, vague, or confusing feedback or provides too much information, that feedback isn't useful because the player can't use it to improve. Improvement is the goal — specific improvement in particular.

Useful feedback is the same whether you're giving positive feedback about what's done well or constructive feedback about how to improve. Positive feedback isn't about praise and making people feel good. It's about defining what success looks like so your employee can keep delivering it. Change your thinking if you're one of those old school managers who thinks positive feedback is about being happy; it's not. It's about setting standards and creating a model for success.

Improving the quality and quantity of the feedback you provide will pay you back in multiples.

Useful feedback has the following three characteristics: specific, action-focused, and solution-oriented.

Specific

Useful feedback isn't general — it's specific. Instead of saying "good job," useful feedback says, "The way you addressed that customer's concerns by listening fully before responding really showed empathy." Instead of "let's improve your communication," useful feedback says, "Your email about the project update was missing some critical information like the new dates for launch and changes to the marketing plan."

Action-focused

For feedback to be useful, it needs to be about actions the person can or did take, not about them as person. By focusing on the actions, you give your employee something to do differently instead of trying to be different. The feedback should outline what specifically worked or didn't work.

Solution-oriented

WARNING

Far too many managers think they're giving constructive feedback when really they're just criticizing their employees' efforts — who are now a whole lot less likely to make efforts in the future. You can even see the mistake in the core foundation of the word. Constructive is based on the word construct, which means to build. If your feedback is just critical, without solutions and ideas for future improvement, then you aren't giving the employee anything to build from.

Uncovering the Seven Sins of Toxic Leadership

When it comes to leadership and managing others, it's easy to fall into some of the common traps. Running a business today requires a lot of effort, so it makes sense that sometimes it's easy to fall prey to cutting corners, with behaviors that ultimately end up creating a toxic environment and hurting your culture. It's easy to miss the signs that the leadership is starting to have a negative impact on the culture until it's done irrevocable damage.

WARNING

To help you remember to steer clear of them, here's a list of the top sins of toxic leadership.

1. **Unaware of energy:** Toxic leaders don't take time to notice how their energy impacts the people around them. They march around the building with negative energy, low energy, or frenetic energy without taking into account how they alter the space when they enter it.

2. **Abuse of power:** Toxic leaders talk like dictators. They treat employees like the employees have to do whatever the leader says. These leaders forget that employees have choices when it comes to investing their discretionary effort with their positive energy, their best ideas, their actual presence, their recommendations, and their social networks.

3. **Creating a vacuum:** Toxic leaders suck the energy out of ideas, thoughts, concerns, and opinions. This is largely due to not having great listening skills and not giving employees room to contribute. It happens because toxic managers think their job is to be right versus being helpful.

4. **Inconsistency:** Toxic leaders are all over the place. Employees don't know what to expect from them. One day they're Dr. Jekyll and the next day they're Mr. Hyde. If the quality of your meeting is dictated by your mood, then you may be a toxic manager. When inconsistency rears its head, employees tend to disengage and play it safe to protect from being the victim of today's bad attitude.

5. **Letting people fail:** One of the biggest sins of toxic managers is letting people fail when they could have prevented it. I'm not suggesting that it's your job (or even productive) to stop employees from making mistakes. A lot can be learned by trying things, failing, picking up the lessons, and using that to improve. But if you see that failure is looming and it may cost them their job, then you need to step in. If failure is evident and you can provide useful feedback, then you need to step in. Managers shouldn't have the right to say "I told you so" when employees fail. Your job is to serve them, help them, and assist them in getting "A's."

6. **Gossiping:** Toxic managers create, spread, and otherwise monger gossip. If your goal is to serve the team, then gossiping just has no place. It crushes trust, ruins relationships, and diminishes your ability to do your job. A surefire way to self-destruct your culture is for you to take part in spreading gossip. This extends beyond your team to other departments, leaders, and the company as well.

7. **Taking credit:** Toxic managers take the credit and don't share it. They celebrate themselves in the spotlight instead of highlighting the efforts of their team and the people on it. By taking credit for your team's accomplishments, you're essentially saying that the work your employees did doesn't matter here. It sends the message to your team that you're the star and you're the one who's going to win, not them. Focus instead on being a servant leader who puts the team in the spotlight.

REMEMBER

Keep in mind that, if you are someone who manages other managers or has influence over other managers in your organization, it is not only your job to be a role model and example to emulate, but to also set the standard and expectation for the people who report to you. As you witness toxic management behaviors, you have to call them out and reset expectations. The same goes for when you see managers doing great management things as well. Appreciation should be shown to everyone in the organization — and success in your managers should be celebrated often.

3

Designing Your Culture for Maximum Impact

IN THIS CHAPTER

» Explaining the distinction between mission and vision

» Knowing why you need an organizational mission

» Writing your own inspiring mission statement

» Finding ways to bring your mission to life

» Uncovering the power of vision

» Crafting your company's vision of success

Chapter **6**

Maximizing Your Impact with Mission and Vision

When most people think of the basics for company culture, they usually find the mission statement recommendation not far behind. It makes sense, right? Part of organizing a group of people is giving them a common cause, a shared direction, and strong purpose. Somewhere along the way, vision statements were added to the mix, and the whole thing got confusing.

This chapter gives you a road map for creating and using a mission statement. I also discuss how vision statements come into view and how to harness their power. By following the outline in this chapter, you will actually start to improve your culture even before you finish the mission statement by bringing people together, increasing communication, and working as a group to help shape these important company culture tools.

Clarifying the Difference between Mission and Vision

What exactly is a mission of your organization? Do you need one? How is it different from a vision? How do they work together? Aren't they both just a bunch of words on a website to make our customers feel good about working with us?

Done correctly, the difference between the two is clear and compelling. Done poorly, they become an easily forgotten bullet point in the employee handbook covered during the new hire orientation and then rolled out once a year during an executive keynote at the company holiday party. Why is it so hard to get right? What exactly is the difference?

REMEMBER

You need both a mission statement and a vision statement to build a great culture full of engaged, informed, and focused people working together to achieve something special. The "statements" are just the written, documented version of your mission and vision — so we will use the terms "mission" and "mission statement" and "vision" and "vision statement" interchangeably from here on out. Here's a summary of the differences between the two:

Mission statement	Vision statement
Informs why	Describes what
Makes a clarifying statement about the business focus	Provides a clear and inspiring image about a desired future
Explains why your company exists	Describes exactly what success looks like at a specific point in time
Points to a destination that a company will strive toward	Acts like a GPS to get to that destination in the future
Could be written on a T-shirt	Needs to be written like a script

Understanding the Real Purpose of an Organizational Mission

As organizations got bigger and we moved from mostly working in factories or working in smaller businesses to working in bigger organizations and brands, it became imperative to share the big goals of the organization, to be able to shine a light on the path ahead, and to provide context for why the company existed in the first place. Savvy business leaders did this with the mission statement set out to provide all those things.

Five reasons you need a compelling mission statement

Before we jump into exactly how to craft your mission statement, let's list some specific reasons you need a well-crafted mission statement.

» **It keeps the team focused on the horizon and provides direction.** As people join the team, it becomes easy for new markets, new opportunities, new ideas, and new leaders to derail the organization without a clear mission.

» **It acts as the magnetic pull in your organizational compass to help center, ground, and orient during difficult times.**

» **It provides a framework for decision-making.** Is it mission-worthy? This helps with delegation. Treat your mission like the compass on a map — always helping to redirect the journey and ensure your efforts are pointed in the right direction.

» **It provides a baseline for alignment.** Without a mission statement, it's easy to spend a lot of time talking about whether something "fits" with the organizational goals. The arguments and discussions become about the merit of the idea and lose the focus on helping the company in its super objective. The mission statement helps to align activities.

» **It acts as a rudder when dealing with change.** As the market, conditions, and environment change, the organization's initiatives and actions need to shift. Having a clear mission that employees have bought into makes it easier to deal with change as it becomes necessary.

Distinguishing a good mission statement from a bad one

But then things got off-traffic. These days, mission statements get a bad rap. They've been wordsmithed to death, dumbed down to the point of making them ineffective and unclear, and cleverly crafted to create a pleasant brand statement that doesn't really say anything and doesn't provide any value to the organization's employees. Some of them focus only on shareholder value or being the marketplace darling. How inspiring or clarifying are the following mission statements?

> "Big Shot Co. is focused on observing the highest standards while maximizing shareholder value and becoming the number one provider in the marketplace."

> "We will become the leaders in all of the markets we serve while benefiting our customers, team, and shareholders."

"We aim for profitable and consistent growth through best-in-class customer service, quality, and commitment."

"To nourish the soul of our customers, our community, and the world one biscotti at a time."

These four mission statements don't really do much to tell you about the path that the organization is on at all. Sentences filled with platitudes won't do much to propel your culture, team, or organization forward. Overly flowery language also won't help anyone get a clear message. Bad mission statements happen to good companies all the time. It's largely because the mission statement becomes something that the marketing department or human resources team has been tasked with wordsmithing to put on a website. There are good intentions about the mission helping to focus the team and provide direction — but they get written, they get watered down, and then they get forgotten.

So, what should an organizational mission statement say?

Your mission statement can be a powerful tool in helping to shape your company culture. A strong mission statement is about providing direction and focus for the organization and the people working within it. It's about describing the purpose of the company in clear language that everyone understands. This isn't some PR puff piece to pop on the "About Us" page of your company website. It should answer the questions:

>> What do we do?

>> Why do we do it?

>> Whom are we doing it for?

REMEMBER

Mission statements are meant to be aspirational and provide guidance toward something bigger. It should be something that can never really be fully achieved but establishes what you're always working toward. The real purpose of the mission statement is not some marketing speak on the website to attract ideal customers (though an authentically crafted one can do just that). The real purpose is to give a shared understanding and purpose to the people within the organization. The mission statement should provide direction for decision-making and for planning, and it should provide a clear purpose. It should answer the question, "Why are we doing all the things we are doing in the first place?" A meaningful mission statement should be enduring and inspirational for the long haul. It doesn't define a specific place or clear idea of success but instead provides the inspiration and purpose for it all.

To build a positive culture, you need a strong mission statement that galvanizes the team, provides meaning to the work, and gives a clear sense of direction.

Crafting a Clear and Inspirational Mission Statement

Looking at the blinking cursor on your computer screen while trying to write "the" mission statement that perfectly wraps up your organizational core can be pretty daunting. It's probably why so many of them end up sounding generic and all-encompassing. After all, it's much easier to say "We are the best maker of things in all the places for all the people" than it is to really get specific about why your organization exists. It doesn't have to be this way. Creating a clear and inspirational mission statement is a great activity to do as a group and can help to further define your culture by giving your team a chance to work together on this important company tool.

Starting with stories

Most organizations have stories to tell — stories about times when things went well, stories about times when they didn't go well, stories about the future. These are the stories that employees tell to new employees when they ask why things are done a certain way. These are the tales that get shared when people talk about "the good old days." It's the one about what sparked a move into a new market or a new product or even the origin of the company in general. Your company has stories — and uncovering them can be the secret to a stronger culture and better mission statement.

REMEMBER

A useful way to get started on working on your mission statement is to get a group of people together and have them start gathering stories. During this phase in creating your mission statement, don't worry about getting the words right or starting to distill a specific type of message. Your group is just going to explore some of the stories that currently exist. You should not aim to get down to the final mission statement in this early meeting. When I work with companies on creating a mission statement, it takes several rounds (or a multi-day retreat) to get it just right — so don't worry about rushing through the process in a 60-minute meeting.

TIP

A story-gathering workshop will take an hour or two and is best led by a facilitator who is currently part of the team. Pick someone who is adept at keeping the conversation moving forward while not inserting much of his or her own agenda. Here's exactly what to do to lead a story-gathering workshop:

1. **Split your group into small teams of three or four people.**

   Try to get a good mix of levels, experience, backgrounds, and roles in each group. It's often helpful to organize them ahead of time, as people tend to stick with others they already work with frequently.

2. **Tell them that you're going to do a few rounds of storytelling around specific prompts.**

   Give each person five minutes to respond, and then call time to move to the next person to share a story around the same prompt.

   Here are some prompts you can use:

   - What does it look like when we are successfully delivering on our promise?

   - What would it look like if we were achieving our ultimate potential as an organization?

   - What is happening when you are feeling totally aligned personally and professionally with the direction of the company?

3. **If someone can't come up with a story around a prompt, then simply have the person make one up in response.**

4. **Ask other people to write down the main points of each story on note cards or large post-it pads.**

5. **Once everyone has gone, post the notes on the wall.**

   - Give each person a marker or highlighter asking them to circle anything they see on other pages that they also wrote down in their notes. They are looking for repeats, themes, and common stories.

   - Then ask them to underline any instance where specific people or groups are mentioned. For example, do you see multiple mentions of creating great experiences for children? Are there several stories about improving the patient experience through empathy? Start to look for clues around "who" you are serving. Underline those instances to use later.

   - Next, draw a box around specific actions that your company or the people in it were taking. Do you see words like *solving, collaborating, communicating,* or *building?*

   - Finally, make note of any specific impact mentioned by your story group. Do you see instances of reduced stress, more college degrees, happier communities, more peace of mind, or greater returns? Pick the areas that clearly identify the impact of your company.

6. **Now, organize all the information you've collected into something you can use for the next phase of the process.**

   Using a whiteboard, shared document, or large paper, re-create the chart shown in Figure 6-1.

Category	Responses from the Story Group
Our Themes *What did we see repeated in our stories?*	
Our Customers/Clients *Who did we serve? Where?*	
Our Work *What actions do we take? What are we actually doing? How?*	
Our Impact *What improved or changed because we took those actions with those people? What specific outcomes did we deliver?*	

FIGURE 6-1: Sample story-gathering workshop outcome chart.

Getting clear on the objectives

Now that you've gathered stories about your organization, the next step in your mission-crafting adventure is to clarify the organization's objectives. In this activity, you'll see some similar things to the previous exercise, but you'll start distilling them into clearer ideas and statements. You can gather the same group of people, a new group of people, or a mixture of both for this exercise. This is a great activity to do in an off-site location to create a different energy and to highlight how important this activity is to the organization. You should plan on spending at least three hours on this work but can also spend a few days working through these ideas together.

When the group meets, you will be talking about the stories and learnings from the earlier sessions and start to get specific about what these things mean. You will work together to uncover the answers to the following questions:

>> **What do we do?** Clearly define the service, commodity, or product that your organization produces and is committed to consistently improving or working toward. This question should fit any organization whether nonprofit, for-profit, retail, manufacturing, agency, or governmental. You can also ask this question specifically of a department, division, or team.

>> **How do we do it?** Now that you know what you do, explore the manner in which you do it. Is the focus on a specific type of remarkable experience? With top-notch current technology? With creative and modern design touches? Explore the ways in which you achieve what you do.

» **Why do we improve the marketplace, our constituents, or our consumers?** In other words, what is better because you exist? What is the impact and outcome you provide to others? Do you increase revenue for others? Do you improve quality of life? Do you help customers achieve something they really want? Do you keep them safer? Why does all of that matter? Why do you care about improving it in that way? Why does the world need it?

» **Whom do we do it for?** Figure out to whom this is all happening. Do you have ideal customers? Do you help patients in New Jersey, bakers in Athens, families in Des Moines? Is your aim small businesses in Boise? Two responses are likely to happen with this question. First, you may say, "We are for everyone everywhere." Then you may say, "We don't want to limit ourselves to [insert location]."

Looking at the first response, you can't be for everyone everywhere and still be able to clearly define your mission. Dig deeper by asking questions like, "Who gets the most value out of what we do?" or, "Who is most likely to need this type of service?" Even big retailers narrow down the "whom do we do it for" question. Think of Patagonia or REI — they aren't for homebodies who never want to leave the house. So while they may be open for business for anyone who strolls through the doors to buy a tent and sleeping bag, they aim their mission at something more specific. You should too.

WARNING

Now let's deal with the second statement about not wanting to limit yourself. If your mission really is to put your insurance plans in businesses across Boise, then that's a noble and great cause. It will also provide a different focus and energy than if you said you want your insurance plan in organizations in 50 countries. If you don't define the difference, then you risk spending a lot of time rudderless later. Your team becomes confused and unsure about where this is all headed. Get specific.

» **Which values do we bring?** Define the specific value you bring. This is where a lot of companies phone it in with generic flowery messages about providing opportunity or improving the lives of others without a lot of clarity around what it means.

» **Who is on our team?** In other words, what types of people work for your organization? Consider the common theme among the people you enjoy working with the most and who do the best work in your company. Who best represents what your company is all about? Think about how you want the people at your company to be known — are they creative risk-takers who push boundaries or is the company full of stable and steady hands? This answer is going to be different for every organization, and there isn't really a wrong answer except for a generic one that doesn't help define the people on your team.

It's time again to organize all the information you've collected into something you can use for the next phase of the process. Using a whiteboard, shared document, or large paper, re-create the table in Figure 6-2.

Category	Responses from the Objective Group	Themes and Common Ideas
What do we do?		
How do we do it?		
Why do we improve the marketplace, our constituents, or our consumers?		
Whom do we do it for?		
Which values do we bring?		
Who is on our team?		

FIGURE 6-2: Sample objective-clarifying workshop outcome chart.

Once this is completed, start to distill and clarify the output. Do you see common themes? You'll notice a theme because ideas will start to sound alike or be focused on the same values or ideas. Someone said families and another said children. Can you agree on a common goal there to simplify things? Did someone say you roast coffee, brew tea, and pour kombucha while someone else said you provide quality drinks? Can those be combined? Begin to combine and organize without losing specificity around the items on the right-hand side of the column.

Constructing the mission statement

It's time to organize all the ideas from the workshop activities described earlier in this chapter into a simple and usable mission statement.

REMEMBER

Remember, the mission statement should answer three specific questions:

>> What do we do?

>> Why do we do it?

>> Whom are we doing it for?

This activity can be done in a group but should be limited to a smaller number than the workshop activities. By working together on this, you start to improve the culture by bringing your team together to start working on something important as a team. This is a chance to listen, to increase empathy through relationship-building, and to create a shared experience around the company mission statement. Those activities are aimed at generating lots of ideas, while writing the mission statement is about refining and clarifying, which is why a smaller, more decisive group should be used. This can also be a solo effort that is then shared with a smaller group. Look at all the information from the story and objective workshops — there are likely several themes that have been identified. Using those themes, organize three to five versions of the following statement:

"We're doing (what), for (whom), because (why)."

For example, here are some clear and well-defined mission statements:

>> We build the best products available for an active lifestyle while leaving the environment and community in a better place than we found them because we believe you can provide growth and opportunity while still being responsible and contributing to a better planet.

>> To help underserved high school students in Los Angeles achieve the dream of attending college through afterschool programming, mentoring, and community leadership.

>> To provide designer footwear at a remarkable price, while creating jobs and opportunity for growth in rural communities.

>> To provide the highest quality healthcare so patients recommend to their family and friends, physicians feel proud of providing, insurers are confident in funding, and employees are engaged in providing because we believe that creates a positive healthcare organization with longevity and a sense of community.

>> We develop technology for local restaurants to grow their online business and connect with their customers so they can compete with big, global food brands because we believe that they are the fuel for our local communities and economies.

WARNING

Don't get caught up in making this something that looks pretty on your website or sounds good to consumers. Your mission statement needs to be helpful, set direction, and create purpose for the people who work in your organization. You can work on your tagline or branding statements in another session.

Testing your mission statement

Once you have your mission statement in a good place using the process from the preceding section, you want to put it on its feet to see if it has lasting power and describes a clear enough path ahead. Does it actually do its intended job of helping to provide purpose, direction, and aim for your organization? Does it really act as a compass for you, your team, and the organization? Use the following questions as prompts and begin sharing your new mission statement around the organization. You can meet with different people in the organization, share the mission statement, and then ask them to respond to these questions:

» Could your competitors use this same exact mission statement?

» Would an employee be able to tell the difference between your mission statement and those of your four closest competitors?

» Does the statement distinguish your company from others? Be thoughtful about language and defining what something means. If you decide that your company is dedicated to security, does that mean that your products are secure or that you make your customers feel secure or that your company is symbolic of what security means? Go around the table and get people talking about what the words actually mean — what would it look like if "we secure"? How many ideas come from that? Are they the right ideas or should they be more specific?

» Would a 12-year-old understand the statement well enough to know what you do and whom you do it for? This is an overlooked part of communication that causes confusion. Your mission statement should be clear enough that it is easily understood. It should be free of jargon, flowery words, and ambiguous sentiments. By giving it the 12-year-old test, you can ensure that your mission statement is meaningful, impactful, and clearly stated.

» Does the mission statement clearly define what you do, even if it pushes you to think slightly out of the box about what business you're really in? For example, if you're a bakery that focuses on southern biscuits, maybe your mission statement expands beyond "we sell biscuits" to "we serve comfort and nostalgia for memories of home." Or if you're a dog-walking company, you might expand from "we take the dogs out" to "we provide dogs and dog owners with peace of mind and a sense of fun."

Bringing Your Mission to Life

I was recently speaking about company culture at a major conference, and I asked the attendees if they were in a leadership role. Nearly the entire audience raised their hands. I then asked them to raise their hands if culture was important to them, their team, and the success of their organization or department. Again, most of the hands went up. Then I asked how many of them had a company mission statement. This time about 75 percent of the hands stayed up. Finally, I asked, "How many of you know and could recite your company mission statement?" One person out of 200 kept her hand up — and she worked in the human resources department. She later told me she was the one that wrote the mission statement, which is why she remembered it in the first place.

This set off alarm bells for me for two reasons. The first is that most company mission statements are generic, boring, and don't help truly define purpose and direction, so they're easy to forget in our day-to-day work. The second is that the mission statement hasn't been incorporated into the company culture in meaningful ways. It's important to find ways to make your mission statement a core part of your normal operations.

If you're writing your mission statement for the first time (or making some edits to an existing one based on the ideas in this book), then it's important that you create a plan for launching it. Following the steps presented in this chapter will help you create a stronger, more compelling mission statement. Depending on the size of your organization and the size of the groups involved in workshopping your mission statement, there will likely still be a lot of people who haven't been part of the process. It's easy at this point to start to feel like it's old news because you've been working on it for a bit. But don't lose the steam! You want to make sure your mission statement makes its way to the people in your organization in a meaningful and impactful way.

The mission statement can be a driver in improving your culture when done well so take the time to get it right. The mission statement will help provide purpose, structure, direction, and meaning to the work your team does, which improves the culture by creating stronger engagement at work.

TIP

Here are a handful of ideas for launching your mission statement:

>> **All-hands meeting:** If your company has monthly or quarterly all-hands, town-hall style meetings, that's a perfect time to announce the new mission statement.

>> **Launch events:** If you don't have any standard group meetings, then scheduling a few lunch-and-learn type sessions can be an effective way to gather small groups at your company to share the news. Order some pizza, gather people in a few sessions, and share the updates.

>> **Annual holiday or summer party:** If your mission statement work happens to be around the holiday season or summertime, consider scheduling a company event to celebrate and announce the new mission statement.

>> **Video:** If your company has a large number of remote employees, think about how to incorporate them via video and live stream.

>> **Mission month:** A really fun way to celebrate the minting of a new mission statement is to dedicate the launch month as "mission month." Announce the mission at the start of the month and then have an entire month of weekly programming around the new mission.

Looking into Your Future Vision

What does the future look like in four years if your company has been successful? Do you have a clear answer to that question? Is the answer so clear that you will actually know when you've made it to that place? If you asked every employee in your organization what success looks like for the company in four years, would you get the same answer? Would everyone have the same shared vision?

How many times have you started a project, hired a new person, or begun a new initiative without a clear idea of what it would look like if everything and everyone was successful? Okay, okay. Maybe *you* had a clear idea — but how often was there a shared vision of future success so clear that everyone could agree when you got there?

While a lot of big organizations have a vision plastered somewhere on their website or buried deep in the handbook, very few have a vision written in such a way that everyone understands exactly where things are headed and what it will look like when they get there. The best company visions act as a GPS — defining a specific destination at a specific time for the company. They are crafted in a way that is easy and clear to understand and that leaves little room for confusion about where that place is and what's happening once you get there.

Imagine you put three people on your team in a car and they left your building, then pulled up to a four-way stop with the goal of continuing from that stop sign in a way that moves your company forward; would they all be able to unanimously decide to continue straight, go left, or go right? Any of those choices may be great choices depending on where they need to be by a certain time. This type of "where are we going" situation happens every day in meetings, in conversations, and in big decisions at your company. Without a clear and specific idea about where things are headed, it takes a lot of effort to determine which option is right. A vision statement provides that clarity. The roads may have detours and potholes, but a clear destination makes it easy to navigate and still arrive at the desired spot.

Creating a vision in the way outlined in this book will help to align your team with common direction. It will allow people to have some autonomy in their work by keeping everyone rowing in the same direction.

Drafting Your Organizational Vision

The vision you create has a specific deadline and is something you can actually achieve. The organizational vision is often best done alone or in a very small group of founders because this group can really speak to what they are trying to create or what they set out to create. In fact, if more than one person is involved, you're better off working alone and then coming back together to share notes so that it doesn't become a process of debate and consensus too early. The vision should be meaningful to the leader and about the future goals you have for your team or organization rather than something crowdsourced and curated.

Deciding on a time frame

To get started with your vision, you have to pick a specific place in the future to describe. For most groups, a time leap of five years will give you solid results. If you're working on a very small team, you can even write one for two years out. I don't recommend going much shorter than that for an organizational vision, as doing so doesn't give you much of a runway.

TIP

If you decide to create a project-based vision or department vision, you can easily do that for a shorter time frame with much success. This doesn't mean you should take a break from creating the overall company vision because really all projects and departments will need that to determine direction.

Getting clear on the wins

Before you start drafting your vision, you want to set out a few specific wins that matter to you. The easiest way to do this is to imagine that future date from whatever end date you chose and then pick a few things that define success within that time frame. Basically, what are some goals that would be good wins for your organization? For example, if you're a wedding photography business, you may have a list that looks like this:

>> Booked for six events a month

>> Conversion rate from interested to booked is 60 percent

>> Being interviewed quarterly by wedding industry magazines and blogs

>> Two working photographers, one coordinator, and one editor

>> Each gig leads to at least one spin-off gig

In this section, you're creating the bones of your vision so you can fill in more details in the next step. Don't skip this part, because doing so will make it harder to get the ideas flowing in the next section.

Drafting your vision

To get started with your vision writing:

1. **Sit down, grab a journal/some paper and pen, put a timer on for 20 minutes, start writing, and don't stop until the timer goes off.**

TIP

   If you decide to do this on a computer, don't use the backspace or delete button during your initial drafting phase. Leave everything you type and just keep adding to it. You can edit, refine, and perfect in the next stage.

2. **Write the date you picked in the first step on the top of the page, along with the word "Draft" to help remind you that this is just a trial run.**

   This whole visioning thing has a way of creating an existential crisis for many folks in your position.

3. **Pretend you're in a hot air balloon floating above your business.**

   Describe what you see and hear in detail as if you're watching it actually happen. Use descriptive words and phrases to define what your customers are saying and doing, how your employees are interacting, what's happening in the business each day. This should be done with enough detail that if someone else was reading it at that date in the future, they would recognize it as what was happening in your company.

As you work on writing all of that into one documented draft of your vision, consider the following questions to help expand your vision more fully:

>> What do you want for yourself, your employees, your customers, and your community?

>> How big is your team? Do you have new locations?

>> What can you do to enrich and improve the lives of your employees and customers? How do you contribute to them?

>> What type of people work with you? Where did you find them? How do they act? How do they work?

>> What is the image of your business? What perception do customers, partners, employees, and the public have of your company? What's the desired image? What do industry insiders, the press, the community, or your suppliers say about you?

>> What's the general (or specific) nature of your products, services, or offerings? What goes into that? How do you deliver on this?

>> What is the level of service you provide? It's easy to say "the best service possible" or "deliver a world class experience," but it's another thing to get very specific about what that looks like. If you were to take a picture of great service, what would be included in that scene?

>> What is the role of leadership? How do managers act in your company? What do they say? What matters? What type of relationship do you/managers have with your/their team?

>> What is different about you from your competitors? What do you do better, different, faster?

>> How do you use technology, capital, products, processes, marketing, and relationships in your business?

>> How does your team make decisions? What's it like to work there each day?

Making edits to your vision

Once you have your first draft done, give yourself a little space from it — say two days minimum. Then come back and read it to yourself. What is exciting? What is missing? What needs more clarity or detail? What doesn't sound that important anymore?

TIP

If you wrote the original version on paper, then go ahead and move the next draft to a computer. If you already have a digital version, then copy and paste the original so you can work on the drafts without editing the original version, which you may want to go back to later.

TIP

A few general tips as you edit and refine:

>> Include more detail than you think is necessary. A company with 30 employees in one office is a very different place than a company with 300 employees in five offices across the county.

>> Look for generic words like "a lot of energy" or "passion" or "serious commitment." If you see something like that, make sure to ask yourself (and then define) exactly how much is a lot? What does that look like in action? What does a serious commitment mean? How will you know it when you see it?

>> Organize it into sections if it's helpful. Often people will create sections like "our service," "our employees," "our community," "our leaders," "our finances," and "our marketing" to help them add enough detail in the areas that matter most. Create your own sections.

>> Give yourself a couple of rounds of edits and then get ready to share it with someone else in your organization.

Sharing your vision for feedback

At some point, once you've drafted and redrafted a few times, you want to share your vision with someone else to get feedback. It will be a little scary, and you may put it off longer than you should for fear of being judged or rejected — but do it anyway. In most cases, the vision you outlined will get other people thinking and excited about what's next.

In this round, don't get too specific with your feedback request. Simply ask people how it sits with them, what they remembered, what they liked best, and what areas needed more information or weren't clear. Sometimes, simply asking people to tell you what they think the vision is in their words is a helpful way to begin to understand what sticks, what was clear enough, and what may need more information. You'll use all this information to decide on a final version of your draft before sharing it with your organization.

Finalizing the vision

Once you have collected all the feedback, reviewed all the ideas, and had more time to think about what you really want to create — it is time to make it final. Using all the information and feedback, spend some time to rework it to the point that it is clear and inspiring. You should end up with a document that can be shared around the organization and used throughout your company systems.

Sharing Your Vision

There are many ways you can approach sharing the new vision — and depending on the size of your organization, you might choose several options from the list in the "Bringing Your Mission to Life" section of this chapter. Before we get to that, some of the things that might come up for your employees once you start sharing the vision is a big focus on the "how" the vision will be achieved. Keep in mind that the vision is about describing the "what" and the "where" — it's totally okay to not know exactly "how."

By leaving room for the employees to help determine the how, you create space for engagement, involvement, and inclusion — all things that can also help boost your culture.

Living Your Vision

Once you've created a vision, it's important that you start to share it in the organization to start moving people toward achieving it. After all, you can't expect people to help navigate the organization in a specific direction if they don't know where that is.

Here are some ideas for living your vision in your organization:

>> **Attracting great talent:** Include your vision as a link with your job postings to encourage candidates to explore how they can help you in achieving it; ask interview questions about how they would help achieve the vision and what specifically stands out to them when they read it; and specifically address how this role has an impact on the long-term vision.

>> **Bringing people into the organization:** Once someone has been hired, include the vision in the new hire orientation process by reviewing it together on their first day; include the vision in the employee handbook.

>> **Using in decision-making:** When a big decision is being made, use the vision you created to help determine which option brings you closer toward achieving the things in the vision.

>> **Developing your strategy and annual plan:** Use the long-term vision to create short-term plans and strategies; with the vision outlined, it's easier to organize quarterly and annual strategies, goals, and plans because you have a solid destination to head toward.

IN THIS CHAPTER

» **Understanding why company values are important**

» **Developing your organizational values**

» **Connecting values to desired behaviors**

» **Creating and launching a values blueprint**

» **Bringing your values to life through action**

Chapter **7**

Setting Your House Rules: Values and Behaviors at Work

Imagine two businesses that offer similar products — cellphones, computers, tablets, and consumer electronics. One is known for its business systems and the other is known for its aggressive, stylish design. Both are two of the biggest companies in the world. Both produce a lot of revenue. Both have celebrity-level CEOs tied to their origin story. Yet we can distinctly differentiate Microsoft from Apple. You can take the same scenario and apply it to Singapore Air and Southwest Airlines, Trader Joe's and Whole Foods Market, Harvard University versus Stanford University, or Uniqlo and H&M. The culture at these businesses varies widely, and yet there's room for them all to be successful.

The values at these organizations are clearly stated and strongly defended. Certain behaviors are "in" and other behaviors are "out." The values and associated behaviors have shaped the cultures of these organizations in a way that makes them distinguishable (and highly desirable to people who want to be part of a team like that).

Many organizations have a values statement somewhere in their employee handbook or deep in a PowerPoint presentation occasionally brought to life for an investor meeting. But for the most part, these values statements are philosophical jargon bombs made to look pretty on a website. They were written at some point, likely with good intention, to promote the ethos of the company externally to customers and investors, and internally for recruiting and retention. But because they were not done well, and not lived through daily practice, they fell into oblivion and failed to capture all they could bring to the cause. This chapter will help you create values that matter and show you the power of moving them from a document to real life through behavioral norms.

Getting to the Truth about Company Values

Picture how a values statement gets created: You can visualize the "values committee" flipping through a thesaurus until they find new and inventive ways to say "integrity" and "service" and "quality." A short sentence to define values is added to the list, and voilà — the statement is done! The new values are plastered around the office, embedded in the employee handbook, and posted on the "About Us" page on the website. At that point, the work is usually over, and everyone goes back to doing whatever they were doing before, never to think of values again. Sound familiar?

REMEMBER

The process of writing down the values of your company doesn't actually change the values of your company. Documenting a list of aspirational words is not the end of the road (and frankly, shouldn't be the start either). Drafting your values is about truth finding and reality setting. What's working? How do we get important things done? Why are decisions made the way they are? You have to examine all these questions to understand the values of an organization.

It's important to get clear on values to start building your culture. They become the visual, physical, and experiential artifacts of your team. Consider them the evidence of your culture in a way — proof that you do care about the things you profess to value. They are the place that allows you to most distinguish yourself from competitors and send out a beacon to your desired customers and future employees.

The alignment of values is what allows your team to operate with a level of consistency and autonomy not available otherwise. In my work with organizations around the world, I often hear about culture fit or a group of employees acting outside of the desired way. When we dig in, what we typically find is that the values at that company aren't clear or are inconsistently applied. No wonder the employees aren't sure what they're supposed to be doing — it was never clear in the first place.

Finding the Value in Values

Values allow you to grow, replicate, and define your brand — from an employee perspective, a customer experience angle, and a marketplace view. Values and their associated behaviors (more on behaviors later in this chapter) truly define your culture because they dictate how people should act, make decisions, and treat each other. Your values are what you'll become known for and how people will place you in their minds. Do you celebrate customer service wins even if they take some extra effort to provide? This sends a clear message about doing the right thing. Do you rework designs that don't deliver the best to the client even if the client wouldn't notice the difference? This sends a clear message about the value you place on quality. Each of these types of daily interactions dictate what you really value.

Whether you state them or not, your values exist, and they speak volumes about your company and you as a manager. In fact, it's not the values on your website that matter but the values that are experienced, seen, and celebrated that truly define your organization. By taking time to get specific about the values that matter and sharing them in a way that clarifies how people in your company should act, you start to celebrate and create expectations around the desired actions of your team. When those happen to be the adopted values at an organizational level, it makes it that much easier to define, teach, repeat, and live inside your company.

Driving culture

Every organization wants engaged employees who are enthusiastic, connected to each other and the work, committed to growth, and willing to deliver on the company's promise to its customers. Culture is the way to get engaged employees. One of the strongest tools in your culture-building toolbox is your values statement, with clearly defined organizational values and behavioral norms spelled out. Your culture depends on people consistently choosing to act in a certain way.

The values in your company define the way your team acts. These values are the ones that dictate how people treat each other, how they approach work, the experience they create for customers, and the way leaders carry themselves daily. Over time, the values of a company become the norm. This norm becomes what you are known for — creating your overall culture.

Defining leadership

At its core, leadership is about establishing the norms for everyone else in the company, but it's easy to get caught up in the rhetoric of leadership, with self-aggrandizing speak about empowerment and helping others succeed. Lots of people really seem to get a kick out of softening the power of leadership by taking on an almost altruistic view of martyrdom around sacrificing for others. It can be exhausting. I could argue all day on either side of this leadership debate. One thing is certain: Leadership is about being an example and about setting the pace for others. The people on your team and in your organization look to you to set the tone and show the way — not just with an inspiring vision or project brief but by showing what is valued and how they should behave. Your values define your leadership because they tell the truth behind what you care about at work. In that way, leadership is ultimately about clearly articulating and living the values of the company.

This doesn't mean that everyone is going to be an exact replica of you and the way you work. It's not that simple. But they will respond to your actions more than anything you write in a handbook. Your employees (and customers) are always watching and assessing what your actions mean, and in that way, your employees adjust their performance to get some desired result. The more consistent, specific, and direct the link between your actions and your stated values, the easier it is to define leadership.

The reality is that you get the perfect result from your team based on the inputs of your values. They literally deliver whatever it is that you've created the conditions for. You can talk about respect all you want, but if you always show up late to meetings, your employees will conclude that respecting each other's time is not important. You can preach positive communication, but if you regularly allow people to cut each other off mid-speech, you'll be saddled with a bunch of rude employees and others who never speak up for fear of being spoken over.

Leading by example is why you can get consistent behavior on relatively small teams. The team sees the leader in action on a daily basis, watches every move and decision, and then can respond in kind because the employees are comfortable with understanding what matters most to the leader. On the opposite spectrum, in larger organizations you can get such varied experiences from different locations or teams. The values are stated one way, but the employees watch the closest leader to determine how they should respond. Leaders drive values. Values drive culture.

WARNING

If you aren't committed to model, measure, get feedback around, and hold everyone else accountable to your values, then don't publish them for the sake of checking the culture box. Whether you clearly state them or not, your organization has existing values today based on what employees and customers see leadership doing. Committing to a new set of values that you aren't committed to at the highest level of the organization puts an entirely different set of values in place. Those values? Hypocrisy, inconsistency, and lack of trustworthiness.

Creating a brand

It isn't a far stretch to recognize that values have the power to shape the way your employees work. The discretionary effort they put in on a project or during a customer experience is based on values and culture. Whether they deliver on those things has less to do with your systems (though that certainly helps ensure a consistent delivery) and more to do with what's valued by your organization. Over time, your customers, clients, patients, passengers, vendors, partners, and the public start to recognize your organization for some specific thing. This is the true making of a brand — not marketing collateral or the font or copy on your website.

Your company becomes known for the things you value. When you think of Volvo, what's the first thing that comes to mind (besides ridiculously stylish Scandinavian design)? You probably thought of safety. Volvo has certainly contributed to that perception of its brand through marketing and messaging, but the company has contributed even more by ensuring that safety is valued throughout the organization through its actions, commitments, and decision-making. This is an intentional choice; it doesn't happen by accident. Your brand is defined by your values — what is in, what is out, and what you're willing to allow.

Reducing risk

You don't need a fancy MBA degree to be familiar with stories of values gone wrong. If you type "company values scandal" into a search engine, you get back millions of results. You'll see companies that had drafted values and well-organized employee orientation programs, but what was really valued and the behaviors associated with success spoke louder. Somewhere along the way, a decision was made that put these companies at risk and led to a crisis that leaked into the public eye and tarnished the brands forever. The values of these organizations might have been stated as one thing, but over time — whether through negligence, lack of intention, or deliberate efforts — other values started to shift the actions of the people within the companies.

Your values have the incredible ability to shift behavior at work and in that way can safeguard you against risk — or drive you toward the brink of an organizational crisis. By having a strong values statement with clearly defined behaviors, you have a better chance of creating the kinds of norms that lead to the kind of culture that protects itself from risk. You create a language and space for people to speak to power. If values speak to how things get done, then this is your chance to make sure your desired actions are explicitly defined for a safer future.

Defining Your Organizational Values

Getting started with defining your organizational values (or redrafting a previous version that isn't really working) is an exciting and somewhat daunting process for a lot of people I've seen in workshops over the years. It's almost as if an existential crisis takes over and people say, "Wait, there is so much to cover. How could I possibly put it all down? I have so many expectations." Sound familiar right about now? The key to getting it right is to do it together, make it personal, and focus on what matters most.

Conducting values interviews

As you begin developing your organization's values, getting ideas and information from around the company can be helpful. Pick about 10 percent of your work population (or at least 10 people if your company is smaller than 100 employees) and try to choose a good cross-section of roles, departments, and levels (some managers, some individual contributors). You're going to interview them to get some ideas for your values work.

To get started in the interview process, let them know that there aren't any wrong or right answers and that these responses are being used to help develop a first draft of the company values. You can record the interviews or transcribe them as the person is speaking. You'll use these later in a group session, so it's helpful to get them into a usable, written format as soon as possible.

TIP

Here are some sample questions:

>> What do you believe are our strengths as an organization? Why do you think we behave that way? What drives that specific way of being and acting?

>> What do you think we don't do as well as we should? What are our weaknesses? Why do you think those things happen? Why do you believe those flaws haven't improved?

>> Tell me about a time when you felt really proud of a decision that the organization made. Why did it make you feel that way? What do you believe was behind that action?

>> Can you think of a crisis or challenge we faced and handled well? How did we respond? Why do you believe we responded that way? What do you think was behind that decision?

>> What has been your most meaningful moment while working here? What happened? Why did it matter to you? Why do you believe it happened?

>> How would you describe our team at its best? How about at its worst?

>> What do you think we will be remembered for? What do we do that makes that happen? Where do you think that comes from?

Read through the next sections to discover how to put the results from these interviews to use.

Getting connected to your own values

You've probably worked somewhere where the CEO or founder couldn't speak to the organization's values — or when the person did, the words coming out were almost painful. If the values of the most senior leaders aren't closely aligned with the espoused values of the organization, then there's no chance you'll actually be able to create value from your values. The actions and behaviors of the leaders speak volumes about what's really valued — who gets promoted, what gets highlighted, how decisions are made. To get started with values, the most senior leader has to be involved, and it has to come from the heart.

In addition to conducting interviews with various members of the company, it's important to get feedback from your top-tier leadership. If you're the senior leader, then keep reading. If you aren't the senior leader, then you'll need to find time to meet with that person and have an interview of sorts. Or even better — send the person the assignment shown in Figure 7-1 to complete. The goal is an authentic and genuine draft of what the leader really cares about and is committed to doing.

Individual Values Assessment Assignment

1. **Write a list of how you want things to work and how you think people should be working together.** Remember, these aren't the outcomes and results you need to produce for the board or the investment bankers. This is about defining what you want people to act like, how you believe people should treat each other, and how you think decisions should be made. Fight the urge to make these sound pretty or website-worthy. Just get the deep core beliefs and desires down on paper.

2. **Drum up a few stories from your past (not even necessarily at this current organization) that really illustrate the points you've jotted down and write those stories next to the items on the list.** It's usually helpful at this point to share this with someone else and ask the person to tell you if he/she can see the link between the stories you shared and the list of things you value.

3. **Refine the list to the values that matter most to you.**

4. **Next to each value, describe three or four behaviors you're committed to based on that value.** For example, if you wrote that you value "hospitality," you might define that in behavioral terms as "create a welcoming environment for others, even when I'm busy or stressed" or "initiate friendly contact with others when I'm within 4 feet of them" or "make calendar reminders about important events in my team's lives so I can reach out to them."

FIGURE 7-1: A sample individual values assessment worksheet.

By having an idea of what matters most to you as the senior leader in the organization, you have a better chance of shaping the company culture and values in a way that is sustainable, authentic, and engaging.

Leading a group values session

Once you've completed the interview work and the individual values assessment, it's time to bring the original values interview group together again to start to refine the ideas. In this group session, your goal is to begin to organize all of the information into one document so you can begin to whittle down to your final version. In this group values session, you will start to define the organization values and develop some clear ideas about what the values look like in action.

Here are the steps to take to lead a group values session:

1. Go over the process.

Explain the process so far, including the individual interview sessions, your own values assessment work, and now this part of the process.

2. Explain why this matters.

Share the reasons for taking action now, which may include a big growth phase, helping to make the right decisions, hiring great people, helping teach new people about how you do things, or helping you realign during a period of disorganization.

3. Define values.

Share some ideas about how values complement mission and vision by informing the way in which everyone agrees to act toward each other, your customers, and the work. If the mission keeps you focused on the long-term purpose and the vision helps you understand a specific destination on the horizon, then values define the manner in which you'll get there.

4. State the goals for today's session.

Highlight what the desired outcomes for this session are, including a discussion about values with everyone sharing and elaborating on each other's ideas, distilling information from the previous interviews and the leader's personal values, and leaving with a drafted version of values to refine.

5. Use the following questions and statements to prompt discussion:

- What does our team really do? Finish the sentence "As a team, we . . ."
- How do we do that differently from other places? Finish the sentence "We are the only place that . . ."

- What values are already in place? What behaviors highlight those?

- The things that make someone successful here are . . .

- I know someone isn't going to be a fit for us when . . .

- The decisions that have confused in the past are . . . because they didn't match up to the value of . . .

- When we are at our best, I see people . . .

6. **Wrap up.**

   Thank everyone for their time. Let them know that you'll be drafting up the core values based on all the information so far and that you'll share the draft with them for feedback and review.

Identifying common themes

Once you've collected ideas from the interviews, the values assessment, and the group values session, it's time to start identifying themes. You'll likely have a bunch of qualitative data points to sift through at this point. Take these steps to winnow them down:

1. **Gather:** Write down the ideas on sticky notes and place them on a whiteboard. Alternatively, you can use software like Trello to create easily movable tiles, or enter the ideas into individual cells in a spreadsheet.

2. **Group:** Review all the comments looking for connections, patterns, and similar points. Doing this activity with a few other people can be helpful, as sometimes the connections between ideas speak to different people differently. Begin grouping comments together based on similar themes and ideas.

3. **Label:** Once you have the ideas organized in groups, see if there's an easy way to label them. Do you have four or five comments that speak to openness, honesty, and clarity? Maybe bundle those under transparency. If you find three or four ideas around service, experience, and satisfaction, perhaps put them under a customer service label.

Aligning Values with Desired Behavior

Culture is the output when values meet action. So the work on your values isn't done yet. You need to add specific behaviors to those values so that people know exactly how they should act. For example, if one of your values is "accomplishment," does that mean I should do whatever it takes to win or does that mean

I should take challenging risks even if I might fail? Getting specific about what you expect is the critical part of this exercise.

Defining your values with behavior

There's a very consistent problem happening around the world at work. I hear it in workshops, advisory sessions, executive coaching calls, and when I step off stage at conferences. I've heard it in Canada, Spain, Des Moines, New York, Los Angeles, and everywhere in between: "How do I manage someone's attitude?" Frustrated managers at every level have asked that question. The simple answer is, "you don't." We don't get to dictate how people feel or decide for them what's going on in their heads and hearts at work. In fact, this book is all about how to create the conditions with culture so that those things happen naturally — which is the only way they can happen.

Instead, you have to focus on the behaviors you want to see. Imagine someone who everyone really likes working with. You might say the person has a great attitude. If you look deeper and ask, "What is that person doing that makes them likable and easy to work with?" you may end up with a list like this:

>> Always treats other respectfully and kindly

>> Makes time to greet coworkers in a friendly way

>> Assumes the positive when thinking about coworkers' actions

>> Gives credit to others

>> Celebrates other people's success

Not that hard, right? I'd imagine you could keep that list running for a while. When you think about it, it's easy to identify observable behaviors that lead to success. The attitude of this likable employee is actually something that can be seen, heard, and managed. If you recognize that this is an important part of your culture and values, you can look for those specific behaviors when hiring, promoting, and giving performance reviews too. The reality is that you can't — and shouldn't — try to manage people's attitudes. But you can focus on the behaviors you'd like to see more of.

Observable behavior

For a behavior to be studied, communicated clearly, and improved, you want to focus on observable behaviors. It's very tricky to have a performance improvement conversation that is useful and productive for the employee's performance if you can't observe the behavior.

For example, telling an employee how he or she feels is a surefire way to off-road your performance conversation. How do you know how the person feels? Is it really fair for you to dictate to people that they should feel a different way than they do? Controlling someone's feelings is a draconian approach to leadership — and is impossible.

Focusing on observable behaviors is a much stronger and more impactful way to approach things. If you took a picture of the employee doing the thing you're describing, what would it look like? What do you see? What can you hear? The behaviors in your values statement need to be observable so you can define, teach, and live your values. Keep refining until they're crystal-clear.

For example, instead of saying "deliver great service to customers," you would say "make eye contact, smile, and greet customers when they are within 5 feet of you" or instead of saying "be respectful of others," you would say "let others finish speaking before jumping in with your own ideas."

Measurable behavior

Defining and clarifying your performance expectations with observable behaviors gives you a pretty good shot at improving performance consistently. Being able to measure it improves your chances even more. When you think about the behaviors aligned with your values, look for ways you can reliably measure them. This doesn't mean that every single behavior is going to have a specific outcome tied to it, like "sold five widgets" or "improved task completion time by 10 percent." But it does mean that you should be able to score the behavior in some way. Can you rank the behavior in terms of low to high on a scale? Can you measure how consistently employees do it with "always, usually, or rarely"? Can someone provide feedback about the degree or level to which someone performed?

TIP

If you find that a lot of your values and behaviors only apply to certain functions, then think bigger and broader. Company-wide goals need to define how people in all roles and all functions should work. Sometimes repeating the behavior part of this for a specific department is a helpful exercise for department leaders. Think about how the desired organizational behaviors apply to your team and give clear examples of them in play — but you should never change the organizational values or come up with specific values for your department. This leads to confusion and typically lowers the adoption rate by your team. Keep it focused on the things that really matter.

Drafting Your Values and Behavior Statement

You can't have culture without behavior. Your actions define your culture. As a leader, the things you do define you. Your behaviors very clearly tell people what you value. Behavior is the focus of all great cultures and is the only way to really shift culture. In fact, this book is about changing behaviors around how you hire, how you communicate, how you train, and how you make decisions.

To help bring behaviors into focus in your organization and really let your values shine, you need to create your values and behavior statement. That can be a little tough to roll off the tongue, so in my workshops my clients typically call this the "Values Blueprint" or "Values Road Map." Whatever you decide to call it, make it shareable and easy to reference.

Getting it in writing

It's time to put pen to paper — or fingers to keyboard, probably. Based on the ideas shared in this chapter, take a stab at writing a first draft. Your goal is to create an original and memorable list of values and observable and measurable behaviors that resonate for your company. Put everything in. Organize it. Then start to move things around to make them make sense. Don't worry about word-smithing at this point. You'll get feedback and make revisions later. For now, just get it all in one place so that it makes sense.

REMEMBER

Some things to keep in mind as you write:

>> **Focus on strengths.** Use this as an opportunity to highlight what works and celebrate the things that add value to your brand, company, and culture. Think about the areas where things are working best. Consider the teams and relationships that deliver the most value. Identify the communication and experiences that drive your culture forward. Name them. Applaud them.

>> **Think of someone specific.** Speak to your ideal employee in your company as you write. Think about the words being shared with the person. Use words and descriptions that are exciting to the person.

>> **Get emotional.** So many values statements avoid evoking any kind of emotions. Don't do that. Get clear, specific, and vibrant. Your review team will dial you back if you go too far (but, in my experience working with organizations on values creation, most people could typically go a little further).

>> **Avoid TLDR.** This stands for "too long, didn't read." Try to really stick to the top three to six values of the organization. When you start moving beyond that, it becomes hard to really defend that these are values and not just a list of

nice-to-haves. Focus on what really matters and what you're willing to commit to, even if it becomes unpopular later. Dig into the core and focus on what differentiates you from other companies.

Putting it all together

The easiest way to get started in organizing your values blueprint is to create a simple document with a chart, like the one in Figure 7-2, with space for the value, a simple definition, and a few defined behaviors for each value.

Values Blueprint		
Value	**Definition**	**Behavior**
Achievement	Create value by delivering more	• Takes on challenging assignments • Asks what more can be done
Ownership	Commitment and pride in the success of the organization	• Holds self accountable for commitments • Follows through • Owns, learns from, and fixes mistakes • Shows pride in appearance • Colors outside the lines to solve customer/client concerns
Teamwork	Collaborates and creates shared purpose	• Shares information broadly and increases others' knowledge of important information • Recognizes and acknowledges the contributions of others • Communicates clear and frequently to break down barriers
Authenticity	Is genuine, honest, and real	• Self-aware and willing to admit mistakes • Open and transparent in communication • Exhibits a sense of humor and is able to laugh at self • Adds to customer/client experience through connection and relating

FIGURE 7-2: An example of a values blueprint.

Collecting feedback and making revisions

It's time to share your rough draft with the original values committee for feedback. Sometimes, people are uncomfortable providing feedback because they don't know how to deliver it in a useful way, so include instructions on how they should provide their feedback to you. An easy way to do that is to ask them for specific feedback. This not only helps them focus their attention but provides a comfortable way to deliver it. An easy way to do that is to ask them what resonated, where they lost interest, and to provide some options for making it better by asking "what if we" . . .

"Resonate, Lost interest, and What if we" feedback example:

>> "It resonated with me when we elaborated on the service value because "service" is such a trite term so I love how our example is specific."

>> "I lost interest when we relied on basic terms like 'integrity' and 'value'."

>> "What if we used less jargony terms and instead said 'ownership' and 'delight'."

Then ask some more specific questions like:

>> Are the behaviors observable? Can you take a picture of someone doing them? Can you hear or see a person doing them?

>> Are the behaviors measurable?

>> Does this list accurately describe what our best people do every day? Does it accurately describe what you see managers doing every day?

>> Can we be more specific about any of the behaviors?

Use this information to perform revisions on the original version. Then repeat this exercise with other stakeholders like your board, the executive team, and other employees in the organization.

WARNING

Avoid using this phase as a way to procrastinate and elongate the process. While you want this to be inclusive and meaningful, you also want to move things forward. Doing too many revisions with too many stakeholders can really slow down the work. This is another chance to get people focused on the observable and measurable behaviors to help create focus and get everyone on the same page. Ask questions like "What does that look like" or "How do you know when that is happening?"

Use this feedback to decide which suggestions are useful and helpful, keeping in mind that "useful" and "helpful" in this context mean more specific and clear. Create a final draft of the values blueprint. Take cues from your brand to decide what the final format should look like. Most of the people I work with like to dress up the values blueprint to create an artifact that can be shared easily across the organization. Work with your design team to come up with something that matches your branding. You want people to read, watch, and interact with this document in a way that engages them and inspires them to connect further with your organization. This should be about creating relationships, developing connections, and deepening the experience people have with your brand.

Launching Your Values and Behavior Blueprint

Things in your organization are probably going one of two ways right now. People have been hearing about the values committee work on defining the values and behavioral norms at the company. They're either excited and looking forward to seeing what has been created or rolling their eyes because they've seen this thing before and feel like it won't really change much. If it's the latter, don't worry. You can change that attitude by what you do next and how you bring your values blueprint to life in your organization.

TIP

Launching your values blueprint is best done as a group effort, so take advantage of a regularly scheduled gathering — a quarterly all-hands meeting, a weekly staff meeting, a monthly celebration, or a holiday party. These are all great opportunities to share your new values blueprint, through both words and actions.

To make a big splash and show that this is important work for the future of your company, you want to gather some of the stories created in the values committee work earlier in this chapter. Look for stories that clearly showcase the desired behaviors and promote the specific value. These should come from a range of departments, perspectives, and roles within the company to help make them relatable. Make sure to invest time in collecting values stories from around the organization for the biggest impact.

Here's a sample values blueprint launch event agenda:

1. Introduce the reasons for creating the values and behavior norms.

2. Explain the vision for the process.

3. Highlight the team involved in crafting the values.

4. Share each of the values and a story about a time that highlights that value in action.

5. Share each of the values and behavior statements.

6. **Tell people what will happen next (incorporate into hiring, onboarding, and other values events you have planned; see the next section for more ideas).**

7. **Thank the values committee for their time and efforts.**

Making Your Values Statement Come to Life

When it all comes down, it's important to deeply embed the values of your organization into the way you actually work together, make decisions, and perform your duties. It should be an all-hands effort to help bring your values to life in your organization. Here are some simple ways to ensure you're off to a good start:

>> **Incorporate into hiring:** Your interviewing can be based around hiring people that align with your values and that have acted in line with the behavior norms. It's much easier to teach someone some of your systems and protocols than to change how someone acts or believes. By asking behavioral questions focused around your values, you can get an idea of how the candidate may work within your organization.

>> **Decision-making:** When considering important decisions, your values and behavior norms can be the guide for choosing between two courses of action. In a meeting around an important decision, use the values to ask, "What do our values dictate we do in this situation?" and "How does that decision line up with our stated values and desired behaviors?" This is one of the key places where your employees and the public will be watching you to see if you really mean what you say when it comes to what you value.

>> **During onboarding:** Use the onboarding and orientation process to include examples of your values in action. Use storytelling around instances where the values were used to shape decisions and how those values have been challenged over time.

TIP

>> **Employee engagement:** Create campaigns around the values throughout the year. Try a #values campaign if you use an online employee recognition or social media platform when an employee recognizes another living the values. Create a values month where different employee-sourced stories about values in action are shared publicly, or make the first Friday of each month a values day, where one of the values is highlighted with stories and examples from around the organization. If you have an employee newsletter or blog, create a values column that highlights an employee-submitted values recognition.

>> **Learning and development:** Align your training and development offerings with your values. If you value innovation, offer an online course around creativity at work. If you value failure, bring an improv trainer a few times a year to teach a workshop about learning how to make the most of mistakes. Have an executive team member give a class or lunch & learn session about the values each month or quarter.

>> **Feedback:** Gathering feedback about your values in action is an important part of living your values. As your organization grows, it will become even more important. You can set up some easy feedback loops to help you ensure things haven't gone off course. If you do 360-degree performance reviews, make the questions about how individuals are behaving in-line with the values. Create a survey about your leaders and ask employees to share examples of your managers living the values or examples of why they don't think they do. During one-on-ones, ask questions about how your team sees others exhibiting the values.

IN THIS CHAPTER

» Understanding the changing landscape of attracting talent to your team

» Developing engaging content to bring in the best job candidates

» Being mindful of your brand and enhancing your website

» Keeping up with the competition

» Using current and former employees in your recruiting efforts

Chapter **8**

Leveraging Your Culture for Inbound Recruiting

Remember the old days of recruiting people to your team? From classified ads to help wanted signs, the power in the world of recruiting has long been tilted toward the employer. You posted the ad, they applied, you sifted through a pile of candidates, interviewed the lucky few, and then selected one. The power was almost completely held by the company — from what the candidate could easily learn about working there to whether the benefits, perks, and salary were competitive with other companies in the area. But that's changed. Today the balance has shifted to the applicants. From being able to apply for any job right from the comfort of their own kitchen table, to being able to research information about your culture online — applicants today are leading the recruiting process.

One of the most frequent questions I'm asked all over the world during workshops and presentations is, "How do I find great talent?" The answer is simple: Use your culture. Stop chasing and start attracting the right people by leveraging the thing most of them are looking for — a positive and rewarding career experience. Lucky you — you've picked up this book to start working on improving your company culture.

With so much public information out there about your company, the candidates coming into your interview process are already pretty informed about what it's like to work with you. The more you can ensure compelling content is available about your culture, the more likely you are to attract the kind of people who can succeed and enhance your culture.

This chapter helps you understand how attracting top talent for your brand has changed and what you need to do about it. You'll create a road map for boosting your inbound candidate pipeline and discover how to maximize your company culture to attract top talent.

Understanding Inbound Marketing

With the majority of the population having access to the Internet and social media, the way consumers look for information about products and services has changed rapidly. Instead of clicking on banner ads that shouted "buy me," consumers were hunting down consumer-produced product reviews. Similarly, consumers became less likely to reach out to a salesperson until they had watched videos, researched options, and understood the landscape. Imagine that you plan to buy a new car in the next few months. Where would you start your search? You'd probably read some online review sites, watch some videos on YouTube, and check out the comments from other people who'd purchased the kind of car you were thinking about buying. By the time you arrive at the dealership, you would have probably learned more about the car than the salesperson.

One of the hottest trends in attracting customers is inbound marketing. *Inbound marketing* is the idea of pulling customers in through content and engagement. It's about helping customers make buying decisions because your company has produced articles, videos, infographics, and other helpful information to aid in their decision process. The same process can be applied to your recruiting efforts to attract great talent. The people you want on your team are out there searching the Internet, researching blog posts, watching videos, and following your brand online to learn as much as they can about your culture and the opportunity you have for them. Are you showing up to answer their questions and put your best foot forward?

A strong inbound recruiting platform includes a thoughtful road map that considers how prospective applicants move from unaware of your brand and culture to aware of it to applicant for your open position to hired for your role and finally to promoting your team and culture. We also know that employees today aren't fooled by slick marketing speak like "this is the best place because we care about our people." Applicants demand the proof. If they can't find the information they want about your culture, you have little chance of ever having them reach the applicant or hired stage of the journey.

Companies who excel at attracting and recruiting great talent are producing blogs, white papers, checklists, and videos and engaging on social media in authentic ways to inform and educate the prospective employee — not just about their open positions but about the whole culture and employee experience. I recently worked with a tech company whose website has information about open positions, videos directly from the hiring managers, infographics and slide decks highlighting their employee programs, videos from their current employees talking about their career growth, and other topics related to the employee experience. Once a candidate has looked at this information, then the inbound recruiter needs to turn those passive visitors into possible applicants.

The world has turned upside down when it comes to how we market, attract, recruit, and close great candidates. Smart organizations realize that finding the best person for the job starts with making their organization as attractive as possible. This chapter shows you how to get started.

Updating the Help Wanted Sign

I remember the first job fair I was ever responsible for executing. We put an ad in the paper clearly defining the expectations we had for employees, posted a help wanted sign in the window with details of our upcoming event, and told applicants that they would have to return to apply on the day of our job fair. We were looking to fill 20 positions. On the day of our job fair, we had over 150 people waiting in line to apply for jobs. We interviewed them to select the best of the bunch and offered them non-negotiable terms to start in the upcoming weeks. They eagerly accepted.

This would never work today. Organizations small and large are left with open positions for long periods of time as job applicants slide into the driver seat. Job applicants today have typically done quite a bit of research before they even apply for a position. They have a good understanding of what working at your company will be like. The separation that once existed between human resources and marketing is quickly shrinking as culture, employee experience, and brand become one interchangeable story.

Where once there were just two major vehicles for announcing that you had a job opening — a help wanted sign in the window or an ad in the classifieds section of the local paper — today there are thousands of opportunities to attract great talent to your organization. From social media posts to employee-generated content, from career-site landing pages to YouTube videos, your company culture is a powerful way to drive talented people to apply to work with your organization. Read on to find out how to use your company culture to draw in the talent.

Creating a culture beacon

Targeted content is about a whole lot more than just plugging some money into sponsored posts on media platforms like Instagram, Facebook, and LinkedIn. Your employer-brand, culture-centric articles, stories, images, and facts act like a central homing device calling your ideal candidates to your company. People are looking for clues to help them make decisions about where to work next. They want to find people they'll like and from whom they can learn. Job seekers are looking for managers to mentor them and organizations full of learning opportunities. Your job is to make it easy for them to find all that in an authentic way that celebrates your culture.

The key methods for successfully leveraging your culture for talent attraction include:

>> **Careers page:** This will be the home for all your recruiting efforts and where future candidates will visit as they do their research about your company culture. If your current careers page doesn't match your brand or simply lists open positions, you want to start improving your careers site by following the ideas in the later section "Giving Your Culture a Home Page." A great careers page should tell your employee story and have a strong employee value proposition that makes the right candidates want to know more about working with you.

>> **Employee-generated content:** Your employees' stories have the most powerful impact on future applicants. Candidates trust the information and connect with it in an authentic away. Not only do your current employees tell the real story of your culture but they also give future employees a glimpse into what working with your team is like. Share your employee stories and narratives via video, written content, and interviews. These can appear in recruiting marketing videos, video job descriptions, blog posts, and listicle-type roundups.

>> **Employer-generated content:** Creating engaging content from the employer perspective isn't dead yet. In addition to the employee-generated content, the company can still leverage information to produce compelling career and culture information. This information can be shared on sites like LinkedIn, your company blog, or your careers site. Future employees will want to hear about programs, benefits, and perks as well as engaging content from your

managers and executives like how they manage the team or their take on industry trends.

>> **Culture-centric videos:** If a picture is worth a thousand words, then videos can really supercharge the message. Your company culture is a content treasure trove full of interesting happenings just waiting to be captured and shared via video. From short-form social media posts to slightly longer employer-brand marketing videos, you likely have the resources and talent to produce videos that can boost your recruiting efforts by highlighting your culture. Having a regular (at least monthly) cadence of new content can help you stay top of mind with your dream candidates.

>> **Simple and easy call-to-action:** A call-to-action is the main action you want people to take once they've interacted with you. There are two best-in-class options when it comes to talent attraction: an "apply now" button and some other kind of opt-in like "learn more" or "get the guide," if you have produced some kind of content the candidate would want to get from you.

>> **Easy ways to stay in touch:** Not all candidates will be ready now to make the jump to your team, and sometimes your team isn't looking for their skill set yet. But you don't want to lose all the effort you put into attracting great people simply because you don't need them today. Creating simple ways to stay in touch that stretch beyond spamming them with job posts is a critical step in using your culture to attract talent. This can be as simple as using the email address to send notifications about jobs that match their skill set or as elaborate as developing a monthly jobs newsletter that highlights industry news and new positions in your organization.

TIP

Watch where your current talent is coming from and go meet them there with engaging content about your culture. You can do this during the recruiting process by asking how they heard about the position and then tracking that information. Over time, you will learn what websites, search engines, social media platforms, or employer–brand content drive the most traffic to your recruiting funnel. Create a spreadsheet where you track this information for each person you interview and review it monthly.

Auditing your current culture brand

An important step before creating a lot of new data is taking stock of what you already have available to you. Sometimes when I've worked with organizations to start improving their employer branding and developing content to boost their talent culture, they're surprised to see how much information already exists. A simple repackaging and more thoughtful distribution plan can bring old content to life in a way that has candidates knocking down your door.

TIP

To gain an understanding of what you may have already in your culture brand arsenal, check out these tips:

>> **Conduct an employee survey:** Take stock of your current employees' ideas about your employer brand. Specifically, you want to ask:

- Where did they first learn about your company?

- When they've recommended someone to join your team in the past, what did they tell the person about your company before the person applied?

- When they talk about their work with friends, what are some of the highlights of that conversation?

- If they were to look for a job today, where would they start their search? What type of information would they look for? What kinds of answers would make them feel confident in applying?

>> **Identify your key competitors:** Having an understanding of how your competition stacks up is an important step to take before you begin developing and enhancing your talent attraction efforts. These are not always the same companies you compete with for customers. Think about the companies where your current employees are leaving you for and the companies who beat you in the quest of wooing a new employee. These are your competitors when it comes to talent. In the "Watching Your Competition" section later in this chapter, you'll learn more about what to assess, but for now, make a list of companies that are after the same talented people you are.

>> **Review employer review sites:** Not much is opaque these days, and the same is true about the culture at your organization. Employees are able to review, comment, and score your company on websites like Glassdoor, Comparably, and even on Google. Take some time to read through and log the information available on these sites. Future employees give a lot of trust to the information available here, so you want to understand what's being said. If you've been intentional about creating a positive culture, you'll likely be pleased with what you see. You'll also probably want to make sure that you're sending candidates and prospects to these pages so they can read the info themselves. If you have a lack of reviews (or lack of current reviews) on these sites, then use the ideas in the "Managing Your Employer Brand" section later in this chapter to improve the quantity of your results.

>> **Assess social media:** Spend some time on the major social media sites to see what's out there about your culture and company. Twitter, Instagram, Facebook, Pinterest, and YouTube all provide opportunities for your employees and customers to highlight their experiences with you. Try doing a search for your company name and then try to add other employer-related words to the search, like "culture" or "work" or "employee." This information will help

you begin to assess where things are currently when candidates are searching for your company.

>> **Take stock of search:** To figure out exactly what future job applicants will find when they start seeking out information on your culture, do a search yourself. Try several different search terms in a search engine to see what comes back in the first three pages. Some ideas to get you started: {your company} + culture, working, jobs, managers, employees, company culture. Additionally, you can do this search within YouTube to see what exists on video about you. You may be surprised by the results.

Organize a list of all the information gathered from the previous points to start to build an understanding of what is currently out there. Take note of the positive and negative information so you can begin to build a supply of material to use for inbound marketing.

Creating Engaging Content

So how do you make sure you're creating content that will pull in talented people?

Focus on what questions future applicants may have. Think of the search engine less like a keyword finder and more like an answer key aimed at your future employees' key questions, worries, and concerns.

Some questions you will want to answer:

>> What is the culture like when you work at XYZ company?

>> What is the interview process like at XYZ company?

>> Does XYZ invest in its employees' growth and development?

>> What type of initial and ongoing training is provided to XYZ employees? How does that training help prepare them for future growth and career opportunities?

>> What is the executive team like? How involved are they? Are they easy to talk to and are they connected to the day-to-day operations?

>> What are the people like at XYZ company?

>> How does XYZ evaluate employee performance, goals, and success?

>> Do people get promoted frequently? How are those decisions made? What's my likelihood of getting promoted?

>> What are the perks and benefits like?

>> Is there a clear direction for employees at XYZ company?

When people start searching for more about your company, make sure that you've provided the answers. The best way to do this is with a multi-pronged approach (see the following sections) — a mix of employee-generated and employer-generated content; a mix of video, articles, infographics, and images; and a mix of social crowd-sourced content and high branded materials. You also don't necessarily need to directly answer the question as if it's an interrogation-style interview. You simply want to create stories and narratives that provide answers to the questions from several different angles and perspectives.

TIP

In addition to answering questions future candidates may have, here are some more ideas for gathering intel on what may be on your dream employee's mind:

>> Document the questions being asked by candidates during the interview process. Ask recent hires what they wish they would have asked during the interview process as well, since sometimes candidates focus on asking very standard interview questions they read online. Dig deep to see what they wish they had asked.

>> Track all the information the recruiting and hiring managers tell candidates routinely and produce content around those themes.

>> Complete a new hire survey at the end of the first week to ask what big questions were answered that week and what the candidate may still be wondering about.

>> Ask current employees what they wish they knew when they first started at your company.

Producing employee-generated content

It's much easier to believe a third party bragging about something than it is when it comes directly from the involved source. It's why word-of-mouth advertising is so impactful. Imagine you meet someone new and she starts telling you how great she is and how much you should want to be her friend. The bragging includes names of other people whom she's friends with and pictures of people enjoying her company. Probably won't take long for you to find a reason to excuse yourself and make a dash for the door.

Now imagine someone else at the party introduces you to the same person. The third party shares why this person has been such a good friend.

In the classic marketing sense, this is called "word-of-mouth" advertising, and it's generally agreed that it packs the most punch when it comes to shifting consumer buying habits. After all, we already trust our friend, neighbor, or coworker who is recommending the product or service, so it makes sense that some of that trust rubs off.

The same tactic is powerful when it comes to promoting your culture and using it for attracting the right people to your team. Your employees can help produce content that increases believability and trust. It can't be overstated that your employee-generated content is going to produce a lot of your results when it comes to attracting applicants.

Here are some ideas for producing employee-generated content:

>> Create top-five lists that help answer the questions your future hires are looking to have answered. For example, you could get five different employees to chime in on their biggest career growth stories each quarter or five different employees to share their favorite parts about working at XYZ company. Doing this every quarter with different employees will give you a lot of shareable content. These can be shared on your careers website, on social media, and via your candidate email lists.

>> Create a thought leader group to help each other write interesting and engaging content in their areas of expertise. For example, someone in your customer support department could write monthly content about your approach to handling difficult customer service situations or someone on your sales leadership team could write a monthly column about his approach to sales team morale.

>> Pick an employee each month to write a retrospective highlighting his last six months at your company. You can create a standard format that the employee uses to help make it easier to rapidly produce the content. This should include information that helps answer some of the questions your future employees may have. If writing isn't his thing, you can interview him and ghost write it or produce a video of someone interviewing him.

>> Organize employee takeover events on Instagram and/or Snapchat where one of your employees runs the feed for a week while sharing a glimpse into his day-to-day work life.

>> Include content generation as part of the job descriptions for different roles, making it an expectation that they will produce one article per month or quarter. The content shouldn't be specifically about your culture, but should highlight this person's ideas, skills, and experiences. As an added bonus, this is a great way for your employees to start to build a portfolio of content that will help them shine in the future as well. Maybe someone on your sales team

writes about his or her approach to prospecting new leads, or one of your managers highlights the way she creates a positive culture during her meetings.

Developing employer-generated content

Once you have a steady flow of employee-generated content, you want to supplement that with information created by the marketing or human resources team. One of the newest roles being added to a lot of companies is an employer brand manager who focuses on curating the employee-generated content mentioned in the preceding section, as well as developing the employer-generated content. This position typically sits somewhere between marketing, PR, and HR. But even if you don't have the budget for a position fully dedicated to this task, there's still plenty you can (and should) be producing that will help you use your culture to drive applicant engagement.

>> **Blogs and articles:** Short-form blog posts (under 800 words) are an effective way to speak directly to your future employees. You should aim to produce an article for all the questions you generated in the brainstorming activity mentioned earlier in the chapter. In most cases, you can write several pieces for each question by taking a different perspective or focus. This is different than the employee-generated content in that it is not just a roll-up of a few people's ideas, but is the company stance on a common candidate question.

>> **SlideShare:** This platform allows you to develop presentations and share them across the Internet as well as LinkedIn. Use this to share short e-book style stories about your culture, team, and workspace. An easy way to do this is to produce a visual slide version in Keynote or PowerPoint for each article or blog post. What images, facts, and keywords would help turn your written post into a visual presentation? If your results around diversity have improved, this is a great place to highlight those efforts and outcomes. If you have an impressive internal promotion pattern, you can produce a presentation on that as well. Your benefits, perks, employee success programs, and training offerings all make for great slides as well.

TIP

Develop and design this content with the same quality you would customer-facing promotions and campaigns. You want to keep a consistent brand between your consumer and employee experience. Far too often companies have a fun, vibrant consumer brand and then leave their employee-focused material feeling and looking bland, which doesn't do a lot to highlight your culture.

>> **Pinterest:** This image-based social media platform makes sharing images easy. The general idea is that you create a "board" to "pin" images around

specific themes. You can create a culture page that highlights pics of your team in action. Or create boards to pin images associated with your different values. Or create a board with images and short bios of your new hires, your promotions, your leadership team, and each individual team in your company. If your brand values customer service, create a board associated with images of your team delivering great experiences.

» **Instagram:** This is a great place for sharing images of your culture in action. Some companies create separate employee and consumer-facing profiles, but you can also just have one that mixes both types of content. These days, consumers are looking to do business with companies that take care of the team, so highlighting that you're a great place to work is a good brand strategy in general. You can do this by posting images of your teams on outings, working together in your office, celebrating big wins, or honoring important anniversaries.

» **Snapchat:** If your employees are in the demographic using Snapchat, then you should be as well. Snapchat allows you to post short videos that develop into a story when watched together. Your content can highlight the behind-the-scenes view of working at your company. This should feel more like a documentary and less like a feature film.

» **Infographics:** These are visual displays of information that make it easy to interpret and understand complex topics. You can use infographics to highlight any of the positive things happening in your company. For example, you might choose to highlight the diversity in your company or the activities going on around the company or the amount of people who have been promoted throughout the years. Think of things that are interesting and highlight your positive culture.

» **Videos:** This is an impactful way to have an employee tell her culture story and help attract your next great hire. You can also show videos highlighting important milestones for the people on your team. Create videos of team outings and affinity group meetings. Anything that would highlight your culture is great for video!

» **Quora:** This platform is based on people asking questions and having them answered by others. While you may not find a lot of specific questions about your company unless you're a major employer, you can start to be seen as a helpful organization, which will lead to more people discovering your content and opportunities. The easiest way to get started is to assign a few people to answer questions on specific topics each week. For example, your marketing team could answer questions about marketing careers, topics, and approaches; your HR team could answer questions about culture and recruiting; and your engineering team could address questions related to coding and development. Over time, this positions your organization in a positive light and drives traffic to your other content.

In addition to answering specific questions about your culture, you can go one step further and provide helpful tools or information in general. Create checklists to help candidates track their job search, develop an e-book with the top questions a job candidate should ask to learn about company culture, or produce a short tutorial explaining how to use storytelling in the interview. Think beyond your company to provide information that candidates may be seeking. This says a lot about your culture and will likely create some positive feelings about your brand.

REMEMBER

Keep your content focused on answering the questions that your applicants are looking for about your culture and company. If you use the brainstorming ideas in this section, you'll never run out of sources and opportunities.

Distributing your culture content for impact

Once you've developed some content, you want it to hit the streets and start to work in helping you attract culture-focused applicants. Getting eyes and shares on your articles and videos is the key to making an impact with your assets.

Here's a list of ideas to help boost your culture content footprint:

» Share on social media and schedule posts for the future. You can use simple social media scheduling tools like Hootsuite, CoSchedule, MeetEdgar, or Buffer to repurpose your content over time. If the article isn't particularly tied to a current date, schedule it for different periods of time in the future to get more traction. You never know when someone may be looking for just the thing you have to share. You can update the image, status, title, and quote to keep it fresh across your platforms.

» LinkedIn is currently the hot platform for career-related content. Use the LinkedIn publishing platform to place some of your written content, such as posts about top tips for interview candidates or your approach to company culture. Post videos on LinkedIn about your company and team and share your content in status updates. You can also leverage your relationships within groups to give your content a boost.

» Leverage the signature section of your company email to share your careers page, which includes relevant content posts. You can also specifically link to certain articles or videos based on the department of the person sending the email.

» Ask new employees to pick a favorite article, video, or infographic from your library to share on their social media pages during their first month. You can sweeten the encouragement by offering a referral or recommendation bonus for anyone they bring to the team.

>> Create an alumni network via a LinkedIn group, Facebook group, or even just an email list. Distribute articles, videos, infographics, thought leadership, and current open job requisitions in a newsletter format.

WARNING

Make sure that you aren't spamming people with information about your culture and company. It doesn't help you achieve your goals if people are receiving information that isn't helpful or relevant to them. Focus on providing useful and helpful information to the type of people you are trying attract.

Managing Your Employer Brand

Good or bad, people are going to talk about your company on places like company review sites, such as Glassdoor, Google, or Comparably. While you can't completely control what your current and former employees say about you, you can help encourage and boost the conversation by setting up the following reminders asking for their input on the platform you're trying to build. Use the following instances to reach out and ask your employees to visit the site you are trying to add more reviews to with a link to your company's page on that site:

>> **Pre-orientation:** As part of your onboarding experience, ask newly hired employees to review their interview process.

>> **Orientation:** Ask during orientation if the new hire used one of the sites to learn about your company. Encourage the person to share his experiences now and in the future as well.

>> **90-days:** Automate or set a calendar reminder to ask for a review when the employee hits the 90-day mark with your company.

>> **Leadership:** Send out a request twice a year to all the managers at your organization asking them to submit a review.

>> **Post-event or news:** If you've had a big company event or recent positive news, send a request to employees.

>> **Annually:** Schedule to send an email request once a year to all employees asking for them to review your organization.

TIP

These notes can be simple: "As you know, XYZ platform is often a job applicant's first stop when considering working with us. Can you take a few minutes now to visit this site (insert link) and leave a few notes about your experience as an employee?" They also could be more specific like: "I had such a great time in our office. It was so much fun getting to know you and to be able to talk so openly about who you are and what you'd like to accomplish here. It's part of the transparency in this company that I personally love so much. We'd love it if you took this opportunity to talk about your experience on Glassdoor."

WARNING

Your goal is for these reviews to be authentic and honest. Don't encourage your employees to write anything specific or to lie in any way about working at your company. Just encourage them to share their experience. If you've been building a great culture, this will show in their comments.

A few ways to supercharge your efforts and company profile:

>> Set a specific goal regarding the number of reviews you want during a specific period of time and then post updates to the team. Maybe you want to hit 50 reviews by the end of Q1 — share that goal, post it, and update it regularly to help encourage employee participation. Remember, don't set goals around scores or positive reviews. The goal is to encourage participation, not to game the system in your favor unfairly.

>> If your scores are high and comments positive, include a link to your review page on your careers page, email signatures, and other job postings.

>> Write an article with a summary of some of the top comments and the programs your company has in place to support employees in that way. For example, if you have several comments about training and development, then pull those quotes, link back to them, and write an article about the training and development programs at your company.

>> Contribute to the conversations with comments. You can typically register your company's page so that you can respond to comments. If you choose to do so, avoid being defensive or abrasive. Instead, use it as an opportunity to boost your culture. In general, treat this with the same empathy you would a customer review.

>> Ensure your company's profile has all the information possible. You can often add photos, articles, and other information. Invest a little time to make yours match the experience you'd like applicants to have with you.

Giving Your Culture a Home Page

Take a look at your careers page on your website. Does it feel like your culture? Could a future employee look at it and instantly get an idea of what working with you would be like? Does it share information about your company, team, culture, and opportunities? Or is it simply a list of open positions waiting to be filled?

TIP

The careers page on your website is often the most wasted opportunity when it comes to using your culture to attract future talent. People show up on this page to learn more, and often it just shares a generic, bland job description. To create a stellar careers page, include company culture highlights and content, stories about your successful employees, videos about your jobs, information about your application and interviewing process, a call-to-action, links to your social review sites (like Glassdoor.com), and other helpful resources you've developed.

The following sections give you the lowdown on just how to make your home page *the* place for potential talent to find out information on everything your company has going for it and bring that talent to your doors.

Setting up a careers landing page that works

In the world of marketing and sales, a *landing page* is a place where prospective buyers end up. These pages typically have one purpose and one function — move the buyer along to the next phase in the relationship. This may be to purchase something, but it may also be to submit an email address, download a checklist/resource, or schedule a call. Your careers page should have the same type of focus and intention. Your goal should be that someone applies for a current position at your company, submits her information for a future position, or deepens the relationship by joining your network by giving her email.

Engaging with culture

It's a pretty safe bet that if someone has landed on your careers page, she is interested in working with you or at least learning about what working with you is like. So why not share all the content you've been creating? Use both the employee- and employer-generated content to answer the questions your prospective employees are looking for. You can organize this in categories or simply serve up the information based on the most frequently asked information.

At minimum, you want to include the answers to the following questions somewhere on your careers page:

>> What is it like to work at XYZ company?

>> Is XYZ company a good place to grow my career? Why?

>> What kinds of people work there? How do they communicate, make decisions, socialize?

>> What's the interview process like at XYZ company?

Telling your employee story

In addition to all the culture-themed content, your careers page should highlight a few employee stories. These can be videos, blog posts, Q&A style posts, top-five roundup posts, and so on. The goal is to give the website visitor a little glimpse into the day-in-the-life of your employees.

A couple of things to keep in mind:

>> If you have specific areas that are difficult to recruit, then create specific content that is search engine–optimized for the keywords those types of candidates would be looking for. For example, you might interview a few engineers or designers if that role is hard to fill. If you're struggling to find bartenders or chefs, then highlight those stories. You want the prospects to say "that sounds like me" when they read or watch.

>> Video is powerful when it comes to storytelling, so if you had one area to spend a little more time and money on, it would be creating day-in-the-life type video content.

Asking the talent to apply

You won't get the sale if you don't ask for it, and you won't get the candidate if you don't let the candidate apply. Your application process should be easy and quick. If you have a 30-minute process that requires three passwords, then you're severely limiting quality candidates from applying. If you allow an applicant to submit a resume or LinkedIn profile but still require him to type in all the information into tiny text fields, then you're sending the message that working with you may be difficult.

REMEMBER

As more and more candidates are exploring and researching companies using mobile phones, you have to create an application process that makes it simple and easy for them to submit their information and interest in working with you.

You'd be surprised at the amount of companies that reach out to improve the flow of applicants that have a 30-minute application process in place. This is a clear sign that people are saying "not worth my time."

TIP

If you have certain positions that are either difficult to fill or frequently open, you can simply have an open position that people can always apply for. If your sales team is growing rapidly, then leave a few sales positions open. If an engineer role is difficult to fill, keep a requisition and position open for applicants that come along. You can specifically state that it's for future opportunities as well. You may also want to schedule a monthly review session to process through candidates so that your hiring managers or recruiters can start to develop relationships with any that are a possible future fit. The best time to start engaging candidates is before you need them.

Using a simple call-to-action

Depending on how frequently you're hiring, there will likely be times when you don't have a position that matches the experiences and career path for the visitor to your site. In most cases, this is where the conversation ends. The prospective candidate — who has read your articles, watched your videos, and connected with your social media channels — simply disappears into the black hole of recruiting, never to be seen or heard from again. What a waste of energy and engagement.

In addition to creating an "always open" position for future opportunities, you can also provide some kind of useful content in exchange for an email address and joining your career network. Think about what would be useful enough that people would want to give their email address to receive it. Maybe a short e-book on interviewing skills? Or a short video course about creating a better resume or LinkedIn profile?

Once you have the email address, here's how to keep in touch and keep your company name front and center in a potential candidate's mind:

>> Reach out with a biweekly or monthly newsletter sharing some of your recent articles, current job openings, and other relevant career information. The more helpful you can be, the stronger the relationship you develop with future talent.

>> Deliver the promised information, article, or training right away to establish trust and start building a relationship.

>> Make sure the first email is simple, short, and elicits some kind of response. The best way to do this is to ask a simple question like, "Thanks for connecting. I'm curious — what kind of job at XYZ company would you be interested in?" Applicants' responses will help you tag their email with specific jobs for future direct outreach from a hiring manager or recruiter.

TIP

If you use an email program like MailChimp, you can set up an email campaign that is delivered to new people who subscribe to the list. In marketing terms, this is called an "onboarding drip campaign" because it is delivered in a series of emails to help "onboard" people to your email list. Take five or six of your best performing articles, videos, or infographics and deliver them over the course of two weeks or so. This will increase engagement and deepen the prospect's awareness of your culture.

Watching Your Competition

If you've done the work in this chapter, you'll be working your way toward the top of the pack when it comes to recruiting top talent. Your culture is the number one tool you have and can help to ensure your pipeline is full of people who share your values. But there's still more to ensure that you're keeping up with your marketplace.

If recruiting is to hiring as marketing is to sales, then you need to keep your eyes on what other companies are doing, saying, and offering to stay competitive.

REMEMBER

The companies you compete with to hire talent are not necessarily the same as the companies you compete with for customers. You'll want to think about companies that have recruited your employees away as well as companies that beat you in recruiting someone. Any organization that hires the people you want to hire should be included in the list of companies you are keeping your eyes on.

TIP

Create a spreadsheet or file folder where you can keep track of the companies you are competing with for talent. You can update this monthly or as news comes to your attention. Use the following list to start organizing your competitive analysis:

>> **Press:** Keep your eyes open for press about competitive companies. While any news could be relative, you want to specifically focus on things that improve the employer brand. This can include articles about fundraising or stock prices, employee-centric awards or certification, new office plans, new market growth, key strategic hires, or winning awards like Best Place to Work.

>> **Benefits:** While your culture and employer brand are the greatest assets you have in winning the war for talent, you need to make sure you take care of the basics for your employees as well. Keep tabs on benefits by completing a quarterly benefit update where you check out the latest job postings from your top competitors. Look at the types of perks, medical benefits, vacation offerings, and other employee programs they offer. You can also create a new employee survey where you survey your newest hires in their first few days (or even before their official start date) to see what benefits their previous employer offered or what other companies they were considering offered. Similarly, this exercise can be repeated during exit interviews to see what the package looks like at the company the employee is joining.

>> **Open positions:** This is an easy way to stay in-the-know about your competition. Watch the positions they have open, the way they write their job descriptions, how they position their culture, and the benefits they list with their jobs.

- » **Glassdoor:** You can learn a lot about what's working and what's not working by checking the Glassdoor reviews for competitors. If you're head-to-head with them for a desired candidate, you can use this information to appeal to the candidate's desire to work in a better culture if your reviews are more positive than the competitor.

- » **Social media:** You should create a place to keep tabs on the companies you often compete with for talent. The simplest way to do this is to create a document with links to their social pages and then schedule 20 minutes weekly to see what's happening with them. Look at the types of content they share, the announcements they make, and the places they're showing up.

- » **Google Alerts:** One easy way to keep track of a few of these areas is to set up a Google Alert for some of your key talent competitors. You will receive an email anytime Google gets wind of a new article about them.

- » **New employees:** If one of your new hires was considering another company, you can ask him about his experience and perspective with the other organization and why he chose you.

Employing the Entire Company as Recruiter

In a world full of marketing messages and paid advertising, the secret to a strong employer brand and robust inbound talent pipeline lies in your current employees. You'll recognize throughout this chapter that using your culture is key to recruiting more people, and those people are more willing to trust your current employees than someone in the recruiting department when it comes to learning about your organization.

Here are some simple ways to get the entire company attracting and recruiting more great people to your team:

- » **Social sharing:** Ask your current employees to share relevant news about your company, your culture, and your open positions.

- » **Teach them:** Organize a few group conversations to teach your current employees how to help recruit more great people like them. It's in your employees' best interests to work with other great people, so they're often interested in helping out. Show them the kinds of things that would be helpful to post on social media, the kinds of people that would be great fits for the roles you have open, and how to help you connect with great candidates.

- >> **LinkedIn:** Help your employees boost their LinkedIn profiles by hosting short workshops or video training. Many job candidates will look at other employees' profiles on social media when researching a company. While you can't control what your employees post, you can help them create a better profile and help them communicate your culture.

- >> **Recommendation program:** Create a referral or recommendation program where current employees can receive a bonus if one of their referrals or recommendations is hired for a position.

Curating a Strong Alumni Referral Network

When most employees leave a company, they disappear as if they never existed. All the knowledge, networks, relationships, and cultural capital walks out the door with them. What a shame to lose all that simply because someone has moved on to a new opportunity.

What if there was a way to keep them engaged beyond the exit interview? What if they could continue to be a source of referrals?

Your former employees understand what it takes to work within the culture of your team and in most cases would be happy to see the company continue to succeed after their exit. By creating a simple alumni network, you can continue to leverage their network and relationships. Referrals and word-of-mouth recommendations are important in tipping the scales of attracting great people, so why not let former employees help out too?

TIP

The simplest way to get started is to create an email list or LinkedIn Group with alumni from your organization. Share your content, industry news, and open positions with them. Then ask specifically if they know anyone who would be a good fit for your open positions. To supercharge your efforts, you can extend the bonus program to them as well by paying them for successful hires based on their referrals. You can also continue to include them in company events, special workshops or training opportunities, and celebrations.

IN THIS CHAPTER

» **Making the link between hiring and culture**

» **Establishing the criteria for your ideal candidate**

» **Creating a culture-centric candidate experience**

» **Designing an effective interviewing process**

» **Sidestepping some typical interviewing mistakes**

Chapter **9**

Hiring to Boost Culture

Having spent 20 years of my life in the hospitality industry, I learned a few things about cooking from watching some of the most talented chefs and flavor engineers dazzle guests night after night. As a sommelier, I discovered the world of winemaking that's equal parts art, science, and improvisation. Yet, it was as an executive growing culture-centric brands that I learned that it's the decisions about what gets put in that determine the value of what comes out.

Every time you make a decision about hiring someone, you're changing the recipe and altering the culture. Each new person has the ability to make things better, make things worse, or keep things the same. Hiring is about making decisions for what's needed next from your team based on what's happening currently, and every time you hire, you send a signal about your values, team, and brand.

In this chapter, I discuss why hiring for culture fit is the wrong way to go, how to hire to get the culture you want, and simple ways to improve the hiring process to boost your culture.

Hiring to Improve Culture

Organizations spend a lot of time on strategy, positioning, marketing, and operations. These areas are measured, reviewed, shared, and celebrated in town halls, at holiday parties, in monthly meetings, and in weekly status updates. They are important and help to keep track of the what and the how of the organization, but rarely does as much attention get paid to the "who" of the organization at that same level.

This is a book about culture that doesn't promote happy hours, ping-pong tables, fancy bonus incentive plans, or free lunches. All those are great, but they don't do much to craft culture. One of the big things people want at work is great people to work with. Sitting at a project meeting with people who are committed to doing great work, who communicate clearly and openly, and who do what they say they will do is one of the greatest joys of the modern workplace. It's your job as a leader to provide that experience to all employees. Culture is driven by those relationships. Those relationships come from the people that you choose to bring into the team.

Making decisions about who should be on your team is one of the most important factors in being able to maintain your culture and boost your brand. Culture is about people — arguably, business is ultimately about people too — so who and how you hire is one of the key determinants of long-term, sustainable success. If you fill your organization with people who aren't in line with your values or excited about the core work your organization does, then it's unlikely that you can achieve the results you want. You'll spend a lot of time on damage control, trying to course correct, and spend a lot of energy trying to get people to be what they probably are not.

If your organization is growing quickly, then managers should spend a large portion of their time on hiring. Throughout my career, I've been part of fast-growing brands and in most cases spent something like 30 percent of my time focused on interviewing and hiring. And I've never regretted spending that amount of time (and in some cases more). Make sure that you are carving out time to do the work required to get great candidates — and ultimately hire the right person. This might mean marking specific blocks of time on your calendar for interviewing-related work or leaving certain days open as candidate sourcing and interviewing days. The time spent here will save you in spades later by helping you to avoid making the wrong hire.

Fixing the Recruiting Cycle

Let's just kill the elephant in the room right off the bat. The whole idea of hiring for culture fit is full of bias (unconscious and conscious) and leaves far too much room for interpretation, which ultimately leads to culture denigration. Lots of hiring managers (and sadly, even a lot of talent and recruiting leaders) drank the culture-fit Kool-Aid a long time ago. It makes sense at face value — look for people who look, act, and sound like the rest of the team and you'll make the team better. But that's not always the case. Often culture fit leaves you with a group of look-alike "yes" people who struggle to bring new perspectives and ideas to the table. So, if finding people to "fit" into your culture doesn't work, then looking for people who can add to your culture is the answer.

The other big mistake often made is the overreliance on a poorly designed job description to do the work of clarifying the position needs and attracting candidates. The standard process usually involves copy-and-paste from an old position or even one found online. Then the manager reviews it and signs off that the ideal candidate would fit that description — but there is so much more to consider: like why you are hiring for this role, why not, and what does success look like. Yes, job descriptions are needed for clarity and legal reasons, but you need to move beyond them for attracting great talent.

Fitting into culture

Culture fit is a broken method for finding the right people to contribute to your company. Not only does it leave you in the same cycle of hiring as you've always had, but it's also an open invitation for unconscious bias. When people claim an applicant isn't a cultural fit but struggle to define exactly why, it typically means there is some other kind of bias at play. I've heard people say "I know it when I see it," but the challenge there is that it means you have seen "it" before and that you are probably just hiring only those who look and act like what you already have. Diversity is not simply a nice-to-have moral obligation — it improves results from the bottom line to innovation (see Chapter 16).

When most people talk about culture fit, they're really thinking about someone they'd like to go to happy hour with or chat with around the water cooler. I've heard wayward hiring managers talk about candidates being "too bro" and someone else being too "emotional." Neither of those has anything to do with the job, and neither of them really has anything to do with company culture. Someone won't fit in because they like to play football? It's unconscious bias at play. Not only is it morally wrong, but it's also going to leave your culture at risk of having a lot of the same khaki-laden people with the same ideas and same backgrounds. In some cases, this has kept women and minorities from getting a job. For your culture (and your company) to thrive, you need a range of ideas and contributors.

Hiring for culture fit might not help you get the culture you want either. It's likely there are some areas of your company culture that you want to improve — you are reading a book on company culture after all. To do that, you need to bring more people into the organization that can help with that transition — people who can help you move closer toward the culture you want to create. Stop looking for culture fit and start looking for culture add!

Moving beyond the job description

In the world of hiring, the job description really needs some disruption. In the best cases, job descriptions clarify some of the basics of the role. In the worst cases, they're a bunch of jargon-laden mumbo jumbo that no one really reads. I'm not sure where it started, but somewhere along the way, they become more about compliance than about attracting talent and defining expectations.

This chapter has some ideas for rethinking the job description, but in a broader sense, I have a few ideas for you to keep in mind as you interview. And since your goal in interviewing is to find the right match for the role — someone with the experience, the interest, and the approach that will help you find success together, regardless of what type of job description you're using — using the following list as a catalyst for what to look for in a candidate will be a great tool:

>> What would the company/division/department look like in 12-, 18-, 24-months were this person to be successful?

>> What is their particular role in making this happen?

>> What track record or expertise and experience will they demonstrate that gives you confidence that they can do it in your company?

Defining Your Ideal Candidate

The people you surround yourself with at work determine your culture, your brand, your reputation, and your results. Your goal is to align skills, culture, and values so that your candidate can excel at the business stuff while thriving in your culture (and even helping to make it better). Taking time before you begin the job description, the phone screening, and the interviewing to really think about what you need is an important (and often overlooked) step in hiring the right people for your culture. Sure, most people usually give a little thought to getting the job description done (or finding one online to copy-and-paste), but a much deeper dive is required to make sure you are bringing someone in who adds value to your culture and helps your team achieve the next big thing.

One of the first steps you need to take in the hiring process is to figure out just what you want from your candidate. Visualize what you see this person doing day to day and then write down:

- » **What you need done.** Get really specific about the reasons you are hiring this person. Think about what you hope they'll accomplish and what success would be like in 3, 6, and 12 months with the right candidate. If you are hiring a trainer for your company, do you need someone really good at developing technical training or someone who is great at leading workshops? If you had to choose one over the other, what would that choice be?

- » **What experience the candidate should have.** By knowing what you need the role to fulfill (see the preceding bullet), you can assess if someone can do that through past experiences and possible job testing.

- » **The best way for people to get results in your organization.** Think about what's made other people successful in your company. This is where your culture starts to really make an impact. Does your team respond best to people who are direct, aggressive, and bold or would someone more nurturing, thoughtful, and steady be more successful on your team?

TIP

You should create this list every time you're hiring for a position, even if it's a role you have other people in currently. It gives you a chance to validate your assumptions from the last hires to determine whether your thinking was right or whether you need to adjust your approach a little. It also gives you the opportunity to update your profile for changes in the market, your strategy, and shifts in your culture. Maybe your sales team has a lot of great inbound representatives who are the best order takers in the business who approach sales with a client service mindset, but you need to hire a few "hunter" style salespeople to find outbound leads. This shifts your profile.

REMEMBER

The real question you should be asking is, "Who has the best chance to succeed given how we work and what we need from this role now?"

Creating a clear purpose for the position available

Start with a clear purpose or mission for each open position. This is the high-level version of "what does success look like in this role." The purpose should answer the question, "Why are we hiring someone to fill this slot?" and it should distinguish how this role can help your organization and why it's different from a similarly titled role at another organization. As you interview candidates, the purpose for the role should be present. You should ask yourself, "Given everything I've learned about this candidate, do I believe they can help us achieve that purpose in our organization?"

The purpose can stay internal to the hiring team, but you can also use it in your job description to really attract the kinds of candidates who are interested in doing the work you need.

Check out a bad example of a role purpose:

> Maximize shareholder value through developing and leveraging our core platform while building a team of A-players who can minimize communication issues, drive results, and ensure customer satisfaction.

Umm, what? This is confusing, unclear, unspecific, and loaded with jargon. This isn't going to help applicants understand what they'd be doing, how they'd be held accountable, and how they could be successful. In the same way, it's going to make it hard for the interviewing committee and hiring manager to really understand what they're looking for in a candidate.

Here's a better example of a role purpose:

> Double our revenue in the next two years by building a team of enterprise sales representatives and helping our current small-medium business sales representatives improve productivity. Increase customer satisfaction scores by improving the process between sales and client services.

Pretty specific, right? The goals are clearly outlined. A vision of success is clearly stated, and anyone interviewing a candidate for this role would be able to understand exactly why you're hiring and what this person would be doing at your company. This kind of clarity not only improves the hiring process but also boosts your culture through promoting transparency and communication.

TIP

Use this purpose as you gather your hiring committee, as you plan your sourcing strategy, as you interview candidates, and as you assess the people you've interviewed. This one activity alone can improve your hiring results threefold.

Clarifying the objectives and results

Once you're clear on why you're hiring this person in the first place, you need to get clear on how you'll measure that success in specific objectives and results.

This is typically somewhere between three to five big objectives with supporting results (see Chapter 19 for more on goals).

The goal is to move beyond the typical "requirements" you'd see in a job description and to think more deeply about what really needs to get done for this role. The hiring manager is going to be able to evaluate whether applicants have been successful in their first year, so why not front-load the process with that information to make a better decision in the first place? In most cases, if this information is provided to candidates, they will self-select as well. The more clearly you can define what's needed in a role for a person to be successful and what the person will be accountable for, the more qualified the applicants will be. No one wants to start a new job and realize they have a pretty high risk of failing at it.

Check out Table 9-1 for a way to match objectives and results to the role's purpose.

TABLE 9-1

Matching Objectives and Results to a Role's Purpose

Purpose: Double our revenue in the next two years by building a team of enterprise sales representatives and helping our current small-medium business (SMB) sales representatives improve productivity. Increase customer satisfaction scores by improving the process between sales and client services.

Objectives	Results
Grow revenue	Double revenue from $15 million to $30 million by the end of year two
	Improve SMB rep productivity from 5 deals per month to 10 deals per month in year one
Increase customer satisfaction	Improve customer satisfaction with sales process from 70% to 90% by end of year two
	Launch training around handoff process in coordination with client services team within six months
Leadership	Create strategy and hire five enterprise sales representatives by end of Q3 in year one
	Design and launch sales training boot camp by end of year

Setting the values and competencies

Once you're clear on why you're hiring someone (purpose) and what you'll measure to determine success (objectives and results), you then need to consider "how" you want the person to do get it done. This is where your culture comes in pretty heavily.

If you look at the purpose example in Table 9-1, there are lots of ways employees can get that work done. They can be ruthless and kind. They can be authoritarian or consultative. They can be inefficient or resourceful. Your culture and your values will dictate what you need to think about here.

Consider your organization's values (see Chapter 7 for an in-depth discussion on how to identify values). Make a list of values and behaviors to create a scorecard or checklist to use during interviews. This will help make sure you find not only people who can get the work done but also people who can do it in a way that's in line with your culture.

Additionally, you want to give some thought to the top eight to ten competencies someone will need to achieve success. For example, in the example given in Table 9-1, it would probably be good if this person was competent at building a team through hiring and training. Now that may not be one of your company values, but it's definitely a core competency when you think about a role where someone needs to design training, build a team, and improve results. Competencies are different than behaviors in that behaviors are the way someone acts (for example, is coachable when given feedback or is thoughtful when sharing difficult information), and competencies are the things people can actually do (such as, use a specific type of software, develop training workbooks, talk about wine in an educated way).

Don't go too far down the road of defining every single thing you'd ever like to see in the most perfect candidate. Stick to the values and associated behaviors and the competencies that someone will really need to be successful in achieving the purpose and goals for this role.

Doing this work at the start will help improve your hiring process, which impacts your culture significantly.

Writing a Better Job Description

Your goal in designing a job description is to bring your culture to the forefront so that applicants can get a sense of what working with you is like. You'll find that more of your applicants are a better fit for your team and needs when you're more specific.

Selling the job

The real goal of a job posted online is to attract the right kinds of people to your team. The best way to do that is to help potential candidates see themselves being successful in the job.

The opening lines of your job posting should be engaging. Think more marketing and less legal. It's important to keep in mind that you can have two documents for this purpose: one that is on-file as the official job description in the HR office and another that is used for marketing purposes to attract your dream applicants. You want to entice people to keep reading. The best way to do this is to focus on the candidate. Let the candidate be the hero in this story. Instead of saying, "We are looking for a digital marketing coordinator. You must blah-blah-blah," you could say, "Are you looking to make your mark through digital marketing? Do you obsess over analyzing digital trends and thinking of the next big thing? If so, then we should talk. Our digital marketing will be {insert purpose from the activity in the earlier section 'Creating a clear purpose for the position available'}."

TIP

If you need help with this, ask some of your current employees. They'll know best what other people like them would be looking for and can probably highlight the benefits someone would experience working with you even better than you can.

In today's tight labor market, you have to focus on what the employee will get by working with you. Consider the first paragraph of your job posting a love letter to your future dream hire. Whether your culture is conservative and steeped in tradition or playful and soaked in fun — writing a strong opening paragraph that captures the attention of your dream candidate is key. If you notice you aren't getting the kinds of candidates you most want in your candidate pipeline, consider making this opening section much more compelling to them.

WARNING

You may want to still have job descriptions that outline your jobs in some specific way according to local and national laws. I'm not your employment lawyer, so seek advice for that. This is simply referring to the way you attract people to the jobs. You can share a full job description later in the interview process as required.

Getting the requirements right

Do you really care about how many years of experience someone has if the person can't do the work? Would you pass over someone with three years of experience who had been successful doing what you need done over someone with seven years of experience but no track record of success with your goals? Similarly, there's a shift in the college-degree requirement, with many companies changing their approach to requiring a specific degree.

Over the years, I've worked with lots of operational leaders who would proudly report that they had 20 years of experience. In a lot of cases, I found they had the same one year of experience 20 times in a row — meaning they hadn't really grown or changed in that time. If you find someone today who talks about his or her long experience as a manager or leader but at the same time complains about the new generation of workers, then I think you've found someone who's living the same year over and over versus someone who has been adapting and thriving.

The best thing you can do to get requirements right is to use the outcomes from the "Clarifying the objectives and results" section earlier to develop the competencies needed. For example, if one of the objectives for the position is someone who can help to launch a new product within their first six months, then a correlated requirement would be that they have product launch experience. If a desired result is to have $500,000 in enterprise sales within six months, then a requirement would be previous enterprise sales experience. Once you have a dialed-in list, use those in your job posting to help clarify exactly what someone will need to succeed.

Crafting the Candidate Experience

Every candidate interaction is a chance to communicate and teach what your organization is about. Imagine that you end up hiring a person and during the orientation you talk about the importance of clear communication, positive interactions, a warm and welcoming feeling, and being on time, but the person didn't experience any of that during the interview process. This starts to create a disconnect right from the beginning between what you say matters and what actually happens.

During the interview process, you'll be evaluating and judging your applicants. And they'll be doing the same to you. Is your office organized or cluttered? Do your interviews start and end on time? Does your team seem stressed and overwhelmed? You should review the candidate experience by filtering each step along the way through your values statement (see Chapter 7). If you state that you value kind and direct feedback, then you need to make sure that the candidate experiences both. This helps strengthen the culture and the candidate experience.

TIP

Every step of the interview process is an opportunity for you to create an impression with your possible new employee. Here are some tips to keep in mind as you review how your candidate starts experiencing your culture before their first day:

>> **Culture first:** If your organization is traditional and conservative, then make sure that's clear in the interviewing process. If your culture is friendly and casual, then keep that at the forefront of your process. This will help candidates have a better idea of what they're getting themselves into and helps to make sure you're assessing the candidate fairly. You can do this by making sure your communications, interview rooms, interviewers, and the follow-up are all consistent with your culture.

>> **Time:** Interviewing should take precedence over other meetings and commitments. Always start and end on time to show that you respect their time and take this seriously.

>> **Organization:** Make sure everyone in the hiring committee is clear about the schedule and the goals. There's nothing worse than a candidate feeling like your team can't get it together to organize a three-hour interview cycle. It may leave the applicant wondering what the rest of the company's initiatives look like.

>> **Communication:** Make sure you're clear on who and when and what will be communicated with the candidate. It's pretty disconcerting to get different messages from different people. It says a lot about your culture if you aren't all on the same page.

Evaluating the Interview Process

Designing a consistent and effective interviewing process will save you time, help you evaluate results over time, and improve the chances that you'll make the right hiring decisions. This doesn't mean that every single person will interview exactly the same or always get to the same place in an interview, but it does mean you have an organized process that can be used to give you measurable results time and time again.

You may be interviewing actual rocket scientists for your team at Space-X, looking for your next social media guru, or hiring a host to work the front counter at your restaurant. Clearly those are going to involve different technical assessments, backgrounds, experiences, and interviewing committees. Similarly, you may be interviewing for someone to join a very conservative and formal culture or an informal and playful one. An engineer interviewing at Apple and Google will find two very different environments, even if both roles are working on cellphone technologies. I'm not here to tell you what you should be looking for in your perfect hire — use the purpose and objectives exercise discussed earlier in this chapter to determine that. I'm not telling you what type of people are best for the culture of your team — use the information you documented in the "Setting the values and competencies" section earlier to determine that. But I do know that a hiring process that's organized and intentional will give you better results every time over one that's haphazard and unfocused.

TIP

While the hiring manager may be the best person to assess the technical skills and experiences of the candidate, other people on the team can be helpful in evaluating the values and behaviors that drive your culture forward. I always recommend that each interview include at least two people interviewing the candidate. Read on for some ideas to help you get your team on the same page when it comes to finding the best people to work with you.

Prescreening for success

Prescreening is a short face-to-face encounter (dropping off an application) or phone conversation focused on a few of the core requirements needs for the position (for example, being able to use specific programming languages or having experience with a certain style of buyer). Your goal is simply to eliminate anyone who isn't a match for the work you need done.

TIP

You can really boost the culture connection by having hiring managers involved in this step of the process. It puts them in the driver's seat in talent acquisition. It also gives candidates an early sample of the manager they'll be working for if they accept the job.

In order to help your screening calls stay focused and intentional, it's helpful to develop a standard list of questions that the person screening applicants can use each time. It should include the following goals and questions:

>> Does this person have the basic experience required? You may be looking for a training manager who will be responsible for writing new e-course outlines. If the candidate has never done that before, it may be best to move along.

>> What's the applicant's schedule availability? If you need someone to work the weekend shifts at the hotel and your applicant is only available on Mondays and Wednesdays, then it's not a match.

>> Do they understand the goals for the position and believe they can achieve them?

>> Are they interested in doing the work you need done? If you've done the purpose and objectives work earlier, this will be easier to assess.

You can usually get to this by asking just a few questions:

>> What made you apply for this position? Why are you taking the time to talk with me?

>> What are your career goals? What would you like to work on next?

>> What areas at work do you excel at?

>> What do you not like doing so much?

>> What do you really love about your company now? What's great about your specific role and projects?

At the end of this conversation, you'll have an idea of how this person works and why she's excited about that work, whether she has the skills and experience to warrant further discussion, and what she's interested in doing next. You should compare this to the needs you outlined in the job description to see if there is alignment. It's not helpful to keep moving forward with a candidate who's really interested in exploring growth-hacker style marketing if you're looking for a brand strategist with big media interests.

Exploring technical skills

Before you dive into whether someone would be a good addition to your culture, you want to make sure the person has the technical competency required to do the work. This will swing widely depending on the technical aspects required for the role.

If you're interviewing an engineer, give him a sample programming exercise and an environment to work within. Give him some time to work on the problem and present his solution. If your engineers work in teams, you could even include some of your current employees in this step to see how they communicate with other people, handle challenges presented by their peers, and what it might be like to have them on the team.

If you're interviewing an accountant, give her some financial statements and ask her to provide an analysis to some of the team who are prepared to ask questions, present challenges, and provide feedback. While it is pretty common to ask financial questions during an interview, it's still important to actually give candidates some data and ask them to show their work. It improves your ability to assess their talent pretty widely.

If you're interviewing someone for a sales role, give him some time with your sales materials and then have him role-play some sales situations. Better yet, have him try to sell you his current product from wherever he's working now.

For a graphic designer, give her a short design task like rebuilding a logo or creating a hi-fi wireframe. Then, ask her to create a few concepts to share with the team who will then ask questions about her design process, the choices she made, and why she decided to present this specific final prototype.

In the hospitality environment, I encourage people to have candidates work a trial shift. This is anywhere from three to four hours with the candidate working alongside others in the company. Recently, a consulting client of mine was hiring people to work in the kitchen and reached out because they kept missing the mark with their hires. It turns out their kitchen was an open concept, with guests sitting right in front of the cooks, which changes the role a bit from being a line cook to also being directly responsible for customer service. We made some changes to the way they hire so that it included a technical assessment of the cook's ability to engage guests with a smile and eye contact.

You get the point.

Regardless of the role, you should take the time to assess the technical abilities. You'll learn more about how the person actually works than you would ever learn through hours of behavioral conversations.

WARNING

Make sure to seek out advice on whether you need to pay candidates for this time. In some jurisdictions, you need to pay them as an independent contractor. It's worth the small investment because it gives you the best sense of their work skills and process.

WARNING

It is important to note that the candidate should not be expected to have gotten everything right and should not be judged on accuracy. After all, they couldn't possibly have all the information that a full-time and long-term staff member has. They should be judged on process more than product.

Testing critical thinking

At the end of the technical interview, you want to take a deep dive into the way the candidate did the work. During this phase, your goal is to learn about the process someone uses to solve problems and think critically. Obviously, the level involved will be different based on the role, but you should always take time to understand more about the decisions the candidate made and why.

Your big questions should be:

>> Why did you make that choice?

>> What have you done like this before?

>> How did you determine that was the best choice?

>> Tell more about . . .

This is ultimately what you're getting when you make the hire — how this person goes about solving problems and delivering results. So spend time really making sure you understand the candidate's process so that you can start to evaluate if it is in line with the needs of the position and matches up to your culture. For example, if you are interviewing someone for a manager position and your company really values collaborative leaders who build consensus, sell their ideas, and serve the team (see Chapter 5 for more about being a servant leader), and the person you are interviewing manages people using authority, power, and dictating to them, then this person wouldn't be a positive add to your culture. By getting specific on how they operate, you can start to uncover the details behind the initial answers they give you.

Conducting the culture interview

The easiest way to do this is to use the values and behaviors you discern in earlier sections in this chapter (and in Chapter 7) as the basis for diving into how this candidate works with others.

Use the competencies, values, and behaviors as a checklist for the interviewers. You don't need to get too creative with questions either. Typically you can focus on asking just a few questions and then diving deeper into each answer provided by the candidate. The initial questions should be framed around some specific competency, area, or desired outcome.

>> What have been your biggest accomplishments in XYZ area of your career?

>> What's been your biggest learning around XYZ in your career?

Then you should dive deeper into the responses provided by the candidate by asking:

>> How did you do that?

>> Who else was involved? In what way? At what level?

>> What was that like?

>> Tell me more . . .

WARNING

As you introduce more people to your hiring process, make sure to take the time to teach them about your approach, including any of the tools, forms, or resources your team uses. You also need to ensure you're covering what types of questions are off-limits for legal reasons. It's typically best to approach this over time by having new interviewers interview alongside more experienced interviewers. In the beginning, the more experienced person should lead the process and slowly transition to the newer person leading.

TIP

Involving more people in the interview process can also help to improve your culture with those team members. Not only does it help create more buy-in and support for the new people you are hiring, but it also can help deepen the relationship the new interviewers have with the culture themselves. By talking about the culture, evaluating people on their ability to add to the culture, and assessing the needs of the culture, it starts to steep them even further in your company culture and helps them connect to it even more.

Leading the interview

In leading an interview, you can really boost your culture and uncover the key components about a candidate that are most important to you and your organization. The biggest thing to keep in mind here is that the interview experience should closely match your culture. If you need a clue into what that looks like, then take a peek at the values and behaviors of your team. Then ask, "How could we apply that to the candidate's experience," or, "What would that look like in the interview?"

At the start of the interview process and during each round of interviewing, the person leading the interview should share the goals with the candidate and make an introduction to the way the interview will proceed. This can be as simple as stating, "We have about 45 minutes together today, and our goal is to learn a little bit more about how you approach XYZ."

REMEMBER

Your goal in the interview is not to intimidate or interrogate the candidate. It's to get an honest understanding of what working together would look like and whether this person could achieve the purpose of this role in a way that's aligned with your culture. Do what you can to make the candidate comfortable and at ease in a way that feels right for your culture. And if your culture is intimidating and full of interrogative leadership, then it may be time to evaluate if that's really working for you. Call me!

Debriefing for success

Once the interviews have completed, it's time to debrief with the candidate and everyone involved in the interview process. This should be done as close to the last interview as possible. In my experience, this is best done if everyone submits their comments, scores, and assessments in writing before the debrief takes place. Once all comments have been submitted, it helps if everyone can see everyone else's comments before discussing the candidate to improve the quality of the debrief meeting. Doing it this way also helps eliminate groupthink or power dynamics, where everyone starts to share the same opinion or the opinion of the person with the most power. It also shows you where people are defining terms radically differently and perhaps misunderstanding culture, skills, or experience requirements.

If everyone was a pass, it will save you a lot of time. If there's one specific area of concern, it will help you focus on that. If everyone makes a glowing recommendation to hire, then you can move forward quickly as well.

In general, it's best to let the hiring manager make the decision. She's the one who will have to work with this person and help the person achieve success in the role.

She's responsible for achieving results with this hire. She should take all the other comments into consideration and make a call.

If you find that people in the debrief are fundamentally at odds, it's typically a sign that there's either a lack of clarity about the expectation for this role and you need to go back to the purpose and objectives activity, or there's a cultural divide around how to get the work done and you need to revisit the values, behaviors, and competency activity from earlier in this chapter.

TIP

If you're scheduling an hour for the interview and find that people are running out of time to submit their notes in writing, then schedule 45 minutes for the actual interview and 15 minutes for the post-interview write-up to help give the interviewers scheduled time to complete their notes to increase compliance.

Making the Offer

You've done it! You've found the perfect person to do the work in a way that contributes to your culture and has the promise to deliver big results. The traditional approach to making a job offer won't do much for communicating your culture and getting your newest team member excited about being part of your team. If part of culture is a shared commitment to values and a common sense of purpose, then you have a big opportunity to spread the message with your offer. Similarly, if your communication and relationship philosophies are the two vehicles that help instill and boost culture, then the offer letter is a chance to say a lot about how things work at your company. Even though an offer letter may sound like a traditional approach, I show you ways to include the basic necessary information as well as ways to really pump it up and showcase your culture.

Covering the basics

Many organizations have a standardized offer letter template that covers the basic details. The idea is to make sure the new hire and employer are on the same page regarding the basic details of employment. Getting all this information out in the open and clear contributes to a culture of transparency. It helps everyone start the relationship on the right foot and with a shared vision.

In general, you want to make sure you've outlined:

>> **Title:** What's this person's job title going to be?

>> **Start date:** When does the person begin employment?

>> **Compensation:** This should include base salary, commission, bonus, and any equity/stock options/ownership.

>> **Benefits:** The basic details about additional benefits should be covered clearly, including coverage amounts and any payments due from the employee.

>> **Terms:** This applies if the offer is contingent upon signing other documents like non-disclosure, non-compete agreement, and so on.

Creating a wow offer

After the basic requirements, how do you really stand out from the pack? Imagine your newest employee being truly wowed by your offer letter in a way that helps him really understand the kind of culture and team he'll be becoming part of on his first day.

The best offer letter packages include:

>> **Brand:** You can dress up your offer letter package significantly by giving it a little trade dress with your company colors, design elements, and logo. Think beyond a standard word processor document and use a tool like Keynote or PowerPoint to really give it some brand appeal. Your new hire will start to get the vibe and feel of your company if his first interactions are consistent with how you want him to feel about you later.

>> **Compensation clarity:** In addition to the details of your compensation, you can include information about how compensation is set at your organization. Do you use market rates to update annually? How will compensation be reviewed and with what frequency? If part of the compensation package includes equity or stock, include a plain language description of what that means, how it vests over time, and some different scenarios.

>> **Office information:** Go beyond the basics. In addition to parking and access basics, you can create a guide that includes favorite lunch options, public transportation stops, and nearby amenities. You can really boost the culture connections by pulling that information from current employees and including pictures, titles, and departments along with their favorite office tips.

>> **First week details:** After leading thousands of employees through new hire orientations over the years, the one thing I've consistently heard is that people wish they had a better idea about what would happen in their first week on the job. Something about not knowing what's coming next is unsettling for people. Include a quick overview of the first week, including any meetings, trainings, or group lunches. This will help settle their nerves and start to get them excited about meeting the team.

>> **Advice from the team:** One of my favorite ideas is to include some advice from your current employees. Send out an email, survey, or conduct some short interviews asking, "What do you wish you knew in your first few weeks about working here that you've learned now?" or, "What's the number one thing a new hire should know in their first month with us?" You'll get a bunch of fun responses and can turn those into a short guide with names, pictures, and titles. This can just be a simple slide deck, infographic, or even a fun video. Not only will the information be helpful but it'll also start to build relationships.

>> **Contact info:** Your new hire will probably have the basic contact information, but give it all to him again in one place. This should include his hiring manager and anyone else he may need to reach out to before his first day.

>> **Organizational chart:** You can give your new hires a little preview of your team by providing a simple org chart with your offer letter. Depending on the size of your organization, you don't need to go into every single person in the company but can just include departments and jobs.

>> **Social boost:** Include a page with links to some of the social media accounts of your company so he can connect if he'd like. You can also include some sample copy that he can use to update his LinkedIn profile with details about his new job. It's always fun when you can connect with new coworkers before you even show up for your first day!

Avoiding the Most Common Interviewing Mistakes

There really isn't one right way to approach hiring. The best way will be determined by your culture, your hiring managers, and the goals of the positions you're looking to fill. But there are a few things that can seriously derail your efforts to improve your culture through hiring.

Letting HR run the show

Most organizations put the responsibility for hiring and recruiting on the recruiters from the HR department. The recruiters are responsible for sourcing, interviewing, organizing, and finally hiring candidates. This is costing you great talent. Everyone in your organization should be helping in recruiting, and your hiring managers should be held accountable for having the talent on their team needed for getting results.

This doesn't mean that hiring managers can go rogue and do whatever they want when it comes to interviewing and hiring. You can still follow guidelines and a process designed by your HR team while also making managers responsible for driving that process. But it does mean that the hiring managers should be the ones reaching out to candidates, doing phone screens, conducting in-person interviews and guiding them through the process, and making the offers. You've got to coach and train them on how to do it best, but it's worth the investment.

If you find yourself competing for talent, this is one of the areas in which you can really shine. Your prospective employees are going to join the company because they want to work with that manager, not because the recruiting team was polite. By putting the manager at the forefront of the process, you send a strong message about the relationships and culture at your company. This can help put you at the top of the list when candidates are considering many options.

Looking for A-players

In my career, I've been very lucky to pretty consistently be surrounded by some of the most committed and talented people. Whether opening new restaurants, launching national marketing campaigns, hiring enough people to double a company's revenue and employee size in a year, or selling luxury real estate, I've uncovered a secret about hiring A-players.

Time and time again, people ask me where I found all these great people. I've heard founders, leaders, and managers lament their "lack of talent" and complain about "kids these days." They think that there is a secret place where great employees exist.

The real secret? Most employees can be A-players if you give them a strong culture, great managers, and a solid team to work with. It's kind of like the talent pool on *American Idol.* If 100 people apply for a position, one of them will be Kelly Clarkson–level talented and is destined to do great things with or without your job. On the other end, one of them will be William Hung — not a match for the role no matter which environment they're in. Chalk it up to whatever you want, but they just keep finding the dark side of every situation. That leaves you with 98 other people who have the opportunity to be pretty good if matched to the right position and put in the right environment. In reality TV, we only see the Kellys and the Williams. The other 98 percent don't make it on screen because they aren't that bad and they aren't that good. In your talent acquisition, you have room to find the 98 percent and then help them deliver great results for your company.

So the secret here is that you need to focus really hard on getting that match right. Then you have to make sure you've created a culture that drives the kinds of conditions where people can succeed. Stop talking about finding A-players and focus on getting clearer about what you really need in each position and what success looks like for that role.

Making new friends

You've probably seen it or experienced it. The interview starts off with some casual chatting about the weather, the Cubs, or the traffic — which makes sense. It's a nice way to make the candidate feel comfortable. But then 45 minutes later, the interview ends and neither party ever really discussed much work-related info.

I'm not suggesting the interview should be an interrogation, but I am suggesting that most of the interview should be about the work — what's been done, how it got done, what needs to be done, and how this candidate would approach it. If you leave the interview "liking" someone but unclear on how that person would approach being successful in your organization, then you need to seriously reconsider your interviewing style.

One of the things that can happen easily with an interviewer who is not skilled at interviewing is that they tend to talk too much instead of focusing on learning about the candidate. This often leads the interviewer to rate the interview and candidate higher simply because the interviewer got to speak more — which most of us like. If you follow the suggestions and interviewing guidelines in this chapter, it will drastically improve your interviews and reduce the chance of this happening to you.

Playing armchair psychologist

I've never actually been part of an interview process that included a psychologist, but I've been nearly fooled into thinking I was on several occasions. I've heard hiring managers talk about how a candidate was feeling inside, making assumptions about a candidate's motivations because they mentioned a childhood trauma, and whether someone was a sociopath in one instance. As an interviewer, your job is not to provide a psychological assessment of a candidate — and frankly most of us aren't qualified to determine this from a job interview anyway. Keep the interview focused on the information you were able to assess based on the interview, the specific results you've identified you need from the candidates, and what you're actually qualified to assess. Determining someone's ability to be successful at the work needed is the goal.

My Favorite Piece of Advice for Hiring

When it comes to hiring, there's no shortage of information out there. Everyone who has had to interview a few folks in their day will usually take some time to give you their advice, from trick questions to gut feelings.

After interviewing close to 10,000 people across industries, from hotels to restaurants to retail to tech startups to manufacturing plants, I've seen one thing to be remarkably and sustainably true:

> If you are not incredibly excited about a candidate, then don't hire the person.

REMEMBER

If you wouldn't bring the candidate in front of your boss, the company, your customers, and the Board of Directors and say, "Look at who I've found! I can't wait for you to see this person in action because I am confident they will be amazing for us," then that is not the person for you. What I've found is that if the hiring manager isn't willing to go out on that limb, then there's only a slim chance that the person would be successful if hired.

Now this isn't an excuse to just throw it all out the window and focus on hiring the people you like best. The reality is, you probably wouldn't stand in front of that group of people and risk possible career destruction for someone you just liked either. You should still use the ideas in this chapter to interview and learn about a candidate. You should always seek to match the real job you need done with the best person to do it. You should always listen to other people involved in the interview process.

After all of that, you should hire the person with whom you have the best chance of winning and succeeding.

IN THIS CHAPTER

» **Grasping the importance of a strong onboarding process**

» **Developing a clear vision for your new hire experience**

» **Assessing and improving your onboarding process**

» **Using the buddy system to help new employees navigate**

» **Tapping technology to improve onboarding**

» **Leveraging your new hires to find more new talent**

Chapter **10**

Onboarding New Hires

You've done the work. You've found that elusive unicorn to join your team in your awesome, talented, and engaged new employee. Now just hand her a cup of coffee, a laptop, and somewhere to store her succulent and you'll have employee success, right? Well, maybe. Perhaps you've found that one special person who just does great stuff no matter what's happening around her. But for most people, the first 90 days at a new job are a critical period of time to build relationships, connect to the organization's values, and begin to develop the cultural know-how to succeed as part of your team. In fact, how you handle their first 90 days communicates a lot about, and has a big impact on, your culture.

This chapter helps you create and execute a new hire onboarding plan — a plan of how to integrate an employee into your organization — that helps drive your culture and improve results. From getting clear on what new employees need most to understanding how to leverage technology to improve the process, you'll be able to design a comprehensive onboarding plan.

Using Onboarding to Set the Stage

You've hired your new employee because you have some specific outcome that needs to be achieved and probably some ideas of how you'd like that to be done from a values perspective. I hear from organizations all the time that their people are their biggest asset, and yet so many companies struggle with creating a strong and engaging kickoff to a new career. New product launches, new marketing campaigns, and growth initiatives include lots of planning, tracking, and execution, yet one of the most important things your company will do — hire talent — gets little attention except for ensuring your new employee has his paperwork completed properly for legal reasons. It's time to improve the onboarding process.

REMEMBER

Without much thought put into it, the new hire onboarding experience usually ends up being poorly managed and under delivers on the opportunity to really define culture and boost your brand. This is the time when your newest additions consciously and unconsciously learn the priorities and values of the organization. What is the experience you create for your new hires saying about your brand?

Did you hire them under the auspice that your company is a creative and innovative driver of change but then have them spend their entire first day reading rules, signing papers, and learning where the emergency exits are? This kind of incongruent, inconsistent, and lackluster onboarding leads to early job abandonment and disengagement — and that's if you're lucky. Imagine if they end up staying with you longer but haven't really been engaged in the work, connected to the company, or clear on the vision.

To create a strong culture, organizations need to improve this bland and wasted first impression and trade it for an experience that helps build confidence, create clarity, develop relationships, and contribute to culture understanding. Without a process in place, you run the risk of unclear expectations, low morale, financial loss, service issues, missed goals, and unnecessary (and costly) turnover.

When it comes to designing a positive and engaging onboarding experience that helps to drive culture and boost employee productivity, you have to include four key areas:

>> **Confidence:** In the early days of the new hire's experience, your job as a leader is to help new employees gain confidence in everything — their role, their knowledge of the company, their awareness of current concerns, and their relationship with their manager. The more employees feel confident about doing great work and their ability to accomplish what's required, the better results will be across the board, including turnover. People don't want to stay in situations where they're anxious and nervous about their ability to

do what's required. In the beginning, more face time spent clarifying and reviewing is a good thing.

WARNING

The idea of leaving people alone to figure things out in the beginning is a really bad one. Lots of hiring managers falsely believe that they should leave people alone to let them settle in, but this often results in new employees feeling confused, lost, and not confident about their new role.

>> **Expectation clarity:** During the hiring process, organizations often write job descriptions that mean so much to them internally, filled with lingo or verbiage known only to them, or based upon history unknown to the outside world. As a result, managers think they are communicating years of knowledge in the job description, but leave the new hire befuddled as to what to do first. New employees are looking for clarity about what to do now and what to do next; they want to understand what's expected in clear language without ambiguity. By stating exactly what's expected and how success will be measured early and often, you not only help the new employee adjust better to the organization but also buffer potential performance issues before they happen. One of the key ingredients in a successful onboarding experience is creating extreme clarity around how success will be measured for this role. Frequent reviewing of the position profile is a good place to start and should take precedence during the first 90 days (check out how to create a position profile in Chapter 9 to put yourself at an early advantage). At the 90-day meeting, you should review the overall expectations again to see how things are going from the employee's perspective and share your observations as well.

>> **Social connections:** Much of an employee's success is based on her ability to get things done with others. The social connections that your employee makes in the early days of her new position are critical to her success and critical to advancing your organizational culture. Through positive social connections at work, new hires will have more confidence, contribute to company culture, become company ambassadors, and remain in your employment longer. Helping your new hires build social connections is an important part of any new hire experience (see the "Designing the Buddy System" section later in this chapter for ideas).

>> **Cultural know-how/why:** You know that feeling when you travel to a foreign country and everything just seems a little, well, foreign? You realize you're in a coffee shop in Rome, but the rules of engagement have changed from the Starbucks near your home. Chances are you're going to still get the coffee, but your experience will be totally different. The way you pay, the way you order, and the way it is served are so drastically different, you can't help but feel out of place. Your employee risks having this same experience if you don't give her a road map for understanding how your culture works. The sooner you can help your new employee understand how things work, how decisions are made, and what to expect, the sooner she can contribute to your culture (and the organizational results you desire).

Crafting a Vision for Your New Hire Experience

In my work helping companies develop and execute highly successful new hire onboarding programs, I've walked into many different scenarios. There was the time I heard the story of new people starting and sitting in the dining room of a restaurant for hours while a busy manager was occupied elsewhere. Or the company that seemed to forget new people were starting and had them sit alone without a laptop or phone at their cubicle for several days before having them shadow other members of the sales team. Obviously, neither of these examples is desirable, but they're pretty common. By creating a vision of a successful new hire onboarding experience, you can help your team navigate the process with success for your team, culture, and newest employees.

Without a clear vision of what a great orientation and new hire experience looks like, it's likely that your team won't be on the same page. It's helpful to really define what a great experience can be and how your organization wants to help integrate your newest people.

To establish your vision, you want to get feedback from some recent hires, incorporate a few hiring managers to help guide the process, and then draft the vision to share with key stakeholders.

Doing research on past experiences

To get started with your vision, survey some of your recent hires to find out how their experience was during their first few weeks.

» Is the job, the team, and the company what they expected?

» Was the position outlined clearly via the job posting, the interview process, and the initial meetings with the team and manager?

» What surprised them positively? What did they like best about the process of onboarding?

» What surprised them negatively? What could have been done to make the process even more impactful, efficient, and positive?

» What did they learn in their subsequent weeks that they wish they had been told during the first week?

>> Were they well prepared for their work? If so, what was most helpful? If not, what would have been helpful?

>> What questions did they have about the company in general that weren't answered? What questions did they have about their role specifically that weren't answered?

>> What would have made them feel even more welcome to the team?

>> What did they learn about the culture and how the team works once they were on the job that they wish they had known ahead of time?

Digesting survey results

Once you've gathered information from the surveys, schedule time to review and distill the information. You'll likely see the same type of feedback from multiple people. Review the feedback with some of your hiring managers and the human resources team responsible for onboarding. During this session, make some decisions about how to improve those areas that received negative feedback. Additionally, do some group thinking around the following questions:

>> What do you want people to say after their first day at your company? First week? First month? Think about the specific quotes you'd like to see. Then explore ideas around what things would make them say those words.

>> How do you want people to feel during their first day? Give it the "story test" by considering what you want your new hires to tell their friends, family, and network when they go home at the end of their first day. It's likely that your new employee will talk to someone in person, on the phone, or over the Internet at the end of his first day. Consider how you'd like him to respond to, "How was your first day at the new gig?"

>> What stories do you want your new people to remember from their first week? Later, you'll develop the actual content for your orientation, but start gathering some of the important stories of your brand, your customers, and your team. The more they highlight your culture in action, the better.

>> How can you apply your values (see Chapter 7) to your onboarding experience? This doesn't mean how can you "teach" them during orientation, though that's important too and covered in the next section. How can you actually show those values to your new hires? If your organization values "creating remarkable experiences," then how can you create a remarkable experience for your new hires? If one of your values is "hospitality," what would it look like to show hospitality to a new employee?

Drafting a vision

With survey questions answered and review data collected, it's time for someone in the group to take all the information and draft a vision. Follow these steps to create a clear vision:

1. **Make a list of key wins for your onboarding experience such as new employees feeling like they were well taken caring of in the time between accepting the offer and their first day or the employees feeling connected to the company by spending time with the CEO in their first week.**

    Use the information you've collected to figure out what's working well and write those things down.

2. **Imagine a date in the future — maybe a year ahead of today — and write that date at the top of your page/screen.**

    You will be using this to develop a vision around how things look at that point in time.

3. **Put 20 minutes on the clock and write until the time is up, describing your new hire onboarding process.**

    Describe things as if they are happening and have happened. What did new hires say? How are they better prepared today? What's changed because of having a better process?

4. **Share that draft with a cross-section of people from the first two activities (the new hire survey and the hiring manager session) and seek feedback.**

    What stood out to them? What did they like best? What's missing? What else should be added?

5. **Make some edits based on that feedback.**

6. **Review and finalize with key stakeholders who are actively involved in bringing this new experience to life (probably the human resources or hiring teams responsible for this process).**

Evaluating Your Current Process

Congratulations! You now have a clear idea of what a successful new hire onboarding experience can look like for your organization. Before you move forward with creating that new and improved process, it's important to take a quick inventory of your current process.

Use the following chart (see Table 10-1) to assess your current process for onboarding a new employee. Each task in the chart includes specific details to help you understand what success looks like for that task. As you look at the feedback you've collected from the survey in section, "Doing research on past experiences," and your current process, take some notes on the action required to help improve your process. This will also help you use the ideas in the rest of this chapter to focus your improvement efforts on the right tasks for maximum impact.

TABLE 10-1   **Onboarding Process Assessment**

Task	Details	Action Required
New hire experience vision	Have a clearly documented vision of what a successful onboarding experience looks like	
Paperwork	Complete required paperwork and compliance-related things before the first day using technology	
Position profile review	Complete a position profile for each role and manager reviews with new hire during first week and then again at 30 days, 60 days, and 90 days	
Announcements	Send an internal announcement introducing new employee including link to LinkedIn profile, some other facts, and a photo	
Welcome Kit	Create a welcome package with company swag and signed card from the hiring manager	
New Hire Orientation Day	Lead an engaging and informative first day orientation that includes company history, customer overview, and product review	
Introductions	Create a checklist to ensure that the first month is full of thoughtful introductions to different people with whom the new employee will need to develop relationships	
Meetings and Conversations	Create a list with all the different people they will be meeting in their first few weeks and the goals of those conversations (for example, meet with Marketing Director Amy and learn about the top priorities for her team; coffee with Sales Manager Melissa to understand the talk about client needs, and so on)	
Feedback	Be sure to always collect feedback from each group of new hires to evaluate the programs around onboarding and orientation	

Combining Vision and Current Practices for Onboarding Success

Once you have your vision clear and a strong understanding of your current oper-ations, it's time to put the core components into place. This involves developing a pre-hire checklist, planning a perfect first day and a strong first week, and gath-ering some feedback to continue to improve the process.

Setting up a pre-hire checklist

Creating a positive and welcoming experience for your new hires starts before they even walk in the door. You can send a positive message by planning ahead and getting the onboarding process started in advance of their first day. Use the following list to create a pre-hire checklist of all the things you should complete so that you can later set your employee up for the perfect first day:

>> Complete necessary government paperwork (federal and state forms, tax forms, and so on)

>> Complete necessary company paperwork (non-disclosure, anti-harassment/non-discrimination, building access forms, and so on)

>> Identify computer needs and place order

>> Set up the new employee's workspace so it is inviting and welcoming — desk, business cards, company water bottle, and even a nice little frame or plant can send a big message

>> Prepare a welcome bag or box with their uniform, supplies, and other company swag if your employee works in a retail, hotel, manufacturing, or restaurant environment

>> Create company accounts (email and other core systems)

>> Send company email, video, or other communication with name, photo, title, and a few trivia facts about your new hire

>> Send your new employee a welcome video that includes a few of his cowork-ers welcoming him to the team and sharing why they're excited about having him join the team

>> Send a text or email on the Friday before the new hire's start

Adopting the PFD: Perfect first day formula

The first day is your new hire's first impression and a big chance to set the stage for a great employment experience. You have the opportunity on the first day to really show the new hire what your culture is all about by the way you treat him. This is called the Perfect First Day, or PFD. It isn't about creating unrealistic expectations about your company by focusing on balloons and cupcakes, but it is about making sure you have a solid system for giving new employees the things they need most on their first day.

A PFD should be filled with a mix of cultural initiation and operation need-to-know information. In most companies, the human resources department will take care of organizing the process, but when adopting the PFD model, managers and senior leaders help set the tone by getting involved in welcoming the newest people to the team.

The investment will pay off huge in helping establish relationships and show your new employee how much his joining the team matters. Culture starts at the beginning.

Use the checklist in Figure 10-1 to help shape your first day and ensure nothing is left behind.

Developing your first week orientation checklist

The first day can be very orchestrated and controlled, and then things can go wickedly wrong once it heads to the department level with busy coworkers, distracted managers, and piles of work to be done. Developing a strong first week plan for your new hires is the key to making sure you set the right impression beyond the perfect first day.

During that first week, the key things to think about are helping the new hire meet more people in the organization, building upon your culture and values training from orientation, starting position and role skills through on-the-job training and classroom sessions, and beginning to develop the employee-manager relationship.

First Day Checklist	
Greeting and Welcome	
Take new headshot with logo	Desk and workspace
Coffee, tea, water	Manager and buddy introduction
Office Tour	
Bathrooms	Office spaces
Kitchen, eating	Meeting spaces
Orientation Class	
Origins, history taught by the CEO or other key leader	Mission, vision, values
Product overview taught by a leader on the sales, product, or operations team	Customer overview taught by a leader on the customer support team
Perks & benefits overview	Handbook highlights
Sexual harassment overview	Compliance overview
Tech & Tools	
Computer walk-through	Get connected to Internet
Overview of key programs	Calendar overview
Email overview	Document storage
Communication overview	How to get IT help
Building Overview	
Visitors	Building access
Safety concerns	Parking
Beyond the Basics	
Have a senior leader greet the new hire with coffee.	Lunch with the new hire's manager or with the entire department/team

FIGURE 10-1:
A guide to follow for any new hire's first day.

While all first weeks will look different based on the position and your company, here are some of the things you want to include to kick things off properly:

>> **Product training:** Allow for your new employee to experience the product several times. If you run a hotel, have him go through the check-in process as a customer would or actually spend an evening in the hotel. Restaurants could

invite the new employee in with a guest to experience what it's like to dine there. Technology companies could have the employee download and use the product.

» **Customer training:** Everyone in your company should have a deep understanding of your customer. During the first week, start to introduce your employee to the customer via testimonials, site visits, and industry reviews. Your new hire should understand what your customers want, why they choose your company, what the competition offers, and how you help your customers succeed.

» **Industry overview:** Create a multimedia training (self-guided or instructor-led) around the industry you work in. Share news clippings, TV interviews, online media, and other key information to help the new employee learn more about the market you operate within.

» **Deeper company awareness:** Curate news articles, press releases, videos, and other information about your company into modules that your new hire can review.

» **Values and culture:** Share your company's mission statement, vision statement, and values and behavior statement. In this session, you should include how you came up with the mission, how the mission is linked to the origin of the company, and why the mission matters in the bigger picture for your clients. You can do a similar activity with the vision by focusing on how the vision defines where you are going and what it looks like. You can ask the new employees to imagine their career at that same point and lead a conversation about how they want their life to look on that date. When you get to the values and behaviors, pull in real-life examples of your employees living these values. Be ready to share stories and highlight examples so that you can bring the values to life for them.

TIP

One of the more interesting things I've helped a company execute was curating lists of videos from sources like TEDx that help to highlight the values and culture of the company. If the company values grit, there's a video for that. If you talk about happiness, there are videos for that.

» **Social connections:** Schedule lunch networking each day for the first week. Create a bingo lunch card or scavenger hunt that the new hire needs to dine with people from different departments.

» **Manager responsibilities:** Review the position profile and outcomes, set up goals, create recurring one-on-ones, give context to important meetings, and so on.

Looking beyond the first week

Once your new employee has started to get the lay of the land with a strong first week, you want to look ahead to make sure you don't lose momentum in helping him get integrated into your team and culture. In addition to your regularly scheduled one-on-ones and team meetings, it's a great idea to create a 30- and 90-day check-in. These can be led by someone from human resources, the employee's manager, or another senior leader in the organization. It sends a powerful message and goes a long way in creating a positive culture when a senior leader takes the time to listen to your newest people.

To get started with these check-ins, copy the following questions to a shared document or intranet site. Then add a calendar invite with a link to the questions during the new hire's first week. This way the check-ins are scheduled and less likely to be overlooked.

> **» The 30-day check-in**
>
> - Based on your expectations before you started at the company and what has actually happened, how are things going? What's matched your expectations? What's been better? Anything that isn't as you expected in a disappointing way?
>
> - How was your initial onboarding and training? What would have helped set you up better? What did you like best? What could we do to make it even more impactful for future hires?
>
> - Is there anyone I can help you get scheduled to spend time with or meet?
>
> - How are you doing toward meeting your goals? Do you have clarity about what's expected now/next? Do you have the resources and relationships to get that work done?
>
> **» The 90-day check-in**
>
> - When you think about our company, our work environment, or our place in the market, is there anything that worries you? Anything you are concerned about?
>
> - Have you seen something recently and thought to yourself, "I wish we did that"?
>
> - Is there something we should measure and share in the company that we currently don't?
>
> - Is there any part of the company you wish you knew more about?

- Are there any benefits we don't offer that you'd like to see us offer?

- Is there an area outside of your current role where you feel you could be contributing and would like to get help in getting that organized?

- Have you seen someone here do great work that's gone unnoticed?

- Are there things you don't know about the company that you feel you should know?

- Is there anything else I can do to help make this a great place to work for you?

Designing the Buddy System

One of the best ways to help new employees navigate their new job and get acclimated (and contributing) to your culture is to create a buddy system. By assigning each new employee an experienced employee as a buddy, you can help your new hire with most of the goals mentioned throughout this chapter.

A new buddy can help them gain confidence by giving them a resource for questions, advice, and tips about navigating the waters during their first months on the job.

By having an experienced employee as a buddy, the new hire will start to build social connections with others around the company. The buddy will help the new hire meet new people, ensure that she is invited to company events, and assist her in finding activities of interest. Read on to find out how to put the buddy system into action.

Selecting a buddy

When I've helped start buddy programs in the past, we've typically seen many employees raise their hands in interest. It's encouraging to see and is a sign of a positive culture. In general, you want to choose buddies who understand your culture and who are well connected with others to help your new hires meet others in the company.

Here are some of the key things to consider in your selection criteria:

>> Does the buddy have the time to meet the commitments?

>> Is the buddy familiar with the work the new hire will be doing? The buddy doesn't need to be in the same role, but having awareness around what the new employee does is usually helpful.

>> Does the buddy communicate positively and effectively? You want to assign a buddy who makes a great impression and is helpful.

>> Has the buddy worked for your organization for a year or longer? In general, a buddy who has had time to settle into the company, meet many others, and have clear examples of your values in action will be able to more effectively help your new hires.

>> Did the buddy volunteer? It's important that the person signing up to be a buddy is volunteering for the work. In some cases, managers or others might volunteer people because they want them to be more helpful or have the experience — but it ultimately needs to be something the potential buddy really wants to do as well. They will be using lots of discretionary effort to welcome your new people — so you want to make sure their interest in the program is strong.

Clarifying buddy expectations

The key to a successful program is setting up clear expectations so that everyone knows what to expect from each other. The buddy is a valuable resource for the new team member but doesn't take the place of the new hire's manager or the HR department.

These are some reasonable expectations for the buddy:

>> Help the new hire navigate her first week by greeting her, helping her find meetings and trainings, and helping to identify resources in the office

>> Provide details about policies, procedures, and office protocols

>> Introduce the new hire to others around the company

>> Lead the new hire on a tour around the office and neighborhood

>> Have coffee and lunch with the new hire throughout her first six months

>> Meet periodically with the hiring manager and HR team to evaluate how the buddy program is doing by getting feedback from the new hires and the buddy volunteers

Structuring your buddy program

The most successful buddy programs last for six months, which is just long enough to help the new hire really understand the company, make connections, and begin contributing positively to your culture.

Provide the buddy with the following outline and let the buddy schedule directly with the new hire so that they can coordinate schedules. By giving a copy of the suggested structure to the buddy, the new hire, and the new hire's manager, you can have the three of them work together to ensure success.

Week 1

» Buddy meets new hire on first day as official greeter (share contact information, set up lunch meeting for one day during the first week)

» Meet for lunch (learn about each other's background, interests, and so on)

» Review the program outline together

» Take new hire on office and neighborhood (if relevant) tour

Months 1 and 2

» Meet weekly for 30 minutes in person or via video chat

» Introduce new hire to other coworkers (create a scavenger hunt or Bingo card that the new hire can check off as she meets people across the organization)

Months 3 and 4

» Check in with employee, hiring manager, and HR rep

» Bring new hire along to a company event or gathering

» Meet every other week for 30 minutes

Months 5 and 6

» Continue to introduce new hire to coworkers

» Meet monthly for an hour

ORGANIZING ONBOARDING WITH TECHNOLOGY

One of the reasons that organizations often fail at onboarding their newest people in a consistent and engaging way is simply the lack of a documented process. When I've worked with organizations to help them improve their culture, this is one of the places we can typically find a quick win. With all the technology resources out there, it's easier than ever to put all the steps outlined in this chapter into a repeatable digital format.

Here are some of the tools available for free to make this easy and simple:

- Google Sheets: https://www.google.com/sheets/about/
- Asana: www.asana.com
- Trello: www.trello.com

To get started with using technology, organize all the things that need to happen for a new hire to be onboarding into a checklist. This should start from the offer letter and should end at the six-month mark when the buddy system wraps up.

Starting a Culture of Feedback Early

The strongest cultures are those that have consistent feedback flowing in all directions around the company. Ideas from the front lines are making it to executive meetings so the people at the top of the organization can learn from the people with the most knowledge of the customers and work. Outcomes and decisions from the latest board meeting are making it to the folks on the front lines so they have the updated strategies, goals, and targets to help them do their best work. At the beginning of your new employee's tenure with you, you should start collecting frequent feedback not only to learn about how the onboarding experience is going but also to start to make them comfortable with sharing their feedback about the company.

Get started by creating a survey that is shared with the employee at the end of "his" or "her" first or second week with your organization. The goal is to learn about how effective and impactful the program has been so far. This will help you improve as you begin to build a stronger new hire onboarding experience.

TIP

You can use an online survey tool, Google Forms (free), or even pen and paper to gather this information.

Feedback Survey: Week 1

» The position profile I applied for matches my experience with the company so far.

» The organizational history, product, and customer information I received was helpful and useful.

» The orientation program was interesting, entertaining, and interactive.

» I've been given enough training to do my job well.

» What topics were not covered this week and should have been?

» What was the most important information you received this week?

» I spent time with my manager and understand the expectations of me. I have a clear understanding of what I need to accomplish in my first 30 days.

» I understand the goals of my department and how I contribute to achieving them.

» At this point, I have the tools to do my job as I understand it.

» I feel welcome and part of the team.

Using New Hires to Recruit More Talent

When employees first start a job, their feelings about a company is freshest in their minds — their LinkedIn profile will change, they'll be talking about their new job, and people will be asking how it's going. There's no better time than this to provide them with lots of great content and ideas to help support your recruiting efforts. People tend to know (and want to work with) other people of the same skill level. So creating a program to help your new hires celebrate their new gig while also boosting your recruiting efforts can go a long way in building your pipeline and celebrating your culture.

TIP

Use these tips to recruit more great talent:

» **Create shareable social media content:** This is easy during the new hire onboarding process. Find a space in your office for a "new hire selfie cam" with a logo in the background for employees to take pictures. Search online for a social media–friendly picture frame that can be used for taking a picture with your logo and company info in the main area of the frame.

>> **Develop written content:** An easy way to get news about your culture and the efforts you put forth to welcome new people to the team is to create written blog-style content for your new hires. During their first week or two, schedule time to do a quick interview with them. The goal is to write a short, engaging, 500-word article or blog post introducing your new person to the team. Consider a "behind-the-scenes" type post. You can share this from your company blog and your LinkedIn account. Make sure to share the link with new hires and ask them to share it with their network.

>> **Record video introductions:** Video is such a fun way to share your new hire's experience. Schedule time at the end of the first week to record a quick interview with him asking about how his first week went, what he thinks of the culture at your company, and what he is excited about in his new career. You can edit these easily for social sharing.

>> **Ask for the connection:** During your employee's third week at your company, reach out to him to share the current positions you have open. Ask him if he knows anyone who is a great fit for those roles. Similarly, you can ask him whom he has worked with before in any position that he thinks would be a good fit for your company. You can add these candidates to your passive pipeline in case a position opens up.

IN THIS CHAPTER

» Understanding how training impacts culture

» Uncovering why training is so hard to get right

» Revealing the truth behind good training

» Developing simple frameworks to improve any training

» Recognizing when training needs an overhaul

Chapter **11**

Better Training to Improve Culture

Company career pages from around the world espouse and promote that organizations invest in their number one asset — their people. Billions of dollars are spent on training, workshops, e-courses, and books to help develop talent, propel performance, and find the nirvana of professional growth. With all the energy (and money and time and resources) spent on training, you'd think that more employees would be seeing record-breaking success. In this chapter, you'll uncover why training and learning is an important part of your culture and a requirement for sustained business growth. You'll find out why so much of it isn't working, where it went wrong, and how to fix it. You'll get a road map to help design better training on the fly.

Impacting Your Culture

No matter which company you look at, one of the most common things employees are seeking is professional development. They want career growth, skill development, and experiences to propel them to new levels in career and life. It's one of the reasons people choose one company over another — they choose the one they believe will give them the kind of work that allows them to gain skills they don't currently have.

When you have a training program that not only teaches the skills and information required to do the job (like onboarding training) but also teaches the skills required to advance in that role, move into other roles, or just generally become a more proficient professional, you get higher levels of engagement, commitment, and loyalty. You're also a lot more likely to improve bottom-line results by creating a knowledgeable and informed team that has the skills required to do the work today and the ability to develop the skills required for the work of tomorrow.

The next sections show just how a successful training program will impact your culture.

Attracting and keeping great talent

Finding and keeping great people is on the top of most managers' lists as one of the biggest issues facing them at work today. It's costly to lose people and downright dangerous to lose people who contribute highly to your organization. By creating training opportunities that give employees one of the things they want most (growth and skill set development), you'll be able to leverage this over your competition to bring great people into your organization. Once they get there, you can double down on your odds of keeping them by continually giving them chances to sharpen their skills.

Developing your bench

Promoting from within helps ensure your culture continues to grow because those very team members who have thrived in your organization will become leaders and evangelists to your newest, most impressionable staff. After all, who best knows how things work, what values and behaviors are desired, and has a history of working with your products and services than the people who've been doing it all along? You can also think about it as the longest interview ever or even the deepest reference check. You've been able to see this person performing in his or her current role, you know what you're getting, you know what to expect from the person, and there are going to be fewer surprises. As they develop both expertise in their roles and mastery of your culture, promoting them builds and strengthens your bench by showing to all that this is what it takes to move up in your organization. You can do this through training by creating a program that helps you get the person ready for the next level. It's a great way to solve your pipeline issues and safeguard your culture as you grow.

If done well, your training programs should:

» Create a pool of promotable employees ready for the next level. Imagine if every time a new role opens up or a management position becomes necessary, you have a group of people waiting to apply who you've seen in action.

» Help you know who's most ready for promotion through their progress in learning. While it's always a good idea to have internal candidates go through an interview committee (see Chapters 9 and 16), you can also tell who's ready for promotion by seeing their progress through learning. If someone is struggling with a specific skill set, then you know that the person may not be ready for the next level if that skill is required for success in that role.

» Ensure your newly promoted people have the skills required for the new job before they move into the new responsibilities full time.

Driving engagement

You've likely seen all the scary stats about disengagement at work. You've probably picked up this book because there are some places where your culture isn't fired up and engaged. Bored employees who don't feel like they're growing in your company create an environment where cultures crumble. By creating learning and development opportunities, you can change all that.

Interesting learning options, opportunities for self-assessment and growth, and engaging development events can be an effective way to spark engagement in your team and then keep the fire burning by providing more and more skill development over time. It keeps the boredom, drudgery, and feeling of apathy at bay.

Boosting bottom-line results

Creating a strong training platform can help produce real business results. Not only does it help to keep employees and save big money in recruiting, onboarding, and turnover costs, but training done right can also improve sales, reduce costs from unnecessary mistakes, and boost overall production. The gains you make in employee production, efficiency, improved sales, and reduced turnover create real value for your business.

Training Is Hard

Let's get this out of the way: Training is hard. Rather: Effective, efficient, engaging training is hard. Even more so: Training is pretty difficult and only made worse by the inefficient, simplistic way we keep subjecting people to learning.

In offices, restaurants, hotels, conference rooms, hospitals, and classrooms around the world (right now), people are being talked at, presented to, walked through, and demonstrated for. Then they're asked to memorize, recall, perform, and execute. Tests, exams, and certifications are administered. Yet so little of it changes behavior.

So little of it actually produces the result desired. Why? Because we keep approaching training with a simplistic view of how people learn, but it's not based in what we actually know to be true from our own experience and from the latest in learning science.

Consider your own experience with learning a new skill set. Read over the following list and see which statement most resonates with your preferred way of learning something new.

Do you learn best when:

>> You watch someone else do something OR when you're able to go hands-on to try it yourself?

>> You sit in a classroom with someone presenting information to you OR when you're involved in a two-way dialogue with the speaker?

>> You're simply told how things happen OR when you get to experience how things happen?

>> You're in a structured learning environment (such as a classroom) OR when you're in a more informal setting trying things out and getting corrective notes along the way to improve?

>> You attend day- or week-long conferences or training OR when you get short bursts of learning followed by actual application and feedback?

>> You review books and pages of content OR when information is minimal, engaging, and organized based on the way you need to perform the tasks being taught?

>> You understand the importance of the training to the company, the customer, and the process OR when you see the benefit for yourself in doing things a specific way?

LOOKING BACK TO LOOK AHEAD

Think back to the big things you've learned in your life. Think about how you learned to do them. Consider how much classroom instruction, live demonstration, experiences, activities, and feedback you got about each one in order to be skilled at it. Examples include:

- How to walk
- How to drive
- How to speak your native language
- How to speak a second language
- How to make your favorite dish
- How to do something you're great at professionally
- How to fold a fitted sheet (just kidding — no one knows how to do this)

Without being in the room with you, it's a pretty safe guess that you chose the statement following "OR" in most of the examples in this list. After training hundreds of people to be better trainers and leading train-the-trainer sessions in several industries — regardless of skill level, role, experience, age, education, or job type — I've seen that people typically choose the "OR" statements.

You may be thinking to yourself that this isn't a huge revelation. Of course, the actual doing of activities and experiencing what it's like to perform in a new way are far more effective than just sitting and listening to someone talk about how to do something. Most of the stuff you're good at probably happened because you learned a little, experienced a lot, got some feedback, and kept working until you could do it well — speaking our native language, riding a bike, eating with a spoon. All things that wouldn't have been possible by just listening to someone and never trying it yourself. You can't really learn to make bread by watching videos of someone doing it all day and never actually trying it (sorry Food Network). It's one of the reasons I loved being a wine trainer — we actually had to drink wine! At work!

Understanding the Basics of Training

It's likely that when you think about training, you have a specific response and experience that comes to mind. Maybe it's some on-the-job training you experienced working in a hotel. Maybe it's some classroom learning you took in an effort to pass the bar exam. Maybe it's a workshop you went to about creating a better company culture or being a better manager. Before we jump into how to improve the training at your team, it's important that we get on the same page about exactly what's meant by training.

Getting clear on learning

Learning is the cornerstone of training. It's about transferring information from an expert (which could take the form of a book, course, or workshop) to someone else so that they can perform a new skill or can improve on a current skill set.

If the ultimate goal of all this work is learning, then what is learning? Learning is about change — changing your perspective, changing your framework, changing your performance. Regardless of the "thing" you're trying to communicate, you can't do it if people can't learn. If your efforts at training people on sales, service, production, or leadership work, then it means they've learned a new way of being. It means you've changed them.

Defining your approach

So if it all comes down to learning and learning is really about creating change, then does the format matter? Is there a difference between training, facilitating, instructing, and educating? Would it be beneficial to understand these differences before you embark on upgrading your training programs? You've probably guessed that the answer to these questions is "yes"; otherwise, I wouldn't be prepping your brain for what comes next.

Training

While most learning programs (and the title of this chapter) fall under the category of training, training is just one part of a comprehensive approach to learning at work. Training someone to do something is about getting the person to do it the same way each time without variation. This is great for things that require specific ways of operating, like selecting the right forms to submit for a client intake conversation. The goal is that training should make the person more accurate and efficient at selecting the right option. At work, there are many times when training is the right choice because we don't want variation:

>> Following all the steps in shutting down equipment

>> Properly setting up a new customer account

>> Slicing vegetables for a popular sandwich

>> Using the right billing code for a patient

>> Blocking out a group of rooms for a wedding party

Training in this way should make things easier by helping your trainee do the right thing with minimal effort because there's only one right way to get the thing done.

Instructing

If everything at work could be as simple as having a definite right answer, it'd be pretty easy to focus on training to ensure a positive result every time. But for most roles this isn't possible. It takes more than just rote memorization and exact execution to do many of the things required in our complex business world. This is where instruction comes in. Instruction is about creating some framework and models that allow people to apply the learning to more situations than just the ones that can be defined and practiced.

Some places where you may see instruction:

>> Using sales skills to help a retail customer make the right choice

>> Delivering a great customer experience

>> Finding a way to get a customer package (or the customer herself if you work in travel) from Point A to Point B during a snowstorm

>> Listening as a manager to an employee's concern and coming up with ideas for solving it

The aim of instruction is being able to take a few generalized scenarios and learning to apply them in various situations that may occur. Instruction is different from training in that there isn't a way to define exactly what it should look like each time. This is why a lot of customer service people and sales people struggle with conversations — they've been trained with very specific protocols but not instructed in how to more generally approach the goals.

Facilitating

Great trainers often get bundled into the role of being a facilitator. It makes sense — a great trainer is able to read the room, help shift energies, and guide a group of people through a process. Facilitating is less about training someone to produce a specific result and more about guiding the group through the steps to get to a solution. The facilitator's role is to make the exchanges among participants easier and more productive. Common instances of facilitating in your organization may include:

>> Leading a session around the benefits of improved service and finding opportunities to deliver it for your brand

>> Exploring ways to improve management skills on your team

>> Identifying critical issues with your product launch process

In many cases, the right answer isn't apparent at the start or is widely disputed by participants in the meeting, and the goal is to use the time together to find some options for doing things better or finding a common ground to move forward with a decision. So it's a learning opportunity for the group in that it will create change, but it's not a training instance.

Educating

Educating involves informing a more broad, long-term approach to changing the way your people do things. This takes times and usually involves some combination of training and instruction. Take leadership, for example. In management training, you teach how to properly handle vacation requests, submit expense reports, and approve budgets. Through instruction, employees learn how to have difficult conversations, work on succession plans, and lead better team meetings. Through education, they adopt a positive approach to being a proactive leader where they organically and naturally approach other employees with thoughtfulness, candor, and accountability. They learn how to recognize potential concerns and naturally navigate around how to resolve them. If this was a university scenario, then training and instructing would be the specific courses you take and education would be the aim of the entire four-year program. Some times where education may be the right call:

>> Being a great manager

>> Empathetically handling customer concerns

>> Being a great listener as a salesperson

>> Confidently speaking in public

>> Staying on brand with values

REMEMBER

Education is the longer play of the bunch because it isn't as simple as training or as universal as instruction. It requires time, effort, and coaching to do all the things required. Role models and other leaders help communicate how these things look. It takes commitment, context, and getting the conditions right for education to happen. Typically the education efforts are in a series over time and include real-world work to get better and master the skills. For example, learning to be a great manager takes time. Sure — there are classes to give instruction on specific frameworks and training on specific programs, but becoming a great manager takes commitment and long-term effort. Often what it takes to become a great manager is not measured on a monthly basis or easily rewarded with bonuses. In this way, education can be harder to pin down. However, education is the thing that — over time — really creates change in your employees.

Learning about Learning

Often when I work with a team to improve their learning and training experiences, I discover that the trainers, facilitators, and workshop leaders are experts in their subject area, but don't often know much about how people learn. Trainers are picked because they're experts (and often because they're available and willing). But there's more to effective transmission of information than one person having it and the other person needing it. There's a way to learn about learning.

Visioning a better learning experience

If you want to get focused on creating change through learning, then you have to create a vision for better learning exchanges. For the training to be effective and impactful (both of those defined by actual performance change taking place after completion), it has to have three qualities: be learner-focused, be performance-based, and be engaging.

Focusing on the learner

Great learning should be focused on the learner — what do they know, think, need, and want? It doesn't start with content and objectives but rather with a learner-focused deep dive to determine what's in it for them. You're asking them to change, and people hate to change. So consider the world from their perspective to make sure you're creating a compelling case for change. Think about their jobs, their tasks, their experiences at work, and expectations in the area you're teaching. Transformation always starts with where they are, so make sure you know what that looks like first.

Basing it on performance

If you're clearly in the training, instructing, or facilitating side of things (and most corporate learning is), then you really are trying to change performance. So why all the talking? Why all the slide decks? Great learning experiences are performance-based. They help the learner to do something different, and the only way to do that is to let them try it. Your goals should be tied to changes in performance, not in "knows XYZ" or "understands ABC." Make sure that you're thinking about your objectives in this way: Measurable, tangible, visible, audible performance changes occurred because of this training.

Aiming for engagement

If the learning experience isn't engaging, then you're shooting yourself in the foot. If your learners are bored, unstimulated, and passive, then they aren't actively learning. They aren't experiencing the change. Engagement is about leaning forward in the chair, trying things on for size, examining how the new information jibes with previous knowledge, and inspiring action.

Presenting doesn't promote learning

Why does so much training at work follow this horrible recipe that over-relies on talking and presenting? If actually doing something is the best way to learn, then why do most corporate training programs focus on the trainee listening to other people for hours without any practice?

It's because it's really easy to forget how you initially learned to do something once you become an expert. As you've moved up the scale in ability and performance, you don't remember the things you did to get there and instead overly rely on the fact that you have all the information in your head that the new person needs and that if you can just say enough of it in a specific order, then he or she too can become an expert like you. Wrong. It's time to approach training and learning at work with a new mindset that's focused on teaching the way that people learn — to stop talking, showing, and describing and to start experiencing, sharing feedback, and performing.

Making Training Successful

For training to be successful, you have to understand a little bit about how we learn so you can know how to teach.

Different types of knowledge

Corporate training usually comes down to types of knowledge: descriptive and performative. *Descriptive knowledge* is the ability to talk about, describe, explain, and name something. This is the kind of knowledge used when someone asks about specific ingredients in a dish or recalls the cities in which you have locations. *Performative knowledge* is being able to take action, to do things, and to perform. This is the kind of knowledge used to design things, serve customers, drive a car, or write code.

Sometimes, both types of knowledge are used — you can both describe how to set the table and actually set the table. But in other cases, it's much harder to be able to use both descriptive and performative knowledge at the same time — or at least with really clear and precise language. Think about teaching someone to drive a car — it's nearly impossible to describe exactly what your body is doing, what your mind is thinking, and how you're balancing all the stimuli. But you're able to perform it pretty well (unless you live in Los Angeles, of course).

Knowing the difference is an important first step in thinking about designing better training. If your trainer has a ton of performative knowledge, then using descriptive methods (talking, telling) will be difficult for the trainer to do well because they can be ineffective at transferring the knowledge. Think about how you want your trainee to perform afterwards — is it something the person needs to say or explain? Or something the person needs to do? Get clear on that and then make sure the method of teaching matches the style of knowledge required. For example, if your employee will need to recite something verbatim upon command, then you should focus the training on hearing, memorizing, and practicing the script in different scenarios. If your employee needs to have a general understanding of your competitors but won't need to use this information, then a brief presentation can do the trick. But, if the trainee is a salesperson who needs to speak about the benefits of your brand over the competition, then you should include some performative exercises so he or she can practice and master that skill set.

Ingredients for approaching training design

Great training design starts with the same specific ingredients regardless of what's being taught, the industry you're in, or what types of knowledge are required. Before learning can occur and training can be designed, you have to have clear ideas about measuring ability, scaffolding knowledge, and motivating change first.

Measuring ability

Can learners actually do the thing you're attempting to teach them currently? Are they able to complete the task and just need some specific training around how to do it at your company or is this a new skill they need to learn from the ground up? If it's the latter, then your approach is going to be significantly different, since you need to teach the basics first. For example, I'm not a runner, so if you attempted to teach me to complete a marathon in 30 days, I probably couldn't do it right now. While we all have the ability to adapt, transform, and grow, the learning has to be around something that's within physical, intellectual, and emotional reach. A savvy trainer will adjust training for ability by giving more time for certain activities, breaking learning down into more digestible chunks, and providing a range of levels for people to achieve over time as ability improves.

Scaffolding the knowledge

What does the learner already know? Is there prior knowledge that can be used as a baseline for adding more information? Just like the scaffolding on a building, you can use this to reach advanced levels of learning. The more readily you can access prior knowledge, the quicker you can build up. It's why learning a second romance language is easier after you've mastered the first one. Effective trainers will investigate what their learners already know before planning a training event so that they can tailor the program to the audience. Sometimes you can even leverage articles, videos, and pre-training questions to start to get the learners to think about the content of the upcoming training program.

Motivating change

The employee has to have some reason for learning. Remember, real learning requires change on the part of the trainee, and we don't like change. So there needs to be some motivating factor to get the trainee to make the effort. The common issue I see here is the "they will change if they want to keep their job issue." This is usually followed by the "I can't keep my employees very long issue," so I recommend looking for other motivators. To boost motivation for training, dive deep into figuring out what's in it for them, focus on the benefits from their perspective, and create a more engaging, positive learning experience. For example, if you were organizing some training about learning to use video for marketing and sales purposes, you could say the following points:

>> Video has become a critical part of many buying decisions with buyers researching, comparing, and studying product offerings using online video.

>> In the absence of video, buyers are less likely to trust your brand and do the necessary research to enter into a sales conversation.

>> Having a strong video presence will make you a more effective, efficient, and influential seller.

>> Learn to make the top three videos that your buyer is looking for online.

>> Create a video content creation calendar.

>> Develop a system for measuring the impact of your videos.

In this scenario, you are explaining to the trainee why video matters for sales and how this training will help him in his role. At its core, this is really the part of the training design where you are thinking like a salesperson yourself by asking "What would make people really want to come to this training session?" and "How can I make sure we position this course to help solve the real problems our target group of employees are facing?"

Creating Better Training Programs

Designing better training programs is the key to being able to use training and learning as a culture-boosting activity. How you design your program will determine if you get employee engagement and manager buy-in. It's the design that governs whether real change occurs.

Four principles of training

Every great training program — whether performative or descriptive knowledge is learned — shares the same four principles. You can use these principles to improve your customer service training, leadership training, product training, compliance training, and pretty much every other learning experience.

Finding the why

The first thing we have to do is move beyond "because I said so." Adults like knowing why they have to do something (clearly kids do too because that saying is still popular after centuries). Training should already start with some really clear reasons for change. To uncover the reasons for the training, consider the following questions from the trainee, the company, and the client/customer perspective:

>> What are the experience benefits of this training? Does it deliver a better customer experience or employee experience?

>> What are the efficiency benefits of this training? Does this shave off a few steps, make the employee quicker, or help produce a specific result in less time?

>> What are the financial rewards for this training? Do I sell more, make more, or save more? Do customers receive a higher perceived value?

>> What are the team or group benefits? Do we collaborate better, create solutions together more effectively, or build better relationships?

>> How did the need for this training come up in the first place? What was going on in the business that urged you to create the training? What was the cause of it? What was the outcome of that? Often you can find a few good reasons why if you dig into these questions deeply enough.

TIP

Before starting any training, make sure you speak concretely to why it matters in the first place. Speak to the specific benefits and reasons for creating the training. Underline and highlight the expected benefits and outcomes for the trainees and company.

Defining the what

You don't want your training to feel like an aimless pursuit of some vague performance expectation on the other side. That's a surefire way to get bad results and limit performance change. Instead, make sure that there are clearly defined objectives for your learning. Learners (and trainers and the learners' managers) should all have a shared definition of what the training is trying to achieve. In fact, all training (and lots of meetings) should include a statement that starts with "by the end of this session, you will be able to . . ." followed by specific outcomes. These are your performance objectives. Consider this the contract you're making with learners — if they attend your session and give their time, then they'll be rewarded with these new skills.

WARNING

Avoid these words, which are passive and immeasurable:

>> Consider

>> Know

>> Understand

TIP

Instead, use these words, which are measurable and visible:

>> Build

>> Choose

>> Convert

>> Create

>> Design

>> State

>> Write

For example, if you were designing some training around the launch of a new line of cars, instead of saying "Understand the four new Volvo models," try "Explain the difference in features of our four new Volvo models." The first one is passive, hard to test or examine, and difficult to give feedback for improving. The second one is much clearer. You could create a page with the four models and then a list of features to be matched to the correct model. You can create a role-play where someone plays a customer asking questions about it. It's much easier to measure success when you get specific about what the trainee should know and be able to do after the training.

Structuring activities

The training program has to make sense and follow a structure. The activities selected should be related to improving in areas connected to the objectives and should follow an outline that makes sense in progress toward objective attainment. If your training includes talking or presenting, then consider that an activity as well. This is where you'll find exercises, role-plays, interactions, and discussions (two-way discussion).

The more your learners have to be engaged during the training, the better your results can be.

TIP

Use these ideas for training activities:

>> Build in short pop quizzes

>> Create opportunities to recap sections

>> Fill in a blank

>> Solve a problem

>> Debate and discuss

>> Brainstorm

Evaluating and providing feedback

In feedback lives growth. Feedback is a critical part of learning — it's how we learned to walk, talk, and drive. We got a response, either from another person or the environment, and then were able to use that to make corrective action. For feedback to help in training, it should:

>> Be focused on the task or action and not the learner, which would zap the learner's confidence and motivation

>> Happen as quickly after an action as possible

>> Be specific and clear with corrective actions

All training and learning experiences should include evaluation and feedback to determine whether the performance objectives have been met. This can be by way of written tests (good for descriptive knowledge) or by competency checks, role-plays, and live demos (best for performative knowledge).

People don't hate being tested if they think they can win; your job is to lead them toward success so they can achieve the thing they've been working on. You stand aside and let them perform.

Use constructive feedback to focus on improvement. This isn't about telling them what they did wrong and what they did right. It's about giving them specific notes on what worked and what didn't with the steps for improving it. For feedback to be useful and constructive, it has to be specific, clear, and inform future action. Let learners help determine the feedback so they're involved and can improve performance. Let them be able to review their own performance in the future. For example, instead of saying "You need to be more clear about the differences of the new features," try "I struggled to follow your explanation of the differences in features. Next time it will be more effective if you do an overview of all four Volvo models, then highlight how they compare to each other when it comes to features. Want to try again using that framework?"

Structuring your training

Great training is the result of great planning and a solid structure. This chapter discusses how to get clear on why you are training, defining what specifically the trainee will be doing differently afterwards, how to structure activities to focus on real skill development, and how to evaluate whether the training was effective in helping your employees gain the skills desired. In this section, it's time to put it all together. Using the worksheet shown in Figure 11-1, think about one of your training sessions and fill in the section that says "Your Content" by reading the columns to the left first. As you do this, you will start to get more clear about your training and find areas to get more specific about the why, what, and how of your program. Come back to this sheet any time you are thinking about designing a new training session to help you start with a strong structure.

The essential five training programs

As you start to review your current training offerings, there are a few specific courses that every organization should have to help employees do their best work and to improve culture. Additionally, having this foundational knowledge will help your employees connect to other training later. For example, if I am learning about changes to the way Apple is regulating how an iPhone application works, then it would be helpful if I had the foundational knowledge about how the product works. While each position, department, and location will have specific training needs, the essential five training programs described in the following sections help to create a baseline understanding of the company, the products, the culture, and how the employee fits into it all. If you are just getting started with offering more extensive training to your employees, then start by developing these five training programs. These can be part of your onboarding experience (see Chapter 10) or can be done throughout the year on a rotating basis.

AREA	GOAL	YOUR CONTENT
Find the why	Explain why they should learn this, how it applied to them, and what's in it for them	
Define the what	Describe what they will be doing afterwards	
Structure activities	Find things for them to do that will allow them to experience the learning	
Evaluate	Measure the learning and ability to execute the what above (testing, role-play, live demo)	

FIGURE 11-1: Training structure worksheet.

Learning your product

Create a training experience that teaches your employees about what you do and how you do it. Every business has some type of product, offering, or service, and your employees should have a deep understanding of yours. The objectives for a great product, service, or offering training might look like the following for a technology company:

>> Able to order products using our mobile app

>> Identify three uses for our product

>> Explain benefits of our three core features

>> Name the markets where our offering is available

Experiencing your values

Far too many new hire onboarding experiences focus on a presenter talking about values and highlighting organizational mission. Every employee should have training around your values and mission. But it shouldn't focus on slide decks and one-way communication. Instead, create an interactive experience that helps your team define, describe, and deliver on your values. Instead of talking about how you value honesty, present your employees with problem sets and have them choose the correct actions someone should take. If values are about behavior, then have them role-play and practice those behaviors (see Chapter 7 for more on that topic).

Understanding your customers

No matter what you call them, you have customers of some sort. The people you serve, the patients you care for, the constituents you guide, the clients you deliver for — all are versions of your customers. Your training should include a deep dive into who your customers are, why they choose you, what they really want, and how you believe they should be treated. This isn't another "customer service" training but rather your company's approach to serving this very specific set of people. Everyone in your company should know this regardless of how frequently they actually speak to customers. Performance objectives might look like:

>> Can pick three ideal customers for our product

>> Able to apply our rules of service to common customer requests

Targeting your competitors

With an understanding of your product and customers, a well-rounded training program also includes a glimpse into your competition. All your employees should understand who else does what you do for the customers you serve. This training should include a look into their product, market share, and benefits. Your employees should be able to explain how you're similar, different, and why customers choose one over the other when they do. All this will help boost your culture, create community, and inform your team so they can make better decisions in the future.

Making money and running the business

WARNING

You'd be amazed at the number of employees working in organizations that have no idea how the company survives. Sure, they know you sell some stuff and make some stuff, but they don't have actual ideas about how it all works. In my mind, this is the first step toward disengagement. If they can't explain how you make money and thrive, there's no chance that they can understand how they clearly contribute to the company winning.

Similarly, if they don't know who's responsible for what and how that gets done, then their ability to collaborate and communicate with empathy is greatly diminished. Great cultures are full of employees who understand team structures and key roles in the organization.

The performance objectives for a class like this might be:

>> Identify the top three metrics that matter most to us

>> Accurately link product lines to the revenue streams

>> Explain your role in helping the company achieve more financial growth

>> Name the teams responsible for X, Y, and Z

Recognizing When It's Time to Upgrade

As you think about your current training or start rolling out some new options based on the ideas in this chapter, it's important to keep in mind that you're changing to create a more learner-focused, performance-based, engagement-aimed learning experience. When I've worked with organizations to improve culture using some of the training programs, we often uncover the same five things that should have had an impact on the content in the training. Often the training becomes less useful over time because it is lacking the real-world connection due to being out-of-date, based on ineffective training methods, or not getting real-time feedback from participants that could be used to improve things. This section helps you understand when it might be time to review your programs to ensure you are getting the most from your training efforts.

Changing with the business

If your business operations and opportunities have changed drastically, then you probably need to review your training to make sure it's still delivering the performance changes you desire. Often, the product or market will shift but the training stays the same, which makes it irrelevant and unhelpful.

Reframing memorization

If your training program requires lots of rote memorization and studying of facts for regurgitation, it's time for an upgrade. Being able to memorize lots of information has very little real life usage. If a learner is memorizing just to be able to respond on a test, then you need to improve the course. Find ways to make the training performative by finding ways for the trainee to use the information being memorized.

Talking, telling, and presenting

Time your training program to see how often the trainer is speaking. If most of the work is being done by the person in the front of the room (or on a video), then it's time to find more opportunities for your learners to experience the objective being presented. For example, in a training about your prospective customers and target market, give employees some foundational information about who your ideal customers and clients are and then have them do an exercise where they have to accurately identify ideal customers from a list of prospects. The more interactive you can make the training, the better chance you have of creating the performance change you are looking for with your training.

Opting out

If your training is voluntary and you're seeing low enrollment, then it's time to upgrade the training. Maybe the outcomes aren't clear enough. Maybe the rationale isn't strong enough. Remember, learners have to see a clear idea of what's in it for them. Perhaps the training needs some activities and engagement to keep things interesting. People love to learn and grow, so if sign-ups are low, it's time to work on the content.

Staying the same

WARNING

The number one sign that it's time to overhaul and rethink your learning opportunities is if people aren't changed afterward. If you're taking time, energy, money, and resources to focus on learning, then you owe it to the organization, yourself, and the participants to make sure it's impactful. This is the number one sin of training — and one you won't make again after reading this chapter.

4
Managing Your Culture

IN THIS CHAPTER

» Assessing how communication impacts culture

» Mistaking mere information for communication

» Communicating with clarity and engagement

» Ameliorating staff meetings

» Creating opportunities for employees to connect

» Dodging some typical communication mistakes

Chapter **12**

Improving Communications

W hen a culture is in trouble, it can frequently be linked to communication. It's a rare organization that actually has bad managers, horrible products, and insidious strategies. The real culprit behind all these things is communication — whether unclear, lacking specificity, inaccurate, or missing altogether. You have done the hard work to articulate your culture, you have gotten buy-in from top to bottom, and you've hired in ways that will boost the culture you're working to create. Organizational leaders assume that everyone understands what's happening, and front-line employees expect that leadership is sharing what matters most. If not done well, that causes a lot of misaligned activities, which lead to cultural problems.

In this chapter, we explore how communication is a critical component for developing your culture's potential. You'll learn about strategies for improving company communications so that your employees are on board and engaged.

You'll also learn a handful of ideas for improving the communication between your team members.

Communication Is the Cornerstone of Culture

When it comes down to it, so much about building a great company culture relies on communicating. From who you are as a leader (see Chapters 4 and 5) to what matters most to your organization (see Chapter 7), from defining a shared destination (see Chapter 6) to promoting a sense of belonging (see Chapter 10), communication is the foundation from which culture is developed. With communication we create a shared language, express empathy, establish relationships, and negotiate ways forward.

Communication is always happening, even when we don't think deeply about the message we're transmitting. In the times that we don't communicate intentionally, something is still being communicated to the people around us. If employees are worried about their jobs during a merger and the management team doesn't speak to the concerns, then the communication can be interpreted as "we don't care enough about your future to clarify what happens next" or "we are hiding the fact that you will all be losing your jobs shortly."

REMEMBER

As you check in with the other chapters in this book and start to bring more intention and clarity to creating culture in your organization, it's critical to communicate in a way that helps you make the most of those efforts. In the absence of great communication, your employees will "fill in the blanks" with a narrative that helps them make sense of what's happening.

At the core, communication is a two-way street between the person speaking and the person listening, between a leader and the team, and between the company and the employees. It's about the person with information or a message getting clear, intentional, and inspirational when delivering it to the intended audience. This is the key to being able to deliver a message in a way that people are influenced and engaged.

You live in an era when attention is the most expensive thing for sale. Attention is the thing we all get to control for ourselves — where we focus, who we give focus to, and what we decide to engage with is all tied to being able to pull attention. Your communication at work has to be compelling, authentic, and engaging to really connect with your employees. You're competing with millions of messages, most of them more entertaining and better designed.

Addressing the Main Issue with Communication

The biggest error in communication is the inaccurate thinking that information equals communication. How many meetings have you been in where there was plenty of information being shared but very little actually sinking in for the participants? Did the meeting have impact if the rest of the people in the room didn't completely understand and interpret the information accurately? Is there any chance that they can actually execute on the information if it was largely misunderstood?

You don't have to look far to see information given being mistaken for communication sharing. For example, leadership gives a quarterly update to employees highlighting the wins and losses from the previous quarter, sharing goals for the upcoming period, and celebrating key contributions from the team. The objective is to create a call-to-action among employees. Everyone claps and cheers. Then nothing happens. The leadership team gets frustrated because employees "don't get it." The employees are stuck between trying to remember what was said way back when and the reality of the day-to-day operations.

Often when I help executives and leadership teams with culture, the first place we start is with communication. It only takes a few minutes into a keynote address or all-hands company meeting to see why the employees are confused and disengaged. When leaders dump information on employees in a way that isn't focused on the actual exchange of information, including meaning, understanding, and comprehension, then nothing happens.

Communication is only as effective as the depth and quality of its reception, level of understanding, and willingness of the listener to take action afterward. If the communication isn't creating the reaction you want, then don't blame the employees. Find ways to improve the communication so that the message sticks and creates the kind of change you want.

REMEMBER

If you really want to improve communication, you need to understand that information shared is not always information received. Focus on making sure that your employees are grasping the message by framing it better. Think of each communication opportunity as an experience and ensure the message is repeated through the organization multiple times.

Improving Communication

Organizations, teams, and people can always level-up and improve in the communication department — and it remains as one of the true differentiators of great managers and leaders. This doesn't mean that everyone is walking around completely clueless, clumsily spilling information in ways that don't work very well. It means that finding ways to help our employees connect to our messages can pay back in multiples. As new technologies, new generations, and new ways of working continue to disrupt the way we lead our organizations, you can avail yourself with new ways of communication and increase skills to leapfrog the competition by focusing on improving the way you deliver messages.

To communicate with clarity and engagement, read on.

Choosing a focus

Different types of communication have different goals. You may be communicating to inform, to inspire, to transform, or to rally. Work communication likely falls into one of these categories:

>> **Communicating to inform**

- Status updates

- Shifts in strategy

- Program shifts

- Product launches

>> **Communicating to inspire**

- Annual kickoff or wrap-up

- New market launches

- New product categories

- Company vision announcements/changes

>> **Communicating to transform/change**

- Mergers and acquisitions

- Process improvement

- Strategy shifts

>> **Communicating to rally**

- Weekly meetings
- Pre-shift meetings (restaurants, hotels, retail)
- Annual/quarterly all-hands

These are just a few examples of different times you formally communicate with your team. During each of these periods, it's important to get really clear on the reason behind the communication. Too often leaders start organizing slides, jotting notes, making bullet points, and talking without understanding what they really want from the audience (employees).

Take some time before your next conversation, meeting, announcement, or speech to ask yourself what you really want from your employees. What outcome do you want to have happen? Is a department going to produce something different? Can customer service answer questions in a new way? Is the sales team able to more accurately speak to how your product helps your customers? If you're communicating in a performance review, does the employee have a clearer vision of what's next? Big or small, one-on-one or one-to-many, each communication experience is an opportunity to connect, inspire, and create change.

If you can't define the main outcomes desired for your communication, keep working before you decide to deliver the message by taking time to really get clear on what you are hoping changes because of the message. Ask yourself what happens because this message has been delivered. Think about what your employees will be doing differently and why that matters.

Defining a strong call for change

Change is hard — small-scale change, big-scale change, your change, my change. It all requires mental, emotional, and physical energy to shake up the status quo and move into something new. There are endless opportunities for change at work, so getting adept at helping people enroll in the desired change is a good skill to master.

If you want to be a good communicator at work, you have to be good at communicating the reason for change. Much communication at work is about change — new programs, new launches, new processes, new employees, new departments, new markets. You're probably inundated with requests for change. But usually the only person excited about change is the person calling for change. Everyone else is worried that the effort won't be worth the payoff.

To get employees on board with the change you're proposing, you need to explain why the current way of doing things is outdated, uncomfortable, ineffective, or otherwise not beneficial to those you're delivering the message to. Really think about what employees will gain by buying into the change, such as putting wine glasses in a new area of the restaurant to improve traffic flow or changing the client proposal process to save on time and resources. Once you have an idea of how to get employees on board with the change, you need to make sure this is expressed in how you deliver the message by first focusing on the state of the current world. The goal is to highlight the reasons why a change is necessary in the first place. This can be a few statements that help to make your case followed by your ideas for something better.

WARNING

This is usually the part where the old school, command-and-control type folks think, "They'll change because I told them to. I pay them to do what I ask." Not only is that attitude inaccurate — you don't pay them to do what you ask but instead typically pay people to deliver some specific result (service, products, and so on) — but it's also not working. Sure they might change, but they won't understand, adopt, and internalize the change, so it will be short-lived at best, or lead to leaks in morale in other places and a long-term turnover problem at worst. That's why you have this book in your hands, to help you find a different way of communicating! Avoid the old-school-thinking monster and focus on finding the benefits of change from your employee's perspective.

Crafting a better tomorrow

You have a call-to-action, you shared how the change is going to make things better for the team, and they are on board. Don't leave people hanging. Be ready to guide your people in the right direction.

REMEMBER

This is the promised land for communication — getting specific about the positive road ahead, what the future can look like if changes are adopted, and making it all sound like the kind of place we want to be in and the kind of work we want to achieve.

This may sound like fodder for someone trying to create systemic global change but not the kind of stuff you need to think about in this week's staff meeting. It's sometimes hard to realize that improving customer service or making a procedural change should require this kind of communication, but isn't it worth it to help ensure you get the desired result? I'm not suggesting that everything that comes out of your mouth (or pecked away on a keyboard by your fingers) needs to take hours of deliberate planning to land correctly with your intended audience. I am suggesting that it's worthwhile to get clear on what you're trying to create each time you share.

Here are some questions you should answer in your communications about change:

>> How does this change positively impact the employees involved?

>> What does it look like when things are going well? What's happening when you are successful?

>> Why is this important for the future of the organization?

>> What are customers and clients saying about you when this is all happening?

Establishing clear next steps

"The current world sucks! The future world is better! We get it! We buy in! What next?" Establishing what happens next is the key to getting your team into action. There's nothing worse than feeling fired up for change and then not knowing what to do next.

Without giving some clear next steps, you run the risk of your team being so engaged in the process that they move forward in a way to guarantee disaster. At the end of each meeting, update, email, or message, make sure to clarify what happens next. Sometimes that's as simple as stating that no action is required. Other times it will be organizing a team to organize the project plan. Either way, make it clear.

Here are some things that your plan should answer to help establish next steps:

>> Who needs to know about the change?

>> What is the most effective way to tell them?

>> What information is still needed before moving forward?

>> How can you test assumptions to make sure you are taking the right steps?

>> What happens next?

>> How can you measure whether things are working as planned?

Enhancing Staff Meetings

Each week in companies around the world, employees gather for the weekly (or biweekly, or monthly, or on whatever period yours happen) staff meeting. Maybe the meeting is hyper-focused on a very current happening (such as a social media crisis kicked off by an inflammatory tweet) or just slowly unfolds with the manager giving some news from the company before closing the meeting without any real engagement or call-to-action.

In almost every organization I've encountered, managers at every level seem to struggle with how to organize and lead better staff meetings. Both sides of the table seem to abhor the existence of the meeting — the person leading it starts to dread it, and the employees attending it view it as a waste of time. Yet we feel this compulsion to keep it on the calendar. You may see other departments doing it with success. When done well, the regularly scheduled staff meeting can be a huge benefit to keeping the team engaged and focused and a terrific way to share communication. So how do you get it right?

Creating better weekly meetings

A great weekly staff meeting has four primary goals:

1. Updating each other on the status of key projects and metrics

2. Creating time to share other important information that doesn't naturally come up during status updates and metric reviews

3. Clarifying the actions and goals for the upcoming week

4. Promoting a sense of community among your team

REMEMBER

The weekly staff meeting isn't the place for major project decisions, strategy-shifting debates, or post-mortem event reviews. All those are important enough to require their very own conversations. Your weekly staff meeting is about meeting the four goals in a consistent and organized way. Maintaining a place for this kind of weekly check-in is an important part of galvanizing your team.

Leading your weekly staff meeting consistently and positively each week goes a long way toward boosting your team's culture. It's a way to create trust and establish relationships, and it ensures everyone is tuned in to what's going on with the team.

Conducting better team meetings

Each week, managers and employees are subjected to painful, ineffective meetings that do little to drive the culture or solidify results. The agenda is inconsistent (or completely nonexistent). Topics seem to be reviewed ad hoc and based on whatever happened before the meeting started. Follow-up is unclear and left to chance. People are put on the spot to present things they weren't prepared to share.

SHAPING UP DAILY MEETINGS

For operations teams across industry, the daily meeting is a common occurrence. In restaurants, retail locations, hotels, manufacturing plants, airlines, and other operations-heavy environments, it's critical to get the daily download and upload of information to effectively carry out the day's work. Here are some ideas for better daily meetings:

- Keep it under 10 minutes.
- Lead it while standing up to keep everyone's focus up and energy high.
- Spend equal time clarifying the day's focus and getting feedback from the staff.
- Let the team take turns leading the meeting so that different people lead it each week/day.
- Spend 1–2 minutes of a 10-minute meeting focused on skills, information, or other trivia. You can even use prizes to keep engagement up.

It's actually easy to put together a well-organized staff meeting. By following a consistent agenda, you can better prepare for each meeting, and employees will feel at ease knowing what to expect. The best weekly staff meetings have these four components:

>> Review (15 minutes)

>> Listen (15 minutes)

>> Identify (20 minutes)

>> Appreciate (10 minutes)

Getting ready to review

During the review portion of the meeting, the key metrics are given a chance to shine. These should be documented on some sort of scoreboard or dashboard with the same numbers reviewed weekly. Your team should know exactly what to report on and should update the scoreboard ahead of time. Don't get too caught up in making it so fancy that you don't get started. A simple spreadsheet with the key numbers your team should track is enough to get value from this portion of the meeting. Set a reminder for your team to update the scoreboard before the meeting. During the meeting, review the numbers. What worked and why? What didn't and why? What's off track and needs more attention? What's going better than planned?

Figure 12-1 shows a sample for what a simple weekly review scoreboard/ dashboard could look like for an HR team.

Metric	Owner	Period 1		Period 2		Period 3	
		Goal	Actual	Goal	Actual	Goal	Actual
Average time to hire	Candice	28 days	21 days				
Average cost per hire	Andrew	$4000	$3800				
Voluntary turnover	Kristine	5%	5%				
Involuntary turnover	Kristine	0%	0%				
eNPS score	Kristine	50	55				

FIGURE 12-1: Sample HR team scoreboard.

Figure 12-2 gives an example of what a simple weekly review scoreboard/ dashboard could look like for a sales team.

Metric	Owner	Period 1		Period 2		Period 3	
		Goal	Actual	Goal	Actual	Goal	Actual
Closed opportunities	Chris	640	688				
Open opportunities	Chris	500	480				
Average deal size	Gracie	$78k	$82k				
Average win ratio	Katie	62%	55%				
Sales team eNPS	Melissa	50	48				

FIGURE 12-2: Sample sales team scoreboard.

Figure 12-3 offers up a sample of a simple weekly review scoreboard/dashboard for a restaurant.

Metric	Owner	Period 1		Period 2		Period 3	
		Goal	Actual	Goal	Actual	Goal	Actual
Average check/guest	Joanne	$44	$40				
Average appetizer/guest	Joanne	.75	.5				
Labor cost	Analisa	30%	29%				
Sales	Analisa	$80k	$78k				
Avg guest rating	DJ	4.8	4.6				

FIGURE 12-3: Sample restaurant scoreboard.

Knowing how to listen

In the listening section of the meeting, you're trying to uncover all the other kinds of things each person on your team is doing that don't necessary fit within the scoreboard section. There are going to inevitably be projects, tasks, initiatives, and happenings that aren't (and shouldn't be) measured in that way. During the listening section of the meeting, each person is given the stage to highlight the other stuff going on: staff concerns, out-of-office topics, a new direction of a key project, and so on. The easiest way to do this is to include a section of the agenda where each person fills in the two or three things that should be known by others on the team. Then during the meeting, it will be quick to review.

WARNING

Avoid the temptation to make the listening section of the meeting longer just because your team can fill the time. In my experience, this is where things tend to get drawn out, making your meeting longer than needed. If more discussion is required on a topic, plan time after the meeting to review.

Identifying discussion topics

In the third section of the meeting, your team will identify other decisions and topics that need discussion. This is where new ideas are surfaced, projects are questioned, results are interrogated, and debate occurs. If you have a really big team (more than 15 people), then this is probably best organized by circulating an agenda and asking for additions in advance. If your team is smaller than 15, you can handle this in an ad hoc fashion.

This is a good time to review customer feedback as well. If you have a way that clients, customers, patients, constituents, or members submit feedback, this is the time to look at it as a group and decide if action is required. Often the feedback will spur creation of a new project or spark some debate, which is a great use of your team's time in the weekly staff meeting.

TIP

During this section of the meeting, allow the team to guide the conversation. After all, this is the staff meeting, not the "come hear what the manager thinks" meeting. As you work through topics in this section, you'll inevitably find that some things are easily handled within the confines of your meeting, and other things are big enough to justify a follow-up conversation. In this case, make sure that next steps are documented and someone is put in charge of the follow-up. Make a note for next week's agenda to follow up.

WARNING

Lack of meeting follow-up is one of the major crimes in most organizations. Make sure that someone is assigned with keeping track of follow-up commitments. These can be reviewed during the next meeting.

Taking time to appreciate

Finally, you should take a few minutes of your staff meeting for appreciations. During this brief section of the meeting, you dedicate time for the team to appreciate and recognize others. It may be someone in the room who helped with something, or someone outside of the room. As a manager, this is your chance to highlight the things that are going right on your team. Maybe one of your employees has done a great job training a new hire, or someone went out of their way to deliver something for a client over a weekend — these are the kinds of things you should notice and recognize as a leader. For more ideas, see Chapter 20.

Calling all hands on deck

While a well-organized and well-executed weekly staff meeting will go a long way toward helping your organization improve communication and culture, sometimes you need to bring the whole group together. In organizations with more than 40 or so employees, the all-hands meeting is a way to keep everyone connected. You'd be surprised at how quickly people start to become unaware of what others are doing. This leads to empathy issues and lack of understanding around why other people/departments are taking the actions they're taking. Hosting a monthly or quarterly all-hands meeting allows you to bring things into the open.

An all-hands meeting helps improve buy-in on decision-making, brings projects to the forefront, and keeps the team connected to the work everyone is doing. It also provides a chance for the employees to ask questions and seek understanding. Politicians have long held these types of town hall meetings to convince the public that the decisions being made were the right ones and to calm concerns by addressing questions directly. Your organization would be well served doing the same.

A great all-hands meeting usually includes:

>> **Presentations:** A few key projects or decisions are reviewed in slightly more detail than can be provided via an email. The team closest to the project presents an overview of what's happening and why (use the earlier "Improving Communication" section to frame a compelling presentation). This could be a new acquisition, a change to the service model, a new product offering, or a human resource program.

>> **Q&A:** This is an open floor session that is typically handled by the executive team. It's a chance for employees to ask questions about anything going on, not just the presentations that are shared. The goal is to provide an authentic and honest answer to the most pressing issues for your employees. When I've coached executives on presence for sessions like this, I typically share much of the information in Chapter 4 to help them create the experience they want for their employees. If this process is new for your team (or trust is low), then send a call for questions ahead of the meeting and allow for people to submit anonymous questions beforehand.

>> **Big goal review:** Since you have everyone together, it's a good time to quickly review where things stand in your annual goals. Don't get too far down the rabbit hole by digging into department or individual goals in these sessions. Keep it focused on high-level organization goals. Share the progress with the team.

TIP

If your company has some way of collecting positive employee feedback or even positive customer comments, this is a great time to publicly praise the people involved.

WARNING

If done poorly, the leadership team can feel great about the meeting because they got some laughs, shared information that mattered to them, owned the agenda, and got a moment in the spotlight. And, guess what? The staff was bored out of their minds. If done well, the leadership often feels exhausted by it, left empty, and not as inspired as they'd hoped the team meeting would make them feel. Why is this? Because the meeting wasn't for them; it was for their staff. If they leave it all out there, and talk about things from their team's perspective, as it relates to the team, and in ways that the team will appreciate and be inspired by, they might find themselves feeling exhausted. But, that's okay. The meeting was for the staff, not the leader, and the energy should flow accordingly.

Helping Your Team Connect

Communication from leadership is key in creating the kind of culture that drives results and doesn't just flow from the top down. Culture lives within every relationship at work. The more that you can help your employees build positive professional relationships, the better able your culture will be to adapt and thrive. Creating opportunities for your employees to share, connect, collaborate, and learn from each other should be a major focus of your leadership and HR team. Check out these next sections for ideas on how to keep communication flowing in different ways, which means more benefits for keeping your culture growing and thriving.

Hosting coffee chats

"Let's grab coffee" is spoken, emailed, or texted millions of times a day. We love connecting with colleagues, networking with new acquaintances, and getting deals done over coffee. It's a low-commitment way of spending some time together. It's also a great way to encourage your employees to learn more about each other.

Encourage your employees to find time to spend together by creating an opt-in coffee chat program. It can be company-wide or department-specific depending on the size of the organization and your role within it. The goal is to get people together with some frequency over coffee to chat.

To start a coffee chat program:

>> Create a way for people to opt in. A simple survey where they choose "yes" or "no" each month is an easy way to start.

>> Create a one-page explanation of the program. Be sure to include the goals (get to know each other better and increase connection), the frequency (monthly is a good start), and guidelines (suggest a length of time and a local spot to visit).

>> Enroll a few people to help you organize it. Someone can make the matches. Someone else can send out the emails/messages to connect matches.

>> Design some suggested questions to help them get started. These can range from ice-breaker type questions to "what are you working on" type questions. Ask your team to help contribute ideas.

#showyourwork sessions

Remember in math class how you had to show your work? It wasn't enough to just get the right answer — you had to show the teacher how you got to the answer. The end did not justify the means — the means mattered too.

The same thinking can create some pretty high engagement on your team.

If the all-hands meetings are a chance to highlight a few high-level projects, then the #showyourwork sessions are a deep dive into someone on your team sharing what he or she is working on. In these regularly scheduled sessions, people on your team share how they work, what they're working on, or the strategy and thinking behind a recent project. This type of communication will go a long way toward helping your team build relationships and learn more about the things going on in your company. It can start to improve the culture by creating more transparency, boosting empathy, and building connections between your team members.

From the design department to the product team, from the operations crew to the human resources squad, your organization is likely full of people doing interesting work that no one else knows about.

Starting book clubs

You'd be amazed at how much a book club can ignite culture and create connections with the people on your team. Reading a book together is a way to help spark conversations and boost relationships — all things that positively benefit your culture and inspire communication.

It's likely that you have a few people on your team who'd be interested in helping to lead a book club. It's as easy as picking a new book each quarter, designing a few questions for each chapter, and then assigning the reading. Schedule a few sessions to meet in person or via video for remote employees. Then allow the book club leaders to facilitate the conversation based on the questions for each chapter.

Using video, technology, and blogs

It's becoming more and more likely that your organization is being called to use social media and technology to communicate with employees. For many organizations, it's the preferred method of communication for the employees. These days, employees are typically comfortable connecting with each other and the organization through technology.

Here's a look at how to take advantage of current technology to boost communication:

>> **Video:** You can use video in so many ways to communicate with your team, from recruiting to training, from announcements to updates. There's no lack of opportunity to use video as a vehicle to share information with your team. Use the info in the earlier "Improving Communication" section and start leveraging this powerful medium. You can use the framework from that section to shape your messages to create the kinds of change you're hoping for from your communication.

>> **Social media:** Create employee accounts to share updates about your company. Encourage your employees to follow and connect with your main brand accounts. Establish employee takeover days where they run the show on your social accounts — answering questions from your customers, creating engagement, and delivering content on behalf of your brand.

>> **Written content:** Use blogs, articles, chat forums, and intranet sites to communicate and offer updates. These types of media can be an effective way to share information with a broad range of employees at once. You can also utilize these methods for sharing follow-up messages after in-person meetings, events, and as a supplement to video messaging.

Regardless of which method you adopt, it's important to be engaged, active, and proficient. Make sure your leadership team is responding to comments so that your employees know this is a valuable way to stay in touch.

Avoiding Common Communication Pitfalls

There are a million ways to communicate, and you likely already excel in some areas. Using the ideas in this chapter will give you a well-rounded approach to keeping your team informed. However, things can go awry. Here are a few common mistakes to avoid.

Cutting out the emotion

When it comes to work, you've likely heard things like "it's not personal, it's professional" or "you shouldn't get upset" or "you shouldn't cry/get emotional." I'm not sure what dystopian world those people live in, but we are humans. Our emotions define our experiences. To ask yourself and other people to strip any type of emotional response to things at work is futile and disheartening. It's impossible to not have emotions and feelings at work, and the more you can learn to leverage your emotions to communicate more honestly, the better you'll be at connecting with your employees.

TIP

Instead of worrying about expressing your emotions at work, focus on making sure that your expression of emotions is clear and connected to what you really want. The truth behind our emotions is driven by something one layer deeper. Bring that to the forefront and share it with your team. For example, if you are communicating a message about changes in the marketplace and are feeling cautious but optimistic — then think about that before you get ready to speak. Often when people go into a conversation or presentation, they forget to remember how they feel about the message. Take stock of that in the few minutes before your next communication.

Overusing email and text

Just because we can communicate at speeds that get ever faster each day doesn't mean we should. Employees are inundated with emails, texts, instant messages, chats, and other forms of quick-hit information dumps that seem more like drive-by-messaging than real attempts at effective communication.

Make sure your use of email and text is intentional. Consider whether the thing you're communicating needs to be shared now or can wait until you see each other in person. Create a list or folder where you can store messages for each person on your team so that your communication can be organized and focused instead of just a long stream of consciousness. Some people do this on paper; others use an app to store notes for later use.

In a world where people pride themselves on getting to inbox zero over doing quality work, we're all responsible for helping to reduce the amount of unnecessary messages we send to each other.

Forgetting to listen

How many times do you think people are willing to contribute, speak up, offer perspectives, and attempt to collaborate without being heard before they just stop making the effort? I'm not sure that there's a scientifically validated answer to this question, but my anecdotal evidence is "not many."

WARNING

If you don't make an intentional effort to hear new hires and seasoned employees out, you run the risk of them concluding that your culture is one that doesn't promote equal sharing of information. You don't get unlimited chances at an employee showing the discretionary effort of speaking up without being acknowledged.

Make sure that you create opportunities for your employees to be heard. Go out of your way to ask questions, to dig deeper, to seek out understanding, and then explore their perspective. Running an organization in an echo chamber is a dangerous way to build culture and safeguard your company's future.

Here are some ideas for remembering to listen more:

>> Ask other people to speak first in meetings

>> Recap what other people say in meetings to ensure understanding

>> Pay attention to the ratio between how much you talk and how much you listen with the goal of listening twice as much as you speak

>> Take notes while others are speaking to you to help you absorb their message and ensure understanding

Chapter **13**

Improvising Your Way to a Better Culture

Think about the start of your week (or last week if it's only Monday). You probably had a to-do list, some ideas about what you needed to accomplish, and an overall agenda set for yourself. Then you got out of bed. A client emails about a change in their new product launch, your star employee emails her resignation, and the coffee pot is busted . . . again. Everything you planned has just changed, and you're making it up from here on out. At some point, you need to improvise each day. The plans we begin with are not the ones we execute. So we have to find better ways to leverage the unexpected to create more together.

In this chapter, you find out about improvisational theater and how it can help your team work better together. From listening better to establishing empathy to finding ways to agree in order to move a project (or conversation) forward, you'll explore how this performance art can change the way you approach management and the way your team works together.

Defining Improv

Imagine stepping out onto a plain black stage. The audience is full of people sitting in uncomfortable sticky chairs and drinking cheap beer from plastic cups, all expecting to be entertained by you. As you walk out, you realize you don't have a script, you aren't in costume, and you have no idea about the character you're going to play. Heck, you don't even know the plot! As your hands get clammy, you remember you aren't in this alone. You've got five other people there to create a show seemingly from thin air. You remember the simple rules that allow you to figure out what's going on as you create it — literally as you speak, you're sorting out the character, scene, and plot twists. One of your ensemble members steps forward and asks for a suggestion from the audience. Someone yells "cornfield" — or, if it were a late night audience in Chicago, like so many of my early shows, they yell something that would make your mom blush and my editor cringe. From that simple suggestion, two actors immediately step forward and initiate a scene. They do this not because they are good at winging it or naturally funny but because they follow a simple framework of rules. If you've ever seen an improv show, then you'll recognize that scenario. If you haven't ever seen a show, well, this is improvisational theater. Every night in theaters like The Second City and Upright Citizens Brigade, actors take the stage and create shows in the spur of the moment.

Improv appears in all kinds of places in the world, from popular TV shows like *Whose Line Is It Anyway?* and *Saturday Night Live* (where they actually use improv to write the sketches that appear weekly) to an ensemble jazz concert. Improv has made appearances in space (remember that scene in the movie *Apollo 13* when they had to figure out how to get the astronauts back to Earth using only what was on the space shuttle?). Pilots use improv to adjust course during flight to ensure you make it to JFK and not LaGuardia (seriously, LaGuardia — let's work on the culture of that airport together). Emergency responders use it every time they go out on a call. Parents use it to deal with all kinds of new and strange requests from their kids. And it shows up in your work and life too.

Living in a VUCA World

One place that may surprise you to find improvisation is in the military. For all the control, structure, and obedience found in the armed forces, they still rely on improvisation. A plan is only good until you face the enemy (or the marketplace in the case of most readers of this book). Soldiers coordinate efforts, make plans, and strategize — and then on the field, they have to adjust to emerging occurrences. The military term that describes these kinds of situations is *VUCA* (volatile, uncertain, complex, and ambiguous). These situations demand flexibility, creativity, adaptability, and agility. It just so happens that these are the same skills improvisational theater instills as well.

From a company culture perspective, these are the kinds of skills and characteristics that highly productive, highly collaborative teams share as well. In your organization, you face times when the marketplace seems volatile, when competition is high, and when circumstances are unclear. Organizations have to be ready to respond to shifting demands, frequently changing regulations, and generational shifts at work. Just like the military, your business operates in a VUCA world that can successfully address shifting circumstances by being able to work better through mastering improvisation.

Volatility

Markets shift, prices change, Mother Nature wreaks havoc, or construction blocks the entrance to your new restaurant. These are all realistic concerns for the modern business leader. The world we operate in is volatile; it's unstable and change is unexpected. To stay competitive, your organization needs to generate fresh ideas and remain agile to respond to new opportunities. Improvisational thinking prepares your team to handle the unexpected and generates ideas for managing the emerging situation.

Uncertainty

Every time one of the popular social media platforms changes its algorithm and approach to business pages, you can hear the sound of marketers and companies all around start to get uncomfortable and cry about the updates. They've built entire campaigns and programs around these algorithms, and now the company has just wiped out an entire budget. The uncertainty that exists in this kind of business decision and pretty much everywhere else in business is the kind of uncertainty that improvisational theater is able to handle so well. Improv allows you to tap into networks and identify new opportunities in a way that sitting in a room banging your head against the wall looking for solutions just won't do. Uncertainty begs for us to adapt quickly and use limited information to make bold choices.

Complexity

Maybe you're doing business in multiple countries and dealing with lots of difficult situations. You may have multiple generations at work or even separate product lines that serve entirely different markets. Whatever business you are in, the environment in which you operate is complex. There are bits and parts and variables and interconnected webs of information and people. With changing marketing technologies, work technologies, and a shift away from the industrial-based economy that marked most of the 20th century — there aren't clear cause-and-effect type answers. As the world becomes more and more connected, the complexity in modern organizations continues to increase. Being able to use strong improvisational skills to help navigate these choppy waters and to find meaning in seemingly disparate occurrences and information is the key to success. By staying open and learning how to leverage emerging trends, data, and happenings, your team will be able to beat the competition.

Ambiguity

Much of the business world today is about facing the unknown and trying to make it known. It's about deciding to go into untapped markets and making sense of information even when it's limited. The new world of business requires you to experiment, to try new things, to fail, and to figure out what to do with all the pieces you've collected along the way. You have to create the kind of environment that celebrates risk-tasking and leveraging mistakes to find a new win. Improvisational techniques can help teach your team to use everything — even the bits that previously seemed like losses. Ambiguity creates an environment of instability because answers aren't clear, solutions aren't obvious, and needs aren't always clarified. Teams have to be able to use limited data to make decisions. They need to be able to trust themselves and each other to take action even when the given circumstances are hazy. To stay on top, you've got to be able to act fluidly. Improvisational thinking helps your team to stay open to possibility.

Applying Improv to Business

If I told you that I had an employee who could help your team find agreement so that they could move forward on projects, reduce the politicking of status and one-upmanship, develop the ability to process on the fly, learn from failure, make each other look good, and create space for others to contribute, you'd probably want that person on your team.

These are the exact skills that training in improvisation can help members of your team develop. From libraries to restaurants, from hotels to tech companies, from marketers to doctors, the core skills of improvisation can improve results in just about every area. Despite all the planning, strategizing, control mechanisms, and policies, business is one big improvisational show. Markets shift, customers change, and regulations, well, regulate — and through it all you have to adjust. You have to learn to use what's available to get things done. Your company depends on the ability of your team to be agile and collaboratively create the future, one agreement at a time.

I've been performing improv theater since I was 21, and I didn't really consider the application to business until much later. After all, I got into the restaurant industry the same way every other would-be actor does — it was the job I took to help me pay the bills while waiting for my big break. My big break came when I realized that the rules of improv theater could help me succeed in business too — that the tenets that created dynamic improv ensembles who could so easily listen, adapt, and collaborate were the very ones that could help my team succeed.

These next sections show you just how improv can be applied to business.

Saying "Yes, and . . ."

When you study improv, the very first rule you learn is the rule of "yes, and . . . ." It's the foundation of all improv theater. It's the rule that helps you figure out where to go and what to do. It says that you will accept whatever the other person has contributed — and then you will add to it, which is where the "and . . ." comes in.

Setting the scene

Consider the cornfield suggestion from the opening of this chapter. The two actors step on the stage and start creating a scene. They haven't had an opportunity to talk to each other, to compare notes, or to plan anything. They literally just start creating something completely improvised together without a script. One of the actors works to create a character, adding a location where they might be together. The other one agrees with whatever the first actor says and then adds details on top of it. It might look something like this:

> Actor 1: "Hey mom! I'm almost done shucking all this corn for dinner — I can't believe we needed 100 pieces for this barbeque."

> Actor 2: "Thanks John. You know how much your Aunt and Uncle love grilled corn when they come to visit us in Des Moines."

This isn't the most interesting scene so far, and that's okay. It doesn't have to be just yet. The point is that the first actor introduced some details to establish the circumstances, and the second actor accepted those details as reality by listening and then adding more ideas to the scene. By continuing in this way, each person is responsible for accepting what the other person has said and then adding his or her own idea. Following this pattern of listening, responding, and heightening will eventually lead them somewhere funny. By following these simple rules, they can make something out of nothing.

Imagine instead that the first actor made the same comments but the other actor said, "What corn? And mom? I'm not your mom." Now they haven't established a base reality and have nothing to build off of. Worse yet, the audience is confused.

Is the first person crazy? Is this a dream? What's happening? Or imagine that the second actor just kept saying "no" to the first person's ideas. That would preclude the scene from going anywhere. Or how about if the second actor just kept saying "yes" to whatever the first actor said, without adding additional details. Wait, that sounds pretty good, doesn't it? Not if you're the first actor, who now feels responsible for adding everything to the scene. This leads to confusion for the audience about what's going on and what's being created — and frankly, for the actors too. Only by saying "yes, and . . ." will the actors be able to create something better together. From this point, I see a scene start to unfold that takes a comedic view at a family reunion with corn-loving relatives.

Putting it into play

Creating a "yes, and . . ." culture in your business is one of the most effective ways to change the way that your team works together. Think about all the meetings you've been in where people just say "no" to each other or where it seems that nobody is building on each other's ideas. It slows down innovation. It makes collaboration impossible. What would happen if your team took a "yes, and . . ." approach to working together? It doesn't mean that they have to have an unconditional acceptance of each other's ideas. It simply means you have to be willing to accept that the other person has an idea and then use that as a springboard to keep adding on to it. In this way, "yes, and . . ." thinking can help your team come up with fresh ideas, new innovations, and a more collaborative, supportive environment.

TIP

The easiest way to get started with "yes and . . ." thinking at work is to share this chapter with your team — and actually practice saying the words "yes and . . ." during your meetings. It will sound a little ridiculous at first, but that's fine — if you're all doing it together, it'll be a fun little experiment. Commit to using "yes and . . ." thinking (and "yes and . . ." saying) for the next week together and see what you can create.

If you think about the VUCA components, consider how accepting the reality of a volatile world is a much more interesting place from which to operate. Being able to accept the world as it is by saying "yes" helps your organization make the most of the current conditions versus trying to fight against what might be completely inevitable. It keeps you nimble and present. In the same way, saying "and" after the yes gives your team the chance to start to create solutions in an uncertain and complex environment. If the role of "and" in "yes and . . ." is to contribute ideas, to heighten the scene, and to explore possibility, then it is directly linked to be able to "think outside of the box" when it comes to responding to change.

Listening to others

Most people don't think twice about how much they really listen to others. They go about their days assuming that they're taking it all in and really hearing what's going on without a second thought. The reality is that many people are hearing but not really listening and, therefore, missing some important information.

It's not that people are complete jerks either. They're busy thinking about how they'll respond instead of listening to understand. In meetings you can see people just waiting for someone to stop talking so they can start talking. After sitting in countless boardrooms and watching many teams try to interact with each other, I know that listening is a challenge for so many people in today's business land-scape. Here are some activities to practice to help with really concentrating on listening:

>> **One-word-at-a-time story:** In this activity, a group of people are creating a story together but only one word at a time. Have people stand in a circle and, going clockwise, ask each person to add one more word to help create a cohesive story as a group. They have to really listen to the people before them to contribute something that moves the story forward.

TIP

Practice listening to the person speaking before utilizing the "yes, and . . ." approach to improv. You're showing that you're listening and accepting what a team member has to say before adding your thoughts.

>> **Last word, first word:** This is a simple activity you can practice alone without anyone else even knowing what you're doing. The goal is that you start your sentence with the same letter that started the last word of the person you're talking to. For example, if someone says, "I had the wildest weekend down in San Diego," then you would start your sentence with a "d" since the last word of the other person's sentence started with a "d." So you could say, "Did you visit that new wine bar?" If you're like most of the people in my workshops and coaching sessions, you'll quickly learn just how hard this is — not because you don't know the alphabet but because it's really hard to stay quiet long enough for the other person to completely finish speaking. Try it out in your next meeting or when you grab your morning coffee. You'll be surprised by the results.

Making statements

If you've ever been in a conversation with someone who constantly asks more questions (unless you're paying to spend some time on the therapist's couch), then you'll understand the power of making statements. In improv theater, we focus on making statements and contributing ideas instead of constantly asking the other person what's going on. For example, in a scene with two students, you wouldn't ask the other person, "How do you feel about the test next week?" but would instead "gift" the other person with an offer by saying something like, "You look really nervous about next week's test." This gives the other person something to build from instead of having to come up with all the ideas himself.

REMEMBER

This idea is useful at work because it makes everyone responsible for contributing ideas instead of just asking questions. This helps move projects, ideas, and conversations forward. By making statements instead of asking questions, you can provide options and opportunities. You give the other person something to "yes, and . . ." back to you. This doesn't mean that there aren't times when asking questions can be helpful; it just means that in most cases, it's most helpful to try to move action forward by making statements.

TIP

Work through the activity of Foursquare. The goal of this activity is to have people practice making statements from different perspectives. This will not only help them make choices and contribute but can also help improve empathy by having them explore other points of view. Here's how to play:

1. **Divide a space into four "squares" and then have each person stand in them.**

2. **Give the team a topic to discuss.**

3. **Give each "square" a specific point of view.**

   Each employee will need to speak from that perspective. For example, you might choose to talk about a new company perk or benefit.

4. **Divide the squares by different employee types or groups.**

   One square might represent employees with children, another might represent your youngest employees, another square can represent your oldest employees, and another can represent your finance team.

   You can do the same thing when looking at other new products or ideas. You can also use this to specifically focus on finding solutions as well. Each square can represent a different perspective or goal for solving a common challenge.

5. **Ask questions or prompt each participant to comment based on the topic from Step 2.**

   Let each square respond in a 60-second time frame. Once each participant has had a chance to respond, have "him" or "her" rotate and play one of the other roles to attempt to gather more ideas, more viewpoints, and to explore new ideas.

This activity is a great way to expand your team's ability to handle VUCA situations by training their brains to look at problems from other perspectives and trying to create solutions to complex or ambiguous issues.

Co-creating something better

Think of all the meetings you've been in that ended by a manager saying something like, "Yes, that would be great, but we don't have the budget to get started." Where can the employee possibly take that? What would happen if instead the manager said, "Yes, that would be great, and we can find some ways to pull resources from other places in our budget." The manager doesn't have to just say "yes" and move on. He or she can contribute to the employee's original idea to build something stronger together.

Try this activity to help get your team into co-creation mode together: Ad Game. The goal of this activity is to get small groups of people to create an entire ad campaign for a fictional product. Here's how to do it:

1. **Break a larger group into teams of three to five people.**

2. **Tell each team to create an ad campaign for a brand new product.**

3. **Ask each team to work together to come up with the following within a two-minute time frame:**

   - A name

   - A slogan/tagline

   - A celebrity spokesperson

   - A jingle

   - A list of features and benefits for this new product

4. **Ask them for a product (something found in a kitchen, something from a convenience store, an item found in a school, and so on) and then ask for a problem some group of people have (senior citizens, dog owners, teachers, and so on).**

   These two things don't need to be (and shouldn't be) related.

5. **Add the product and problem together to create a new product before setting the timer and getting your teams started (for example, a measuring cup that helps quiet unruly students; a protein bar that helps restore short-term memory).**

6. **See what language is used to express and respond to ideas.**

WARNING

   Teams will likely struggle during the first round to get it done within the two minutes. This is because they aren't saying "yes, and . . ." and instead are just accepting each idea. Likely they're saying "no" and judging the ideas as they come.

7. **Give them direction to agree and contribute to each other's ideas by only saying "yes, and . . ." and avoiding "yes, but . . ." or "no" type comments.**

8. **Have them try again for two minutes.**

This activity is a great way to get your team thinking differently about creating something together. In a VUCA world, you need employees who can create things together with limited information and limited resources. Using activities like this frequently can help to build that muscle on your team.

Putting improv to work

Creating an environment built on trust and full of authenticity is the aim of most organizations. Getting employees and managers to a place where they can really listen to each other, find the value in one another's ideas, and then build something better together is the panacea of culture. Learning to communicate with a "yes, and . . ." approach works in any environment and pays big dividends when it comes to increasing a team's ability to communicate, collaborate, and create.

Chapter **14**

Creating a Feedback-Rich Culture

O rganizational leaders around the world say things like "feedback is a gift." Yet somehow, this doesn't take the sting out of getting it or the anxiety out of giving it. If feedback is a gift, then why the heck does it feel so much like punishment? Managers struggle with it. Your peers avoid it. Executives abhor it. Yet it remains one of the ways to most positively propel your culture upwards.

In this chapter, you explore how feedback shifts your culture. You discover the benefits of establishing a feedback-rich culture and discover some simple ideas for improving the feedback in your organization.

Shifting Culture Using Feedback

Creating a feedback-rich culture should be at the top of all leaders' to-do lists. In a feedback-rich culture, employees feel safe to share ideas with each other. They appreciate hearing from others about ways to grow and improve their performance. Managers get notes on what their teams need from them.

REMEMBER

The relationships you have at work are at the core of your job. You simply can't reach your highest potential, be your most impactful, or deliver your best results if you don't have strong relationships. Those strong relationships live and breathe in a feedback-rich culture, and they stagnate and rot in a culture that doesn't celebrate feedback.

Enriching trust

Being able to speak honestly, openly, and supportively is key to building relationships at work. When other people know you have their back and are looking out for them, trust is built. Great cultures rely on trust between coworkers. Think about the best, most productive teams you've been part of — I'll bet that mutual trust was a big factor. But building trust isn't just about following steps. By creating a feedback-rich culture in a way that's positive, you start to show that the people in your organization care about reaching each other beyond the title.

When someone else has your back — which is shown by looking out for each other, by giving the feedback employees need to achieve whatever projects they are attempting and improve their skills — trust is built.

Enhancing relationships

If trust is core to feedback-rich cultures, then relationships are a beneficial outcome. When you develop a culture that encourages, teaches, and celebrates effective feedback, the team starts to build relationships based on mutual trust, appreciation, and shared commitment to getting better. When we display an openness to getting feedback (or actively seek it out), we show signs of vulnerability and commitment to being seen, and both of these boost the chances that other people will connect with us.

Think about the people you've worked with in the past that you had the best, most enduring relationships with. It's probably a safe bet to say that it was the people who were willing to tell you what you needed to hear in order to grow. Your company culture relies on the relationships and communication between your employees to help create the conditions for great work, strong collaboration, and effective service. Creating an environment where the team is able to be honest, direct, and supportive with each other will create those relationships.

Boosting skills

Ultimately, a feedback-rich culture means skills improvement. By getting feedback and taking perspective from others, your employees have a chance to improve skills in ways that people in less feedback-friendly environments lack. In organizations with a weak feedback culture, employees don't get important information about their performance from each other and often not from their managers either outside of an annual review. Feedback is the way people grow, learn, and improve their skills. Getting specific information about how your work was done, the impact you are making, and the results of the things you do is critical for skill development.

Imagine part of your job is giving presentations about the product your company sells. As you go around delivering presentations and sharing information, you don't get any feedback from your peers, your manager, or the audience. You have no idea whether what you presented makes sense, was received positively, or had an impact. Now imagine that after every presentation your manager or a peer spent a few minutes with you sharing notes from the presentation about what was strong, what was really clear, what needs some more background, and a few ideas for connecting with the audience better. If you received that kind of feedback every time you presented, your skills would improve much faster than in the first scenario.

Professional growth and career development are at the top of everyone's list, so creating a culture that celebrates feedback helps your employees improve while improving your retention. Direct and clear feedback is the most efficient way to get notes on how to improve performance.

Understanding the Four Styles of Feedback

Creating a feedback-rich culture requires that you get specific about what type of feedback is expected and desired. You may think it's pretty easy for people to understand what you want, but too many people have been rewarded their whole lives for only being nice and not hurting people's feelings. They've been told "if you don't have anything nice to say, then don't say anything at all" so often that they bite their tongues. Other people have been rewarded for their aggressive and direct approach, an approach that forgets there's another human on the other side of the feedback. If feedback is about helping the recipient improve, then there must be an effective model for doing it. Check out the following four common styles of feedback to help clarify and teach your team the best approach (hint: it's the last one).

Indifferent lies

Lying indifferently is probably the worst style of feedback at work. It lacks any attempt at showing others you care while avoiding telling them what they need to hear. They get neither the positive relationship vibes nor the feedback. This happens most often because you just aren't interested in dealing with the extra relationship development required to be able to give someone feedback comfortably. For example, an employee has just turned in a proposal that you need to finalize for a client. You realize it doesn't look great but because you aren't that invested in the employee's skill set development or his or her personal growth, you just redo the work and send it off to the client. When the employee asks how it was, you say, "It looked great," even though you know that's not true. The difference between this and the next section is that you aren't worried about hurting the person's feelings — you just simply don't care about getting involved in the feedback process.

WARNING

This is a very selfish place to play from. It's a place that focuses on conflict avoidance because it's easier on you. The feedback doesn't get delivered, the relationship doesn't thrive, and your colleague doesn't benefit, all while keeping you uninvolved.

Nice lies

Nice lies are the equivalent of the land of sweet nothings, if you will. This is where you provide lots of love but no feedback. Doing so doesn't give people the honesty they need to improve but makes them feel good about you.

Newly promoted or hired managers love this type. They falsely believe that they need to establish relationships with employees before giving them feedback. Then they get stuck here — living in a cycle of niceties without truth.

These are the managers who end up over-indexing on using policies and HR to manage the team because they haven't been willing to be honest about how things are going. When something finally happens with their employee that puts their job at risk, the employee is surprised and the manager claims that it is "out of his hands." They haven't been willing to get uncomfortable to tell their team what they need to hear more: the truth about how to improve.

Think about the example from the previous section about the employee who turned in a less than stellar proposal. In the scenario, the manager still redoes the work but when the employee asks about the quality, the manager says "It was really great. I could see how hard you worked on it and the time you spent putting it all together. I've sent it off to the client and I'm sure they are going to love it. Great work!" Do you see how this starts to send the wrong message to the employee? It's not that the boss is indifferent like in the previous section — it is that the boss is actually lying because he wants to be "nice." In this way, he is slowly creating a situation where the employee will keep turning in subpar work thinking it is great. This doesn't improve the skills, the product, the culture, or the company. A little bit more honesty would improve things greatly.

Brutal honesty

Ever worked with someone who liked to use the phrase "telling it like it is" or "I'm keeping it real" to excuse their bad behavior? Not tempering your feedback in a way that shows you care about someone is being brutally honest. Brutal honesty doesn't have a place in a positive culture — and it shouldn't in yours either.

Sure, the person who delivers feedback with brutal honesty may be expressing ideas that the recipient needs to hear in order to improve. Yes, doing so is better than lying, but if employees don't take time to build trust, establish relationships, and show that they care, then the feedback isn't going to land. If the feedback is delivered in a way that focuses on the person and not the behavior, then recipients are given little room to improve.

Think about the client proposal example from the "Indifferent lies" section. If the manager was one who practiced brutal honesty, then when the employee asked for feedback, the manager would say something like "It was horrible. You missed some key information that would have positioned our offering as the best choice. I found several spelling errors and a few images that didn't match up. I fixed your mistakes and sent it along. Things need to get better." See how in this example the information is accurate and the feedback is clear, but it is delivered in a way that seems to forget another person is on the receiving end of the message. It's honest, but it's also brutal. The employee is hearing the information he needs to improve but might be worried about losing his job, his manager's trust in him to do it right, or intimidated to ask for help in improving. There has to be a better way, right?

Kind honesty

You guessed it — kind honesty is the goal for feedback at work. The holy grail of feedback for company culture. The vision of success when it comes to giving feedback to each other. Let's break it down:

>> Kind is not nice. *Nice* means saying pretty words to make people like you better. This doesn't help them grow. It's selfish in that it makes you look good, makes you on-the-surface likable, and isn't focused on the other person. Kind is a different story.

>> *Kind* is about being selfless. It's about delivering information in a way that can be heard. It's about saying, "I see you. I care about you. I know your goals."

>> Kindness includes honesty. The honest part is about telling people the information they need to know to improve. It's focused on actions. It's specific and clear. It's not about them as people; it's about the work.

TIP

A simple model to use when delivering kindly, honest feedback is this: "I know you want [insert what you know about what this person wants], which is why I needed to tell you [insert the feedback that will help the person improve]." For example: "I know you care about the way people perceive you as a leader, which is why I wanted to share some feedback about the way you closed that meeting."

Consider the client proposal scenario one more time to see how it plays out with a manager focused on giving kindly honest feedback. When the employee turns in the mediocre proposal, the manager reaches out and asks to review it together with the goal that the employee will get some feedback and make the improvements himself. So the manager starts off the conversation by saying "Chris, I know one of the things you'd like to be known for is creating really strong client proposals. You've shared that that's something important to you. I wanted to review the one you sent to give you some notes that will make it more effective so you can give it one more pass before I send it along to the client. I've marked a few places where I found some spelling errors. It would be helpful to write all the copy in a word processor with spell-checker before copying it into the proposal software. On pages 4 and 6, you've used images that correspond to our consumer positioning. In this case, we are working with a major corporate client who would probably expect to see more corporate-focused images. Why don't you do one more pass and then we can review it together before sending it off?" In this scenario, the manager isn't softening the blow by being overly nice nor is the manager being a brute by treating the person poorly. This is the type of feedback that great managers use to help and develop their team.

Sometimes the reason that people haven't improved is because no one ever took the time to be kindly and honest with them. No one cared enough to be willing to be uncomfortable to deliver the news they needed so they could get better. Be the person who does.

Crafting a Feedback-Rich Culture

Creating an environment where people are openly and willingly sharing feedback with each other takes commitment, energy, and intention. For your employees to feel comfortable doing this, you've got to establish an environment where feedback is taught, expected, and celebrated. This section will help you start to put the pieces in place to develop a feedback-rich culture for your company.

Ensuring safety

Giving and receiving feedback in a way that is kindly and honest requires that your team feel safe. As a leader, you need to create an environment where people have a high level of trust and feel safe to give and receive feedback. Here's how:

- **» Build relationships:** The more your team interacts and spends time together, the higher level of trust they'll have with each other. Make sure you schedule time for people to get to know each other. Small things like sharing about families, talking about weekend plans, and highlighting personal and professional histories can make a big difference.

- **» Don't be scared of getting emotional:** Being able to share and discuss our emotions is an important part of culture development. Don't shy away from it. This doesn't mean that your team needs to spend lots of time sharing their deepest, darkest secrets. But it does mean you need to explore ways for them to share their feelings about things at work. This can be as simple as asking for feedback more frequently and specifically asking people how they feel, how something impacted them, and then making sure it is celebrated when they are honest about their feelings. We are social animals. The way we feel and the emotions we have at work are real things. There are a lot of people who feel that emotions don't belong at work. I'd agree that outbursts, screaming, and crying all day are probably not effective ways to get work done, but sharing that something disappointed you or that you are sad about the loss of a major account is a completely human and acceptable thing to do at work.

- **» Get permission:** Make permission a key part of your feedback culture. Sometimes we aren't in the right mindset to take in feedback. Make sure that the first step in giving someone feedback is asking for permission. Then make it explicit that people can say "no." Being able to postpone the conversations makes sure both parties feel safe and ready to give and receive feedback. This can be as simple as saying something like: "Melissa, I have a few notes for you about the presentation you just delivered. Is now a good time to share them?" Sometimes the moment that is convenient or easy for the feedback giver is not the time when the feedback receiver is in the right mindset to hear it. If the goal of the feedback is truly to help the person grow and improve, then it has to be delivered when the recipient is ready to hear it.

Finding balance

Feedback isn't only about delivering the constructive ideas that help people improve performance. It's also about understanding how to leverage positive feedback to grow. In an environment that over-indexes on constructive feedback, people can get scared of feedback because it's always full of things to work on. It's critical to make sure people also know how to give each other positive feedback. Positive feedback should still be specific and actionable. It should still be focused on the actions someone took and not the person.

TIP

Follow these tips:

>> **Avoid the sandwich method.** This is when you say something positive, then give negative feedback, then end with something positive. It's as if by sandwiching the constructive feedback in the middle, you can soften the blow. But what typically ends up happening is that the person receiving the feedback ends up feeling confused and manipulated. Imagine if you were actually honest with what you were attempting to do: "Andrew, I am going to say a few nice things to you to help you relax and get you ready to hear the negative feedback I've got, now I'm going to tell you something you should work on that needs improvement, and now I'm going to say something else positive to you to make you feel good at the end of our talk." This is an ineffective and unfair way to share important information with people.

>> **Focus on effort, not the person.** Instead of making feedback about the person being great, focus on what the person did that was great. For example, if you notice that someone on your team has gone to extreme efforts to be detail-oriented on a client proposal say, "Phil, I'm really happy with how much effort you put into making sure every part of the proposal was high quality and accurate. You found a few embarrassing mistakes, clarified our language and position, and made some important suggestions for updated graphics." Compare that with, "Phil, you're awesome for handling this proposal so well." Not only is the first example more specific and clear so that Phil knows what to do in the future, it also focuses on the work and not the person.

Making it regular

In so many organizations, feedback is an irregular occurrence. It happens after a big project, during performance review cycles, and when things go wrong. This leads to people fearing it and waiting for the other shoe to drop. Instead, you have to normalize feedback and bake it into your normal day-to-day work life. It has to make regular appearances in the halls, after meetings, when conference calls end, and following presentations. Here are two ways to help incorporate feedback regularly:

>> **Build it in:** At the end of meetings, leave time for people to provide each other feedback.

>> **Go direct:** When employees come to you with feedback about each other, help them prepare to share it with the other person instead of doing it for them.

Going for it

As a manager, you have to take the first step if you want a feedback-rich culture. If you expect your team to be comfortable getting feedback from each other, then you have to show that you're also comfortable with it first. Use the following ways to show how you want to receive feedback as well:

>> **Ask:** Frequently and publicly ask your employees for feedback about your performance. Then listen and thank them for it.

>> **Go public:** Make your goal of a feedback-rich culture known to the people on your team. Explain your reasons why and expectations for receiving feedback from them about your own performance.

IN THIS CHAPTER

» Defining and creating culture pockets

» Understanding how culture pockets benefit your organization

» Establishing your company culture mission, vision, and values

» Encouraging your team to embrace feedback

» Setting up team relationship activities

Chapter **15**

Creating a Culture Pocket in the Org Chart

You've likely seen (or maybe lead) a team that's known for being a positive place to work inside of a company. It's the department that everyone talks about, that everyone wishes would be hiring more staff, and where it seems like every day is a positive day. The team is engaged, fired up, and focused while being supportive, productive, and efficient. It almost seems like they work at an entirely different company than the rest of the organization. You've just witnessed a culture pocket.

Culture is created in all areas of the organization. There can be a macro-culture that guides the overall brand — sometimes this is intentional and other times it is accidental. Sometimes the company has spent time doing the kind of work found in this book to make sure that culture is a differentiating factor, and other times the culture just happens. Regardless of which type of organization you are in, you can make culture a touchstone of your department, team, or division. Over time, when enough managers get on board at improving the area around them — the entire organization begins to benefit. In some ways, this can start to redefine the broader macro-culture as well.

Culture pockets aren't accidental. They're the result of intentionality and focus. And you, too, can create them. In this chapter, you find out about creating culture pockets within larger organizations. You'll see how despite your authority or reach, you can create positive change to your team, even inside of a big brand.

What's a Culture Pocket?

When it comes to organizations, there's always a macro-culture and a micro-culture — the big overriding one for the brand, and the one for each individual team. Maybe your company is known for being an intense and productive place, but some teams are more laid-back and casual. Maybe the retail side of the business operates differently from the corporate side. Maybe the engineering team feels different from the sales team. Yet you can still recognize that they're all still part of the same company. Turn the micro-culture on your team into a culture pocket.

It's similar to how if you visit San Francisco, you notice a faster-paced lifestyle than when you slide up the coast to Napa Valley. Both are unmistakably American, both clearly California, but both have significantly different cultures.

Your company is no different. There are likely tens or hundreds of different micro-cultures that make up your macro-culture. In fact, your culture improvement activities won't work if they aren't adopted at all levels and with all teams. Throughout this book, I give ideas on how to improve the culture from the top-down and the bottom-up. This is because that's how culture really works. It's a prism that can be viewed and altered from all directions at all times.

Here's the truth — you don't even really have "a" culture. You have a bunch of cultures blended together to create something bigger. When done well (by following the protocols in this book, for example), they all form a macro-culture that's productive, engaging, and sustainable.

When creating or improving culture, it's most effectively altered at the local level first — on your shifts, in your department meetings, during your project meetings, and in your one-on-ones. You have the power, ability, and information you need to shift things for your team.

REMEMBER

A *culture pocket* is exactly that — the individual teams, relationships, and departments that intentionally create a culture pocket that enhances relationships and improves results. A culture pocket is created when you align the vision for your team, get clear on the behavior agreements, establish systems that help the group thrive, and focus on fostering high levels of team interaction and feedback. The exchange between the macro-culture of the culture pockets of smaller groups can be a strong force in revolutionizing your brand.

Seeing How a Culture Pocket Makes Your Team Shine

Before we dive further into how to start improving the culture on your team, let's explore some of the benefits of creating a culture pocket within your organization.

Attracting talent

Great talent attracts great talent — or at least knows how to find it. If your team is engaged and excited to be part of your organization, they're more likely to share that with their friends and acquaintances. During a cocktail party, they'll brag about their job, their team, and their boss. On social media, they'll post positive stories and images. They'll write blogs and articles about working together. Ultimately, they'll spread the word and help bring more people to the team.

Top performers typically want to be around other top performers and on a winning team. The more effectively your group works together, the more likely others are going to want to join. It's a classic case of the saying "birds of a feather flock together."

Improving service

This isn't a book about improving customer service, but if that's your goal (and it should be), then improving the culture in your corner of the organization is an effective way to do just that.

Whatever you provide — customer service, patient care, client services, government services — you're doing something for someone in exchange for a paycheck. This automatically improves when your team is part of a strong culture pocket. When your team is functioning at high levels internally, it will function at higher levels externally. Your customers will notice this, even if your real customers are other internal customers (as is the case with most human resources, finance, marketing, and training departments).

Getting a budget and resources

If your team starts to stand out as the place to get things done, you'll get more attention. Organizational leaders will take notice of how well you can get things done. This is helpful when it comes time to look at budgets and resources. You're more likely to get more staff, make a better case for professional development, and carve out some funds for activities if your department is known for making a good return on those investments — which is usually an outcome of a great culture pocket.

Creating a legacy

One of the best feelings is being the manager that people want to follow. In my years running hospitality businesses, it was always a good sign to me that people wanted to follow a manager from a different location or brand even after they'd left the organization where they originally worked together. Since then, I've used that as a litmus test for great managers — I always know that if the team wants to follow the manager, then this is a person who builds strong cultures. People do good work when they work in a healthy environment. They thrive in an intentional culture. If you invest in developing one for your team, department, or crew, it improves your record and helps develop a legacy as someone to follow.

Shifts, Teams, Locations, and Departments: How to Craft Culture at Any Level

As you think about creating a culture pocket, realize that it can be done at several levels and in several ways. You don't have to be the CEO or the General Manager to make a difference and improve the culture of the people around you.

If you're in charge of leading a single shift, then use the ideas in this section to change the way your team works together for those few hours each day that you're together. If you lead a team, then create structure around how your team works within the broader department. If you're a department leader, you have even more space to change the way a large group works.

I've seen this happen in restaurants, in hotels, in retail, on airplanes, on project teams, in departments, and beyond. Small groups can gather, form, and change the way they work. Even yours.

Keeping it below the radar

A quick word of caution: As you start to shift how things work on your team, you may get some resistance. This is normal — people get freaked out by change, they get uncomfortable when people make adjustments, and, sometimes, when the people around them improve faster then they are, it makes them anxious and worried about falling behind. You may find that even your own boss is resistant to your shifting the dynamics on your team. Approach it slow. Make small changes. Modify things in a way that doesn't feel like a monumental slap to the organizational culture. This isn't about creating a coup or revolution; it's just about establishing simple ways for your team to work together better.

You don't need to announce these changes around the organization or to other managers from other departments. No need to say things like "we don't do that on my team" or "we've created our own culture." All those kinds of things make it about you and not about just helping alter the culture. Just focus on your culture pocket and improving the culture there.

Defining your vision

Think about movies in which a group of people band together. From bank heists to saving the earth — no matter the end goal — when people come together for the same purpose, they can succeed at just about anything. Creating a culture pocket comes down to forming a clear mission.

Strong cultures have to be aligned around something specific that brings them all together. There has to be a rally cry, a burning platform, a call for something better. The easiest place to do this is on your team. While the larger organization may struggle to find a unifying cause, your smaller team, department, or shift can more easily create it — and, you guessed it: It starts with an exciting vision.

Defining the vision for your department, team, project, or other culture pocket is critical. You need to define what success looks like for your group. Whether you're leading a project team aimed at launching a new project, creating solutions to big challenges, or bringing new ideas to the market, you've got to establish a shared vision. If you're guiding a department, team, or division, then you need to create a guiding vision for your team that helps them understand what they're aiming for and what you're trying to achieve, and gives them a GPS for their organizational energy. If you're leading a shift, then define how you'll work together, what's been accomplished by the end of the shift, and how the energy feels throughout.

Here are some ideas for creating a vision for your corner of the org:

>> Define how your department is perceived by the rest of the org. What do they say about your team? What are you known for?

>> Clarify what it looks like if you're successful. You can do this for a shift, a project, a department, a division, or a market. Take the time to define what success looks like so your team knows where they're headed.

>> Create a single unifying statement that helps define your value to the organization. If you're a project team, then clearly state the big problem you're trying to solve. If you're a department, state your clear promise to others in the org. You should use this statement when you onboard new employees, when you complete performance reviews, and in your ongoing team communications. It will help act as a guideline for how your team should approach problem-solving within the organization.

Once you have this information, it will start to paint a picture of where you are today and where you want to be in the future. From there, you can start to work with your team to get specific about how to strengthen the things that are working and how to improve the areas that aren't working. Developing this will allow you to more easily focus on your value to the organization, how your group interacts with others, and create a purpose that drives group behaviors.

Sharing values

Whether or not your company has a values statement, your smaller team needs to understand how your team works, what matters most, and how things get done.

If your organization has a values statement, then dive deeper to help define those values further for your team. In my experience, these definitions are often vague statements like "work collaboratively to design great things." Sounds nice, but it won't do much in helping your team understand what to do on Tuesday to work together better. Instead, go one level deeper by defining the specific behaviors expected of people on your team to uphold the values. How does your team interact with that organizational value? Make sure that you help define how your team works together by considering the following questions:

>> What are the explicit agreements people on your team make in regards to how they treat each other, treat customers, and approach their work?

>> What behaviors get promoted, celebrated, and awarded? What actions get coached?

>> What is the team doing when it's working best?

For example, if one of the organizational values is "Take a hospitality first approach," and the associated behaviors (see Chapter 7) are "greet people with a warm reception, assume the other person has positive intentions, and go out of your way to do something extra for others," then consider how those apply on your team and explicitly state the behaviors your team should practice. It can be difficult to figure this out on your own if you are someone in the accounting department, so go the extra step from the organizational values to show how an accountant should practice the value. For example, "be kind and thoughtful in your requests from other departments, make the extra effort to ensure others understand the work you are asking them to do, and attempt to get things done for people before the deadline." These are all examples of how the "take a hospitality first approach" could be defined in your culture pocket.

In addition to helping your smaller team develop a strong culture, this will also bubble up at enhancing and strengthening the macro-culture as well. If each team takes personal responsibility for ensuring they are living the values and expressing the desired behaviors of the company, then the organizational values and culture become even stronger and more integrated.

Establishing systems

As discussed in the opening chapter, great cultures have strong systems and structures that allow them to consistently execute on their values. The systems and structures help to ensure that things are done in line with what's important and create a framework for people to live into the expectations of the culture. Look — work gets busy and taking shortcuts is natural. Sometimes it takes extra work to do things the right way. This is why systems and structures help to make sure you stay on track. Otherwise, the quickest, fastest, easiest path will always win. That's not because your employees (and you) don't care — it's because it's basic human psychology. Our brains want to get things done most efficiently, so when we find a shortcut, it's really attractive. By designing systems for a better culture, you help short-circuit that thinking to ensure you get the results you want.

TIP

Here are some ideas to help you get started:

>> Each month, pick one of the values of the organization (or your team). During your weekly staff meeting, make this a focus by having all team members speak about an example they've seen, an example they've exhibited, and something they're committed to doing this week. This reminder will keep the values at the forefront.

>> The world is obsessed with online videos, articles, and blogs. Assign a team member each month to find a video, article, or blog that highlights something your team is working on, a value you share, or an interesting angle you should explore. Ask the rest of the team to read the content or watch the video (the TED Talks series is great for this). The team member who picked it will plan a mini-review session with questions and discussion topics that you'll review in a group meeting together.

>> Schedule post-mortem meetings for all projects. Use this time to share feedback, pull learnings, and see how the team accomplished the vision (or didn't).

Ensuring a Feedback Culture on Your Team

Psychological safety is one of the cornerstones of a great team. It means that your team feels safe to be themselves, to contribute ideas, and to know that they won't be chastised for speaking up. It's the belief that taking a risk will be supported. In all the organizations I've worked for and consulted for, the best teams had high levels of psychological safety. And while everything in this book will help move you closer to a team with high levels of this feeling, teaching your team how to give and share feedback is one of the quickest ways to boost it (see Chapter 14 for all kinds of info on feedback). You can accomplish this on your team even if the broader organization doesn't thrive on the sentiment.

Here are some ideas to help nurture the best ways of giving and receiving feedback on a smaller team:

>> Teach your employees how to give feedback early in their tenure.

>> During each meeting or project review, add time to the agenda for the participants to review what worked well and what could make the next meeting more effective. This gives people a chance to share feedback with each other and you in a productive way (see Chapter 14).

>> For each project or initiative, schedule a post-mortem.

>> During the interview process, find a way to have the candidate demonstrate something for you. Then give the person some coaching feedback. If he or she is unable to handle the coaching, it's unlikely that this is someone who is coachable, self-aware, and will contribute to a high level of psychological safety on the team.

>> When someone comes to you with an issue with someone else on the team, try to help them find a way to work directly with the other person involved. Give them some guidance on how to constructively share feedback (see Chapter 14 for ideas). Your goal is to help them build a stronger relationship with their coworkers.

>> Be quick to put an end to times when people don't offer feedback in the ways that you ask for. This will help keep the team safe, set boundaries, and clarify intentions around feedback-giving.

Making Time for Your Team to Get Together

One of the things that can really help your culture is finding casual ways for people to improve their relationships, enhance communications, and boost the level of empathy among each other. The easiest way to do this is to find ways to get together. Often, the first thought here is to attend happy hours, and I'm all for that if your team is. But whatever you choose, I recommend that the get-together is just a fun, outside-of-work activity that isn't necessarily considered to be bonding time.

WARNING

Keep in mind that if your team starts to lean toward dinners, happy hours, and other after-work events, this can be hard for people with spouses, children, and other commitments. Just be aware of how often it happens and realize it can put a strain on some people who fear missing out but also have other focuses in their lives.

Exploring the neighborhood

An easy way to get your team together is to explore the neighborhood around your office together. I'm always surprised at how often people haven't explored the space where they spend a good part of their day. Take a walk together at the same time each week. Put it on the calendar as a recurring event. It's a great way to get out of the office, get a little fresh air, and rejuvenate. You can even set a topic for each week so as you walk, you can talk and explore a new area of life. Avoid making this about a new project or turning it into a project status meeting. The goal is to learn a little bit more about each other. I've seen managers organize walks with topics like traditions, first memories, favorite vacations, and other topics to get the conversation going.

Checking out local offerings

Do you ever look forward to when out-of-town visitors come to town because you have an excuse to do all the touristy things that you never make time to do in your regular life? Museums, exhibits, architecture tours, walking neighborhood tours (you can find free ones online in some cities) are all great ways to enjoy your city — and something people rarely do. Check your local spaces to see if they have a local day that's free. Fairs, art shows, special exhibits, and street markets are all good choices as well. Often, museums set aside one day or afternoon a week for people who live in the area. Schedule to do something like this together once a month, every other month, or once a quarter. Doing so will not only help your team connect and bond but it can also be a springboard for new products, new ideas, and creative thinking.

Lunching

Breaking bread together has a long history of uniting people, creating bonds, and being fun. It's likely that your team takes lunch every day, and it's likely they do it at the same time each day. Why not pick a day each week or month for them to do it together? If you have the budget, the company can buy lunch. But if not, just have them bring whatever they normally eat for lunch and dine together at the same time. During the warmer months, take the lunch outside if you're near a park. You might initially need to kick off the lunches with some icebreaker type questions if your team isn't used to interacting casually, but once you get started, things should be fine.

Giving back

The team that gives together stays together. If you can arrange it, have your team volunteer together during a workday. Speak to your HR team to see if you can use work time in this way. If not, see if your employees would be interested in volunteering on a weekend morning. Make it even more inclusive by finding an activity that they can bring their families to as well. This is a fun way to do something positive for the community while also bringing your team together.

IN THIS CHAPTER

» Defining diversity and inclusivity

» Appreciating why diversity matters to bottom-line results

» Recognizing unconscious bias

» Using behavior design in your business

» Achieving transparency

» Fostering a more inclusive work culture

Chapter **16**

Producing an Inclusive and Diverse Place to Work

The news is full of organizations that have suffered, gone toxic, closed their doors, and lost their way because of a lack of diversity. By not having a strong system in place to foster a more inclusive and welcoming workplace, they not only lost the benefits associated with it but also created a negative experience for employees and customers alike. But some organizations are thriving in this area by taking intentional actions to develop the kind of culture that celebrates new ideas, brings more people to the table, and fosters a collaborative approach to work.

In this chapter, you'll discover why diversity and inclusivity are critical components of your culture. You'll also find out why they are different and require different approaches. Finally, you'll explore over a dozen ideas about how to improve the levels of diversity and inclusivity at your company.

Shifting Culture: Understanding How Diversity and Inclusivity Work Together

Diversity is about hiring and bringing more people from different groups into the organization, while *inclusivity* is about ensuring those diverse perspectives and voices are heard from, treated fairly, and provided ample opportunities to contribute.

REMEMBER

Diversity is more than a buzzword. It's not just about a moral obligation to have a specific quota filled to show that your company is making inroads at bringing more people into the fold. There are real bottom-line consequences. *Diversity* is about bringing in more perspectives so your products and services benefit from the perks of different opinions based on a multitude of backgrounds, approaches, and sensitivities. Improved innovation, better decision-making, and more empathetic problem-solving are all rewards of having a more diverse team.

But diversity is also not the same as inclusivity. Inviting people to the party is diversity; engaging them in the conversations and introducing them to people is inclusivity. *Inclusivity* is about making sure that the range of thinking, ideas, and contributions are encouraged, explored, and invited within the organization. An inclusive workplace leads to a positive culture that actively involves more employees to improve business results.

In short, diversity is step one in a two-step process, which isn't complete until attention is paid to inclusivity, too.

Appreciating Why Diversity Matters

There aren't many companies that wouldn't profess a commitment to a diverse team. For a long time, this has been part of corporate communication on websites, in handbooks, and in sound bites. Moral obligation and cultural norm have demanded it. But how many organizations are really committed to it beyond the nice words or elaborate policies? Does a more diverse workforce have real bottom-line impact or is it just a must-have sentiment in a world brought together by technology? Companies today should focus on creating a more diverse workplace, not only because it's morally and socially rewarded but also because there are long-term sustainability outcomes tied to it.

Companies with more diversity have historically delivered better business results including the ultimate measurement — profitability. A study from Bersin by

Deloitte shows that companies with higher diversity had 2.3 times higher cash flow per employee than non-diverse companies. In a 2015 study, global consulting firm McKinsey & Company found that "companies in the top quartile for racial and ethnic diversity are 35 percent more likely to have financial returns above their respective national industry medians."

Expanding recruiting

If you talk to most recruiters, they will tell you that they have a lot of applicants but just not enough of the right kinds of people. The answer to this of course is twofold: Improve your attraction efforts for the people best for your culture (see Chapter 8) and improve the overall number of applicants by casting a wider net. Organizations improve by enlarging the pool of people from which they can hire. It's that simple. More candidates can increase your chances of finding the right candidates, shorten your search period, and decrease the costs associated with attracting, recruiting, and retaining talent. By specifically focusing on improving your approach to diversity, you expand the talent pool you can select from drastically.

Diverse teams lead to improved recruiting because your reach improves dramatically. The more diverse your team, the broader their own networks will be. And, the vaster the pool from which you find candidates, the more comfortable candidates from diverse backgrounds will be to engage in a process where others look like them.

Driving creativity

New ideas, product breakthroughs, and idea generation are all outputs of having more voices at the table and in the room. Original ideas have a stronger chance of being surfaced when people from a broad range of experiences and backgrounds are brought into the fold. Diversity in this way includes not only gender and race but also age, socioeconomic background, social status, and educational background.

Without a diverse culture, you run the risk of groupthink and slowing the production of creative approaches. Think about a team of people who have all had very similar life experiences, education backgrounds, and enjoy the same types of things. This group of people likely won't generate as many new ideas as one with more diversity simply because they all share the same demographics versus bringing new experiences to the table.

Improving decision-making

When you bring more people into the room when decisions are being made and specifically ask for their help in shaping the decision, you increase your chances of getting it right. If you think about an HR decision around benefits or policy, when you incorporate a broader range of people into the decision-making process, your chance of improving outcomes for all types of employees increases simply by having people representing different segments of the employee population. The same approach works when thinking about ad campaigns, product features, and client services. When the team of people working on these projects have a range of backgrounds and experiences, they can bring more viewpoints to the table for consideration. This leads to examining more available options before making decisions.

Boosting customer service

A team of people with varied backgrounds best meets the needs of your customers and clients. Whether it's generating solutions to customer complaints, listening with empathy to customer concerns, or thinking up creative approaches to meeting customer demands, a diverse team will outperform a group of people lacking a broader perspective. Empathy, problem-solving, and idea generation all increase when the service providers have a broader range of experiences and backgrounds. As the global marketplace brings more people together, delivering a better customer experience is a critical priority for companies wanting to maintain an edge over competitors.

Becoming Aware of the Unaware

You've probably been in the position of having to choose between two candidates for a job — maybe it's an external hire or even an internal promotion. Candice and Carla both interviewed well and produced work products that are in line with the scope of the new role. But you liked Candice's approach to presenting new ideas better and think she will get the buy-in of other teams easier, so the job goes to her. Are you aware of any other thinking that got in your way? Did her getting that job have to do with anything besides the reasons you justified?

People walk around with different types of biases at work. The bias impacts decisions around hiring, promotions, project assignment, terminations, and other critical areas. These decisions are being impacted by things that have nothing to do with the quality of the work simply because these biases are left unchecked and managers are unaware of their impact on their decisions.

Exploring origins of unconscious bias

Our brains are hardwired for efficiency. Think about how much stimulus you have around you each day — heck, look around the room you're in now and consider all the different things your brain has to take in. From sounds to sights to touch to your own physiology, your brain is processing a ridiculous amount of data at any given time.

To help keep things from getting out of control, we categorize things, from the very simple — is this area safe or dangerous? — to the more complex — is that person a friend or a foe? The gut reaction we have to circumstances and situations is based on the quick-fire bucketing our brain does. We see a kid and recognize it as a kid. We see a friendly puppy and recognize it as safe. We make all kinds of quick categorizations. We classify people based on age, weight, gender, and skin color. In social and work settings, we also organize people by sexuality, economic status, job title, accent, vocal quality, social status, attractiveness, hairstyle, and clothing.

WARNING

All of this is productive most of the time. But along with all that classifying comes all the automatically assumed characteristics of other people we put into those buckets as well. So that's where the trouble begins. Sure, it can save us some brainpower, but it also may dictate the action we take toward those people. Actions like hiring, promoting, firing, mentoring, and listening. Actions that can have a real impact on your culture and business.

Recognizing unconscious bias

A lot of money is spent in workshops every year trying to train the bias out of people. Energy and time are spent getting policies and statements around diversity and discrimination just right. It's actually against federal law in the United States to discriminate in employment decisions based on race, sex, family status, religion, age, national origin, military status, or disability. In some states, that is extended to sexual orientation.

So then why do we still have such a raging issue around diversity at work? It's because we keep focusing on trying to train the bias out of people. You've already been introduced to the idea that this is a natural part of our brain, so it makes sense that trying to simply stop the brain from organizing things in this way is futile. The training, programs, and policies cover the intentional discrimination but don't do anything to shed light on all the unintentional moments when our unconscious biases impact the way we make decisions at work. They don't help us learn to maneuver around our natural instincts to create better, more diverse, and inclusive company cultures.

The first place to start is in recognizing and accepting that you have many unconscious biases. This doesn't make you a monster; it makes you human, and realizing that they exist is the first step in making sure they don't negatively impact your decision-making.

TIP

Try taking the Implicit Association Test (`https://implicit.harvard.edu/implicit/`), created by researchers at Harvard University, Yale University, University of Virginia, and University of Washington, to help you reveal where your biases might live. Try to move more of your decisions around people (hiring, promoting, firing, compensation, project assignment) to be based on facts, measurable progress, and work product. Stop trying to retrain your brain to be unbiased and instead focus on designing systems around the human resource processes (hiring, promotion, performance reviews, and so on) that illuminate the potential impact of unconscious bias to the final outcomes.

Changing Behavior Design to Create More Unifying Systems

Whenever people say, "I don't have any bias," you can be sure their unconscious biases are impacting the choices they make at work. Everyone has these unconscious biases — the factor is what degree they are aware of how they might be impacting their decision-making. The more management responsibilities those people have, the bigger the chance that those biases have unintended consequences to your culture. We all have bias, and it's by accepting that fact that we can start to think about how to make sure those biases don't have negative, unintentional consequences on our culture. Instead of seeking some utopia where biases don't exist, it's more impactful to ensure your human resources systems are designed in a way that minimizes the risk of the unconscious bias. This is called *behavior design*; instead of focusing on how to make people less biased at work, you focus on removing the impact of bias from your systems, policies, and processes.

Noting how changes to behavior design can reduce bias impact

When you change the design of something, you can change the outcome. This is true for games, products, architecture, and pretty much every other tangible product. But it's also true for the way you design the protocols, processes, and programs you use to make people decisions at work. If culture is largely about establishing normative and acceptable behavior at work (see Chapter 7), then part of the process of defueling the power of unconscious bias comes in designing new norms.

Behavior design is about putting steps in place to limit the amount of non-critical information available in key decisions — this means trying to eliminate unnecessary information so it's not included in the decision. The critical information for making employment decisions is obviously the work product and the relationships employees have with other people that would enable them to deliver the results required. But we often are faced with a lot more information about people than is critical for the decision at hand, so the possibility for unconscious bias to affect the outcomes is nearly guaranteed. Most organizations haven't stopped to look at their systems to remove non-critical information for their hiring, firing, promotion, and compensation policies.

Incorporating behavior design into your hiring practices

Around the globe, the way that organizations pick people to join a team is frequently flawed, typically cumbersome, and largely circumstantial. It's also wrought with the spoils of unconscious bias left unchecked, unmonitored, and unmeasured. For more information about rethinking the way you attract and hire new talent, check out Chapters 8 and 9. Here are some practices you can put into place to revise the behavior design of your hiring practices:

TIP

>> **Use blind resumes:** The practice of removing identifying information from resumes can go a long way in helping to improve the top of your recruiting funnel. By blinding the resume reviewer to gender, age, name, education, and ethnicity, you force the reviewer to focus on what matters most — the experience and work product of the candidate.

   You can easily do this yourself by having your recruiting team strip this information from the resume/application, or you can use a software program like Applied or Talent Sonar.

>> **Design a testing/work sample pre-interview:** This step involves designing a work test or work sample submission (like a portfolio) before the applicant is brought in for an in-person interview. These should be focused on what it takes to do the job and assigned to the applicants you are considering bringing in. A committee that reviews it should be blind to any other details about the candidate.

>> **Use structured interviews:** By having interviewers ask each candidate the same questions, you help ensure that the candidates are being measured

using the same framework. It's easy for bias to step in by asking candidate A easy questions and candidate B tougher questions and then finding that candidate A was better able to perform during the interview. This doesn't mean the interviews should be exact cookie cutter versions of each other, but it does mean the high level questions used to review candidates should be the same, and then the interviewer can dive into asking more specifics from there.

>> **Watch your language:** It's pretty common to hear that the pipeline isn't diverse and that's the cause of an unbalanced workforce. Sometimes this can be true — in areas where the societal norm is that women do the job (nursing, teaching, social work) or men are the chosen ones (engineering, manufacturing, finance). The images on TV, movies, and media reinforce this flawed thinking, and it impacts the real diversity you see in applicants. But there is a lot you can do by looking at the language you use in your recruiting message and employer branding. Some words tend to skew more masculine and others more feminine. An organization trying to attract more women engineering candidates would want to remove words like ninja, competitive, or driven, as they may discourage female applicants, while a hospital trying to attract more male nursing applicants might strike words like nurturing, committed, and collaborative. Work with people on your team to be specific about using non-gendered language in your ads to improve applicant response rates from a wider range of backgrounds.

TIP

You can also check out software like Gender Decoder for Job Ads or Textio, which make recommendations to create a more gender-balanced job posting.

>> **Establish a non-negotiable compensation:** In some organizations, you can easily create a system where candidates are informed ahead of time of the company's policy around negotiating starting salary. In an attempt to provide gender and ethnic pay parity, each person in each role would be paid the same. Lots of men have been able to negotiate higher rates than their equally competent female counterparts simply because they were more comfortable asking for it based on societal norms that reward men for being aggressive and punish women for those same behaviors. By creating a process for designing fair market compensation and then removing the ability to negotiate, you can ensure pay equity exists in your ranks. You should include this in your job posting if you adopt the policy.

Improving performance management with behavior design

The easiest way to approach performance management is to try and use as much data as possible in making decisions around how someone is performing. Traditional performance review programs can be really poor indicators of true levels of performance for the simple reason that they're based on subjective responses about someone's approach to work and generally reflect only the very last project or interactions with the employee. Similarly, it's concerning to think about how an employee's own opinion of his or her work, as happens during the self-assessment part of the review, impacts the overall record of the person's performance. People have varying levels of confidence, which can sometimes be linked to a lifetime of hearing stereotypes about what types of people should be good at the kind of work they do. Impostor syndrome can lead some people to score themselves lower than others even when their work product suggests they perform at or above the same level.

To ensure that your performance review system is achieving its goal of providing a fair overview of performance, make sure the following steps are part of your process:

>> **Increase inputs for subjective reviews:** If your review process is subjective — meaning someone decides a level at which someone is collaborative or at which level someone communicates — then validate the scores with multiple inputs from other people. If the manager's voice is the only one heard in these reviews, there's far too much room for unconscious bias. We've all heard the examples of a female manager being told she was too pushy while a male manager was rewarded for his aggressiveness. The 360 process can help with this when designed to include voices from a diverse pool in each applicant's review (for more on reviews and the 360 process, see Chapter 17).

>> **Use objective data:** Whenever possible, you should use objective data as the leading indicator of performance. It's not possible in all positions and gets harder to track as roles become less production-based, but it's worth finding ways to measure success objectively. For sales professionals, you probably use quota attainment as a metric, but you can also use conversion, time to close, retention, and other areas. For client services teams, you can measure response times, satisfaction scores, and customer retention. For leadership roles, you can measure skill growth on the team and improvements in critical performance areas. In all cases, you can use goal systems and goal attainment to provide an objective view. For more ideas on setting goals, see Chapter 19.

>> **Bring in many data points:** Instead of basing performance measurements on a once-a-year process that is wrought with recent bias, spread your review cycle across the year with a full review every six months and a goal check-in every six months. This way managers and employees are bringing performance to the forefront of their communications at least four times per year. In your annual (or biannual) full-cycle review, bring in notes from the previous cycles, check-ins, and one-on-ones to inform the process.

>> **Limit manager access:** When designing your performance review process, don't allow managers to see the employee's self-scores or the 360 peer reviews before submitting their own scores. The only way to ensure that people remain impartial to group thinking is to limit the information they see ahead of time.

Using behavior design to influence promotions

Promotions are another area that unconscious bias can negatively impact when left unchecked by a solid system. Check out the following fixes for two different types of promotions:

>> **Advanced levels:** When employees are moving from one tier in their role to the next tier (such as going from Sales Rep to Sr. Sales Rep), base it on objective performance measurements as much as possible (such as closed a certain amount of deals, maintained a certain retention rate, and so on). When this isn't possible, bring as much performance data to the table to make these decisions. Don't make people ask for these promotions, which overly rewards confident groups of people.

>> **Internal promotions:** Have everyone apply for internal promotions the same as an external candidate would. You can also have managers and others nudge qualified candidates who might not speak up to apply for the position. Include a diverse group of people in the interview committee and arm them with structured interview questions. Make sure the people interviewing the internal candidates focus on the work to be done for the future role. Have the interview committee provide their notes and final hire decision before they review what the others on the committee said. This will help ensure that people are putting their own perspective down versus falling in line with others on the committee.

Becoming More Transparent

Information made public with consistency has a way of changing the narrative in a positive way. By becoming more transparent in key areas of your organization, you can start to bring more light to areas that are often left opaque and dark. When combined with other efforts around improving your culture, transparency and actively educating employees about your diversity efforts have a way of putting your results in this area into hyper-speed.

Setting goals

Establishing clear targets around your diversity efforts is a critical first step in making sure the efforts you're taking are in line with the results you hope to achieve. Setting goals and targets around this area will also help make it easier to report on successes and setbacks. Many different goals can be right for you, so the first step is to consider what you're trying to accomplish and then take a look at current results in that area. You can use the list of targets following to collect current information from your human resources team.

Some ideas for targets:

» Percentage of women as part of total new hires

» Percentage of women/minorities in technical roles

» Matching the ratio of female employees to female managers

» Ratio of male to female promotions

» Number of blog posts/articles written about your culture by women, minorities, and/or LGBTQ employees

Publishing results

If you're going to make a dent at improving your diversity and inclusivity, then you need to frequently share the results without sugarcoating them. They should be presented during all-hands meetings, town halls, and business review sessions. Making this an HR scorecard metric is a mistake — the entire organization is responsible for these metrics. They should appear alongside every other important business metric and be tied to each manager's business review cycles because reaching these goals will improve the bottom line of the entire organization.

The goal isn't to provide a pretty picture with a bunch of diverse faces. It's to show that as you measure success, implement new systems, and make adjustments, the actual diversity at your company improves. And, it's to show that it's not a "would be nice" goal, but central to your business success. Make a commitment to share and teach about your diversity metrics. Post the information to your website to show candidates that it's an important part of your organization, and don't wait for the numbers to be impressive before sharing. The impressive part is the commitment to measuring, the transparency in sharing, and the efforts to improving.

Bringing people to meetings

One of the ways organizations become less welcoming for diverse groups of people is that decisions are made further and further up the organizational hierarchy without representation from a broad group of people. Consider creating a few employee seats on your executive team and inviting employees into key decisions by specifically asking for their feedback during decision-making meetings and conversations. Bring employees into conversations around benefit program planning, market strategies, and other key business decisions. This will not only help your team make more informed decisions that are inclusive of more perspectives from around your company, but will also increase the transparency among the team so that it doesn't feel like decisions are being made at the top in a vacuum.

Creating a fair compensation structure

Gender pay equity has been an issue for a long time. By developing a policy around compensation, your organization can greatly reduce the chance that this will happen to your team. Document your approach to compensation decisions, including how initial compensation is determined, when pay is reviewed, and how merit increases will be decided. Also, utilize the impact of compensation bands to minimize the risk of people being paid drastically different for the same work, and create a committee that's responsible for making compensation decisions. Publish this information alongside your other employee handbooks and documentation.

WARNING

Make sure that you don't leave it up to your employees to ask for a raise. This is one of the ways that gender pay disparity starts to spiral out of control. Establish a process that all pay increases go through and consistently apply it across the board.

Creating a More Inclusive Culture

Creating an inclusive and welcoming culture that encourages a range of people to apply and stay takes intentional work, but it doesn't always have to be an expensive process overladen with benefits and perks. In fact, much of what fosters an environment where people belong is typically achieved with some simple actions and thoughtful effort. Once you've done the work of finding and fostering a diverse workforce, you have to do the extra work to find ways to include everyone in the organization. The ideas that follow will help you increase the likelihood that you can benefit from the advantages of a diverse workforce.

Designing parental leave

Parental leave policies are one of the hot-button issues that affect employees considering a family. The United States ranks pretty low with federally mandated leave when compared to other developed nations. Some companies are making efforts (largely in the tech industry) to improve on that and use parental leave as a way to attract talent and retain a diverse workforce.

While the absolute number of weeks your company pays for parental leave is a complex issue, you should spend the time to make it as generous as possible to keep would-be parents in your ranks. Additionally, you should ensure that the policy is outlined as primary and secondary leave to cover non-traditional family structures and adoption.

Many organizations are even adopting a transition-back-to-work program that slowly acclimates new parents back to full time after parental leave. In these policies, at the end of covered parental leave, the employee slowly ramps back up to full-time hours over the course of 60 to 90 days.

Allowing flexibility

In most types of business today, there's room to be flexible around work hours. While there are still many people working in shifts, large numbers of people aren't required at their desk at a certain time in order for business to happen. Flexibility can be a way to encourage parents to apply and stay with your organization by giving them flexible start and end times to better balance childcare needs, attend school events, and be an active participant in their child's life. With so many people able to work from a laptop or smart device, you may not even notice they've stepped out a little earlier than normal. The extra benefit is that a lot of people would enjoy this extra flexibility, so it is likely to increase your overall recruiting success as well.

Controlling the narrative

Take stock of all the collateral being used in your employer branding, website, and office. Are the subjects primarily men? Are they primarily white? Make sure that the images, videos, and photos are representative of your team and your commitment to diversity.

Likewise, look at the stories you tell during orientation. Do they represent your commitment to inclusivity? Do they highlight stories of diverse groups doing big things together? What story are they really telling your new hires?

Does the signage in your office support your commitment? Does the bathroom use inclusive language (for example, "for people who identify as . . ."). If your meeting rooms are named, do they include equal ratios of women, men, and underrepresented minorities? Do the books on your corporate bookshelf represent authors from a spectrum of backgrounds?

What about the music in your lobby? Is it positive or misogynistic? Be careful with the "explicit" label because it can catch curse words but won't stop negative messaging and other derogatory terms against women, minorities, and LGBTQ people.

Ordering swag

Make sure that the clothing you order includes women sizes as well. Women shouldn't have to wear little boys' sizes or custom tailor their company track jacket to feel like they're part of the team. When you place an order, don't assume that everyone will be male. Consider the types of women's clothes you purchase as well. Companies with normal fitting crew-neck shirts for men and skintight, low V-neck shirts for women are not sending an inclusive message that women are respected as peers. Same thing goes for sizes — make sure you keep a full stock of options around so that your employees who don't fit into a size medium also feel welcome and included.

Reaching out

Plan your outreach around the areas where you lack diversity. There are so many events for employers these days, from college fairs to job fairs to conferences. If you're struggling to hire women in tech positions, then show up at college campuses, recruiting fairs, and conferences aimed at them. Looking to boost applicants from minority groups? Find the places that they gather and go create a welcoming environment to start developing relationships. When you have a specific group you are trying to increase representation of in your company, type that group name and the words "conference," "events," "job fairs," or "recruiting" into a search engine. Use that to begin exploring opportunities to include your company in these events.

Mentoring the next generation

Establish an internal mentoring program where people in leadership roles are available to mentor other employees. Encourage women and minorities to seek out mentors. Provide the mentors with some outlines to help in these conversations and to set goals. It doesn't need to be too organized to be useful — you just want to avoid the mentors and mentees simply talking about travel and Netflix all the time.

By having your leadership team develop relationships and provide mentorship, you not only increase the mentee's confidence in applying for future roles but also improve the chances that the mentors also confront (and change) some unconscious bias in themselves in the process.

Celebrating holidays

You send a clear message if your company only celebrates Christmas, Easter, and Presidents' Day. Make sure that your holidays and other celebrations are inclusive of underrepresented minorities. Create programming for Black History Month and Gay Pride. Celebrate influential women alongside the men.

Setting up affinity groups

Creating affinity groups for your employees is a positive way to help them organize, celebrate each other, and establish community. Affinity groups can be organized around anything (running, gamers, readers), but in this case we're specifically thinking about affinity groups related to representing the diversity in your organization (LGBTQ, minority groups, women, parents). This doesn't mean that only women or only LGBTQ would join those groups — but that the groups are about celebrating and creating community around those areas.

In addition to allowing and sponsoring these groups, you can also leverage these groups as employee resource groups by organizing contact info, meet-up schedules, and events in one place for all employees to access. You can also use these groups as resources for getting advice on policies and for making recommendations for improving the sense of belonging at your organization. You can include the groups in new policy development to ensure perspective.

TIP

Some other ideas to foster affinity groups:

>> **Movie nights:** Host movie nights or buy tickets to see important films related to the groups.

>> **Book clubs:** Host book readings around books related to the groups.

>> **Local events:** Sponsor participation in local events like Pride parades, festivals, and other cultural events.

Scheduling events

Don't schedule happy hours and team outings on weekends and during the evening. Often when consulting with startup companies, they're surprised that the parents and married people in their organization don't feel included. Yet all happy hours, company events, and other employee activities are scheduled at night and on weekends, when those groups want to be home or have other commitments. Scheduling your events after work hours, even if they're optional, sends a message that "you aren't wanted" when the employee can't attend due to family obligations.

Calling it out

It takes a commitment from everyone to make the push to create a true sense of belonging at work. It's not just about programs, perks, and policies. It's about relationships, meetings, and norms. Here are some ways you can call out non-inclusive behavior:

>> **Point out when people interrupt women:** Make it your cultural norm to stop people when they interrupt. Women are more likely to be interrupted during meetings than men. The only way to stop this is to stop it when it happens. Make your commitment public so that everyone knows it's everyone's responsibility to call it out. In fact, create signage for your meeting spaces that sets "rules" for productive meetings.

>> **Point out when someone repeats someone else's idea:** It's pretty common for a male employee to repeat something a female employee has said without attribution or credit. Make it the norm that you call it out. Simply say, "I think that's what Laura was just saying. Isn't it? Let's let her clarify it for us."

>> **Create a "guys jar" to extinguish the use of gender-specific language used to reference "everyone":** Put a jar in meeting rooms, and when people use "guys" to refer to people who do not identify as male, they put $1 into the jar. Once the jar gets to $100, the money is donated to a cause.

Making More Inclusive Decisions

Bringing more people and data into the mix is a positive step in making sure your decisions are coming from a more inclusive place. This involves not only getting more voices and perspectives but also using better systems to make decisions in the first place.

Writing better job descriptions

Job postings that are strong on unnecessary requirements and low on real definitions tend to result in more men applying than qualified women. By changing job postings to focus on the results required for the position, you level the playing field for inbound applicants. Additionally, this focus on results allows the interview committee to base their feedback around whether applicants have the ability to get the desired work done instead of around how much they meet some arbitrary requirements. For more on job descriptions, see Chapters 8 and 9.

Using goals

By establishing and sharing goals and objectives for each employee, you start creating visibility into the expectations across the team. Employees can compare themselves to their peers, understand each other's impact, and more accurately assess standings. It makes it easier for employees from minority groups or underrepresented groups to see that their work is on par with their peers from majority groups instead of falling into the standard stereotypes or suffering from imposter syndrome.

Goals also help to give managers more objective ways to measure performance by having clear performance targets. This eliminates a little bit of the risk that unconscious bias will negatively impact performance management. For more about goals, see Chapter 19.

Organizing interview panels

When interviews are only done by a small group of people that all look alike, you're doing little to increase your chances at improving inclusivity. Instead, make sure that your interview panel includes a cross-section of people from the organization. There should be women and members of underrepresented groups in each interview committee. It minimizes the risk of unconscious bias, increases the chances that you give a fairer interview, and improves the odds of bringing more diverse talent into your team, as well as making current minority employees feel included in the decision-making process of bringing in new people.

Having better meetings

There aren't many organizations that don't have some type of standard rotation of meetings, making them a good place to start to bring more inclusivity into your culture. Here's how:

>> **Rotate leaders:** Trade off each meeting with a different person leading. This helps encourage more involvement while also showcasing different styles. It also gives the manager a chance to see people in a different light and ensures that it doesn't minimize the voice of underrepresented groups.

» **Circulate the agenda:** Some people need more time to think about things and are less likely to speak up until they've had a chance to prep, while others are okay speaking off the cuff. Make sure both sides get a chance to be represented by sharing the agenda ahead of the meeting.

» **Conduct round-robin feedback:** Make it the standard that instead of someone having to fight to be heard, you will each get a turn to speak on the topic at hand by going around the table in an organized way. Make it okay for an employee to "pass" if he or she has nothing to add, but make sure that each person is given the floor to speak.

» **Write notes first:** When thinking of brainstorming or ideation type sessions where you want input from people, ask them to write down their ideas first. Present them with the question or topic and then give three to five minutes to put notes on paper. Then ask everyone to share what they wrote or ask them to trade notes with someone else and then share what the other person wrote.

5

Disrupting Performance Management

Chapter **17**

Reviewing the Performance Review

N o other shoe has dropped louder when it comes to company culture and sacred human resources protocols than that of the performance review. A once much-revered process for organizing, understanding, and rewarding employees, the performance review has been called to the court of corporate opinions to stand trial for inefficiency.

In your own experience, can you think of a time when you received a performance review and left feeling that you had a solid understanding of how you really contributed to the company? Can you say that you left with really clear ideas about what to do next? Did you have a succinct vision of how success looks in your role and exactly what that means to others? I'm taking a wild guess that the answer to most of those questions starts with "n" and ends with "o."

This chapter helps break the myths, find the truth, and create a positive way forward for the performance review. You will learn why performance reviews are critical for creating engaging performance conversations, how they can be used to boost transparency between coworkers, and ways to leverage them to boost your culture by improving relationships between managers and employees.

Hating the Performance Review

Performance reviews have gotten a bad reputation from employees, managers, the business press, the HR teams, and pretty much everyone else in modern organizations. The promise of performance reviews is exciting — a way for managers and employees to talk about performance in a way that uncovers a better path forward. But the reality is so far from that. In some companies, the performance review is so feared and disliked that managers never started doing them in the first place, but also never replaced them with something else to help foster those development conversations between manager and employee.

Trading up from traditional ways

There was a time when measuring everyone against the same predictable outcomes was the primary goal for establishing productivity. Employees needed to produce a certain amount of widgets to keep production in a plant on track to reach goals. The performance review seems to have been born to help establish a way to predictably address performance. The system allows organizations to hand out annual increases in a regular cadence, so many companies keep it even though it doesn't effectively do its main job, which is to create an engaging conversation around past performance so that a plan for future performance can be developed.

Exiting from nonexistent systems

On the other side of the spectrum, some organizations have no performance systems in place at all. Whether they simply haven't taken the time to establish something as their fledgling startup becomes a small company, or they simply think things will fall into place, many organizations I've worked with don't have established performance management systems. This leads to an unfocused, chaotic, and inequitable approach to handling performance. In this environment, employees are left to question how they're doing, what's next, and where they stand in the eyes of their manager and the organization.

The reality is that even companies with no formal review do actually have a performance management system in place — it's just not defined, consistent, or effective in most cases. If a key goal for employee engagement is tracking and sharing progress, then the companies without performance management systems are leaving a lot of discretionary effort and engagement on the table.

Creating a productive performance review should be at the top of every manager's "must-achieve" list. When done in an effective manner, the review has tremendous benefits to the employee's work life and the company's culture.

Finding fault with the performance review

The performance review process has long been distrusted and disliked. Not only is it often a cumbersome and bureaucratic process; in many cases it has been promoted as a way to spread a survival-of-fittest approach throughout the ranks.

Four issues with the standard performance review process include:

WARNING

- >> **Primacy:** We often continue to think of people as we originally perceived them. That good ole' first impression factor can make our opinions of people slow to change. What's worse is that sometimes a manager will have little direct awareness of how an employee's performance has shifted over time, so the manager's ratings are based on what he or she originally expected from this person based on first impressions.

- >> **Recency:** This is one of the most common issues in dealing with performance reviews. Managers often recall their most recent interactions with employees when completing performance reviews. Had a good six-month run and then bombed the latest report presentation? Gonna have to mark down your presentation skills. It's hard for us to divorce ourselves from our most recent interactions when sitting down to ink out a review. It's also not a fair way to assess a year in the life of employees if the process allows their most recent actions to negatively (or positively) alter the overall impact of their work.

- >> **Latency:** The distance between someone's performance snafu and the performance review is often way too long to be an effective way to address a concern. I'll never forget the time my manager gave me feedback about the way I presented information, which I did nearly weekly for a year. I had never heard anything from her about my performance until it was time for our review, when she told me how ineffective the way I shared something was every week. I remember thinking, "How dare she sit there and watch me do this every single week and never tell me. I could've made it better 11 months ago!" Therein lies an issue with the way most performance reviews are designed. The space between an action and a post-action review is often too broad. The feedback loop needs to be tighter to help employees deliver great performance and to create a culture of positive improvements.

- >> **Forced ranking:** In some companies, the performance review process is used to rank employees against each other. In this process, the top employees are rewarded and the bottom employees are penalized and sometimes terminated. This process ends up creating stress and undue competition and promotes risk aversion for fear of failing. On some teams where the employees are ranked against each other, the team can attempt to keep top performers from joining their rank for fear of lowering their own status on the performance chart.

Connecting reviews with performance

There's little link to actual performance improvements based on reviewing what happened in the past. This cataloging of past behavior doesn't seem to be the secret toward motivating future behaviors at all. Employees are often left unclear about how to actually improve, what success looks like in the future, and which of their behaviors are truly damaging to their careers and which are just simply nice-to-haves. They're fixated on the past versus clarifying what should happen in the future.

Is the manager the best reviewer?

In this world of command-and-control style leadership, it's assumed that the manager is best able to assess each person's performance. In today's workplace, this is often not true.

The world at work has changed — where team members are responsible to other groups, where managers are often disconnected from the day-to-day work of their team, and where results aren't easily measured by Industrial Age style production metrics.

It's time to include more people involved in the employee's performance in the review process. It needs to include the other people that the employee works with in the company. It should include lots of data around goal achievement and results.

We don't run our marketing and technology functions with systems from the 1800s. Why are we still managing people that way?

How expensive is the process?

The performance review process is not only outdated and antiquated but also expensive. Think of all the time that's spent developing the tools, systems, processes, checklists, rollouts, launches, follow-ups, and validation meetings. Now consider the amount of time lost in productivity from employees stressing about their scores and ranks.

It seems like something this expensive — of time, of resources, of morale, of energy — would need to provide a huge ROI to maintain power in a world obsessed with bottom-line results, right? Yet there's surprisingly little evidence of the old rank-and-file style performance reviews doing that at all. In most cases the things measured in the performance review process are the tactical and measurable production goals, leaving out all the other things that someone does to add value to the organization (and typically improving the culture overall). Someone may get rewarded for the amount of calls they were able to process in the call center, while someone else who had lower production but focused on helping new representatives get up to speed would be scored lower because the traditional review process only takes the tactical goals into mind. Can you see how quickly a culture can crumble if this is the only metric that's measured?

The typical performance reviews amplify shortcomings and emphasize what "needs improvement" over the positive feedback about what's working and how to get more of that from the employee. This leaves the employee feeling everything except excited about doing an even better job.

Loving the Performance Review

Many organizations have started to put the performance review in the unemployment line. For all the reasons I mention in the preceding section, the process has been slowly losing support and administrative steam. The billions of hours spent cataloging, organizing, ranking, and pushing paperwork don't add up to many improved results. But don't throw away the baby with the bathwater quite yet. Taking time to periodically review performance, reset expectations, and plan for the future is a valuable process. In fact, there's something almost ritualistic about it.

When it comes to running an organization and continuing to improve productivity and achieve goals, there needs to be some way to check in on the progress of employees toward those goals. In fact, most employees want to receive feedback, and if they aren't getting the information they need to boost their professional skills, they will start looking for it in a new employer. One thing is clear when it comes to employee engagement — it starts with performance and career growth.

Imagine two employees:

Employee A: The first one is given very little feedback from his manager. He comes in every day, sits at his desk, completes his work, and then leaves again. Each day seems like the one before. Each week becomes indistinguishable from the last. He sees his friends at other companies making progress on their goals, updating their LinkedIn pages with new skills, and seeking promotions with the confidence that they are prepared to excel in those roles. If you want to know why engagement is an issue at work, look no further than exhibit A.

Employee B: Our second contender is getting frequent feedback from her manager. They chat about performance in one-on-ones, they meet quarterly to review goals and set new ones, and twice a year they get together to do a quick review of her performance. During those conversations, the employee and manager sit on the same side of the table while they review feedback from peers and key stakeholders. They review the results she has achieved as well as the way in which she achieved them. The manager has prepared some notes on the impact the employee has made and the impact she'd like to see her make in the future. The employee has done the same. Based on all the information, they both have a clear picture of the impact this employee has had on the organization as well as some ideas about what's next. Together they prepare a vision for future success that covers the next 6 to 12 months. This becomes their working orders. At the end of the session, the employee is clear on what's working, what would help make her more impactful, and where she wants things to be at the next review cycle. Side of engagement coming right up!

Could your organization do with a little bit of example two? Do your managers and employees spend this kind of time together having discussions about where performance can go and how to get there?

REMEMBER

This might seem like a lot of work, but as your employees are more engaged and more productive, you will find your time freer than when you had to intervene and micromanage their activities.

Here are some main points to love about an updated performance review:

>> **It guides and measures success.** Employees love a sense of progress and a vision of what success looks like in the future. The performance review process when done well can help employees get clear on what's working and where they can continue to expand their professional skills and gain new experiences. It gives them a chance to define career success and then work with their manager to outline a plan to achieve their goals. As we see generational shifts demand career progression and professional clarity, the performance review can be an important milestone in measuring success along the way.

>> **It puts players on a level playing field.** The presence of a strong performance review process can help to eliminate the appearance (and occurrence) of favoritism, promote a sense of transparency, and promote a higher level of accountability. It can help managers and employees create a shared language in which to assess how things are going, what's needed next, and what success looks like for each role.

>> **It provides opportunities for growth.** The process can help managers understand what their employees want to achieve to help develop activities, projects, and opportunities for the employee to gain those experiences and build those skills. In a world of work where employee engagement seems to hinge on providing positive career growth and a clear sense of progress, it seems that a well-designed performance review process can not only boost culture but also go a long way in improving organizational results across the board.

>> **It provides a way to link business success with employees' efforts.** Organizations have to meet tactical goals and deliver on the promises they've made to the customers. Hitting daily, weekly, monthly, quarterly, and annual goals is a critical part of being able to keep customers happy and create a sustainable future for the business. So it makes sense that there's a way to measure progress toward those goals. It seems prudent to track employees' progress and outcomes in creating results for the organization. The performance review provides a chance to reflect on an employee's impact.

>> **It joins the whole team together and leads to future goals.** Great leaders have the power to galvanize each individual team member's efforts in achieving a bigger goal. The performance review done well can contribute to that by aligning the manager, the employee, and the organization. If used to energize the employee toward the future versus simply evaluating the past, the performance review can be a powerful tool in creating positive results, engaged teams, and a strong culture.

>> **It gives managers a chance to be heroes.** Most people want to improve, they want to get better, and they look at their boss as a person who can help them achieve more and grow professionally. In my work with employees across industries, organizations, and international borders, I've seen that employees are seeking mentors and opportunities to upsize their professional experiences and skills. A great performance review provides a perfect opportunity to do exactly that.

WARNING

All this positive light on performance review doesn't mean you should put down this chapter and assume the process your organization is doing is delivering on that promise. Keep reading to learn about how to shape an entirely different process that can help you get all the benefits outlined in this section.

Recognizing the Goals of an Effective Performance Review System

Like all good programs, an effective performance review system starts with a clear vision of success and some intention around the goals. So before you run off to redesign the performance tools at your organization, let's take a few minutes to outline some of the goals of your program design:

>> **Improved culture:** A performance review process that is designed to enhance the relationships between your employees, their work, and their manager will help to improve your culture.

>> **Longer tenure:** When employees feel like they are getting important feedback for their career development and making professional progress, they stay at your company longer.

>> **Improved profits:** With the lower turnover, you benefit from decreased costs from recruiting, training, and other costs associated with employee turnover. If your employee directly impacts important cost or profit centers, then a better performance review process can help to boost his or her performance in those areas, which will positively impact the bottom line.

>> **Creating professional development and career growth:** Your performance review plan should give the employee and manager an opportunity to track progress on professional development with a strong focus on defining upcoming opportunities for the employee to learn new things and gain new skills. Employees have the ability to choose from many employers in most markets, and professional growth is one of the most in-demand benefits that they're looking for in an employer. Use your performance review process to further your organization's ability to grow your team and keep your employees from leaving for your competitor.

>> **Seeking all available information:** The modern workplace is one where employees interact with each other, with partners, with vendors, and with other stakeholders besides their manager. It's a shame that so often that goes unrecognized in the design of the performance review process. Gathering information from other parties who are closely linked to the employee's performance provides the best vantage point from which to review performance holistically. The 360-degree approach to performance reviews allows for collaborative feedback sharing (see the later section "Going 360").

>> **Establishing goals and aligning resources:** The employee and the manager should both walk away with a clearly documented understanding of what's expected and what resources are available to achieve those goals.

>> **Writing the future with a clear vision of success:** Taking all the aforementioned goals into consideration, a great performance review should be a dialogue between the manager and employee in which they're focused on creating a shared vision for the future. It should allow them to co-create a definition of what success looks like when viewed from some vantage point in the future. The conversation should focus equal parts on "how am I doing?" and "where am I going next?"

By keeping these primary goals in mind and sharing them explicitly with everyone involved in the process, your organization has the opportunity to turn the dreaded, misguided, oft–maligned, and typically ineffective performance review process into one that both employee and manager look forward to each cycle.

TIP

In general, you'll find the most success scheduling a performance review cycle to occur once an employee has completed his or her initial training, at the end of the first 6 months, and at the 12-month mark. If you don't have an initial training outline, then schedule around the 60-day anniversary of the person's hire date. Also, be thoughtful about the other times of year you schedule them so that they don't happen during the busiest times of year for your business.

Curating a Better Review Process

For those of you with a long-entrenched and disliked (or even just ineffective) performance review system, don't throw the baby out with the bathwater; improvement can be as easy as simplifying or refocusing. For those without any system, lucky you. Starting from scratch with the right goals shaping the process is even easier than fixing what's broken.

First things first: Stop using the term "performance reviews." That's not what they are. They are performance enhancers. So, why not rebrand them by focusing on future improvement, based on lessons from the past and looking towards future expectations.

In this review process, there are four critical steps:

1. **Seek peer feedback to include a broad range of experiences and perspectives on the employee's performance.**

2. **Provide employees time and prompts to reflect on their performance and to begin shaping what they'd like to achieve next.**

3. **Provide the manager's feedback on performance and outcomes with a focus on establishing what's needed to achieve the next set of objectives.**

4. **Develop a shared vision of future performance so that both manager and employee have a clear understanding of what success looks like going forward.**

TIP

Keep in mind the information given in this chapter up to this point as you set forth to put pencil to paper (or finger to keyboard!) and reconfigure, or create from scratch, a new process for reviewing performance.

Setting standards

Something strange happens to people when you start to rank them inside of little boxes based on how well they executed some desired behavior or outcomes.

Knowing that a manager is going to mark down an employee's approach to work as a 5, 4, 3, 2, or 1 makes people squeamish, plus it's antiquated and inaccurate in a world where work is based on the application of knowledge and not on the production of widgets. When the scoring becomes the focus of the review process, the employee focuses on getting a higher score instead of hearing the feedback and focusing on the growth opportunities.

That makes sense, right? You, after all, are scoring them. Why shouldn't they focus on defending the reasons that their performance deserves an above average score versus an average? This starts one of the most painful and ineffective parts of the classic performance review. The manager and employee are both focused on the wrong thing — they're looking backward and trying to validate their thinking around how six months of performance can be summed up in a simple multiple choice option on the review form.

The goal of reviewing performance is to improve performance for the future. To do this effectively, you must also review previous performance to see how the standards set have been met previously. This will allow you to make a more strategic plan for achieving them in the future. To get clear on exactly what was supposed to have happened, you should use two specific areas when considering outcomes achieved:

>> **Goals:** What specific goals have been outlined for this position? In a great organization, goals and objectives should be front and center in the employee/manager relationship, so it should be easy to review progress made. For more information about setting goals and how they impact culture and performance, see Chapter 19.

>> **Values and behaviors:** One of the key points to making your performance review process a critical driver of culture is to have a robust conversation about the values of the company and the desired behaviors associated with those values. If you've followed the guidance in Chapter 7, you've outlined clear and specific values and their associated behaviors (if not, head over there and check out the info!). With the desired behaviors clearly drafted for each value, you can have a conversation with your employees about how they have displayed those behaviors, which ones they have struggled with, and how they'd like to improve in specific areas going forward. In a company where the stated values are clear, specific, and being used to hold everyone accountable for contributing to the culture, these conversations can go a long way toward helping the employees not only improve their performance but also further the overall culture as well.

REMEMBER

A solid performance review always balances reviewing past performance with setting intention for future performance. Likewise, it should be a balance of reviewing *what* the employee achieved and *how* the employee achieved it.

Going 360

One the goals for the performance review process should be getting more voices, opinions, and perspectives to the table. The lone manager reviewer system is full of flaws, from unconscious bias to absentee managers. It's just not the way most modern organizations work these days. The impact that an employee has moves far beyond the employee-manager relationship. Consider using a 360-degree review style that brings in feedback from other people impacted by the work of the employee for a broader lens into performance and what can help drive future growth.

The problem with most 360-degree reviews is that they rely on the same outdated scoring modules as the rest of the process. You're asking employees who don't typically review performance to figure out how to score someone in little boxes and then left with the big question of whether Lisa in Accounting and Roger in Sales distribute their "3" in the same manner. Another waste of time and opportunity. Instead, make it easier and more impactful by keeping it simple and future-focused.

Choose five people who work closely with the employee and seek their feedback. You can use a survey form from Google, SurveyMonkey, or some other tool, or you can ask them to reply to an email with their feedback. Include a simple statement saying that you're preparing for the employee's performance review cycle and would like to seek feedback on performance. Ask them to be specific in their examples and to provide concrete observations that are measurable and observable. Confirm that the feedback is confidential and will be treated as such. Then ask a few simple questions:

>> When you think about (employee's name) performance, what do you consider to be his/her biggest strengths and value to the organization?

>> If you think about our values and behaviors (you can share them again here but avoid asking for a score), which ones do you see (employee's name) exhibiting in clear ways?

>> As you have worked with (employee's name) over the last 6–12 months, what did you like best about working together?

>> As you have worked with (employee's name) over the last 6–12 months, what suggestions do you have to improve that?

Once the information is received back, then the manager will organize it all into one document that's provided to the employee. It's helpful to let the employee know who was involved in giving the feedback but not necessary to tell them who specifically provided which feedback.

Setting the self-review

Reflection is an important part of improving, and that's true for the performance review process as well. Giving employees a chance to consider and share their own feedback on their performance is a critical part of moving forward toward their next professional accomplishments. The typical model of scoring yourself on a 1–5 scale is once again not part of the modern performance review cycle. It leaves employees trying to figure out where they stand in relation to desired outcomes and their peers without a true rubric for making that decision.

The better process is to keep it simple, with equal parts looking in the rearview mirror at past performance and through the windshield at the future. Can you imagine trying to navigate the road by watching the rearview mirror? Sure, it's nostalgic to see where you've been, but you have little chance of getting where you're going safely without looking ahead. The same is true in this process.

To start the self-review, send the employee a survey form or just a simple word processor document to complete. I've often encouraged people to use Google Docs so that the files can be shared and organized easily. Make sure the employee is clear on how to prepare for the review and give clear instructions for completing and submitting the self-review. In the self-review, ask the following questions:

- **»** What do you see as your three most significant contributions/accomplishments in the last 6–12 months?

- **»** What's been the best feedback/recognition you've received in the last 6–12 months? Why was that so impactful?

- **»** What challenges have you had to overcome to achieve those goals? How have you made progress on the areas we identified to work on from the last cycle?

- **»** As you look ahead, what do you believe you need to work on? How are you seeing this, hearing this, or recognizing this today?

- **»** How is your current workload? Is there anywhere you feel stuck or are facing obstacles?

- **»** As you consider the next 6–12 months, what impact do you want to make on the organization? What actions do you need to take to achieve that?

>> To achieve your goals, what professional development do you need to seek? How can you do that?

>> When you consider your relationships with others at the company, which ones are the strongest? Which ones are not as strong? How are these relationships impacting your work? How would you like to focus on those in the next 6–12 months?

>> What else should we both know and talk about in your upcoming feedback review session?

>> What did you hope to accomplish personally and professionally when you came to this company? Have you, and if not, why not?

Reviews, when done poorly, disengage employees. However, when done well, they increase employee engagement. By creating a system that encourages the employee to be an active participant in the conversation around his or her performance, you can improve the culture and quality of the review process. What better opportunity, then, to influence your corporate culture through a process in which employees are deeply engaged?

Preparing for the performance review

Of course, it's important to gather information from other team members and from the employee himself, but the manager needs to weigh in as well! (Check out Chapters 18 and 19 for one-on-one framework and goal-setting outlines.) It's important for the manager to organize her thoughts around the same areas as the employee by answering the following questions:

>> What has been the most impactful work this employee has done over the last 6–12 months? How has this employee positively impacted the culture and values of the organization? This should include any milestones, major goals, or customer interactions. Use your notes from one-on-ones and goal review cycles to bring in previous success. Aim for three to five accomplishments.

>> In what ways has this employee improved since the last review cycle? Look back at the last review to see what areas were outlined for the employee to work on and consider improvement made in those areas.

>> As you look ahead, what do you believe the employee needs to work on next that would provide positive impact to others and business results? How are you seeing this, hearing this, or recognizing this in the employee today?

>> As you consider the next 6–12 months, what impact do you want the employee to make on the organization? What actions does the employee need to take to achieve that? How can he or she have a more positive impact on the culture? What values should he or she exhibit more frequently? What would be the impact of that?

>> To achieve those things, what performance changes will need to be made and what new skills developed?

>> When you consider the employee's relationships with others at the company, which ones are the strongest? Which ones are not as strong? How is that impacting the work? How do you think that can improve over the next 6–12 months?

>> What else should we both know and talk about in your upcoming feedback review session?

TIP

If you're leading the process, take some time to touch base with your energy before heading into a review conversation. Take time before the review begins to focus on your energy and intention. This can be as simple as a few minutes of intentional breathing or visualization of how you'd like the conversation to go.

Leading the conversation

Once all the information has been collected (see previous sections), the manager will organize it all into one place for easy review. The simplest way to do this is to create a document that includes the following sections:

>> **Opening statements:** The manager should draft a summary paragraph that outlines the achievements of this employee for the review cycle. Consider the results achieved, the outcomes delivered, and the relationships developed. Likewise, include some of the areas that have been a challenge — goals not achieved, previous performance improvements not met. The goal is to provide a balanced overview before getting into the specific.

>> **Last review:** In this section, copy and paste the "what to work on next" section from the previous review cycle with a few notes about progress that has been made. This is simply to highlight and track improvement over time.

>> **What's working best:** In this section, organize all the feedback you've received from peers, the employee, and the manager's feedback. This should be a bullet point list based on all the feedback. It should highlight what the employee has achieved and the impact the employee has been able to make on others.

>> **What to work on next:** In this section, organize all the feedback around what can help this employee be even more impactful in the future. This is where the suggestions from peers would go. You would include the self and manager

review notes around areas to work on, workload concerns, actions to take going forward, professional development, and any relationship-building opportunities. This section should read more like "here is what's coming up" and less like "this is what you have been doing wrong." The goal is always improving future performance during this process. Think windshield, not rearview mirror.

>> **Other feedback received this year:** This is where the manager will incorporate feedback from peers, awards, performance conversation notes, one-on-one notes, and other documented performance discussions.

>> **Final notes or summary:** This section is a roll-up of all the information from the previous sections of the review.

>> **Key follow-up dates and action items:** This section helps to create a clear follow-up plan that includes action items and dates. These should be logged on the calendar so that the manager and employee can check in on those dates.

REMEMBER

It's tempting to use language like "positive" or "negative" in the review to identify what's working best and what needs improvement, but these words typically cause employees to get defensive and feel as if they've done something wrong. This is not the goal. If they had been doing something wrong, it's the manager's job to have already dealt with this. The performance review is not the time for surprises or dealing with ongoing performance issues.

Figure 17-1 gives an example of an ideal review form.

Putting your words to good use

Here are some helpful things for the manager delivering the review to keep in mind during the conversation:

Things to focus on:

>> Positive energy and self-awareness for the manager

>> Eye contact

>> Specific behaviors, examples, and results

>> Clear deadlines with observable, measurable results

>> The future goals versus the past actions

>> Defining a personalized plan and vision for the future

Employee Name: Cara Thomas
Overview
Cara has been able to take a stronger leadership role on the team since our last feedback review session in June. We identified that it would be helpful for her to work on her communication in group settings and during presentations. I've seen huge improvements in the way she organizes information, prepares for a presentation, and includes others in the prep work. The outcomes have been much more clear data review sessions and more organized meeting agendas. The next phase of growth for Cara in this area will be around follow-up and organizing projects. Several times in the last six months, Cara has struggled to organize and follow through with the group assigned to do the work. Focusing on this during the next six months would provide a large benefit to the team and provide Cara with professional growth opportunities.
Last Review:
Based on the feedback from your peers and my own observations, it appears you have been able to improve in the areas we outlined in your last review. I've seen a positive change in the way you present information and in the way you include others in your process. In our last review on 06/01/2017, we outlined the following areas to work on between then and now:
• Cara often seems under-prepared in meetings and unable to communicate her ideas in groups.
• She struggles to deliver information in a way that is easy to understand and take action on.
• I'm often surprised by the things she is working on and wish I had known earlier that she had something in progress that would impact my own work.
What's Working Best
• Her presentations are so easy to understand and always include clear action steps.
• I really like the way she provides digestible information in her work. It makes it easier to make decisions because the information is clear.
• Cara has been really helpful to me as a newer employee. She is available to answer questions and has shared resources with me that shaved a lot of time off of my work.
What to Work on Next
• Sometimes it feels like we have clear action items after a meeting but then I'm surprised that we don't receive any follow-up to ensure the project is on track.
• I'm often unclear on who is doing what and when it is due when we leave a project review meeting. I've noticed that we struggle to stay on track because Cara hasn't captured those commitments and scheduled follow-up.
Other Feedback Received This Year
• Cara is a great example of our "be a good citizen" core value. I see her often volunteering to help new people and is always the first to jump in when someone needs help.
Final Notes or Summary
During our next review cycle, Cara will have made improvements to the way she organizes projects and creates strong follow-up. She wants to see comments like "Cara always ensures we have a road map for project completion and schedules follow-up so we are all clear on who is doing what and by when."
Similarly, Cara wants to spearhead a project around putting a resource center together for our new team members. The goal is to help them get access to the most important information they need to do their job. She will have this launched by the time we complete the next six-month review.
Key Follow-Up Dates and Action Items
• Complete project management online training course (due 01/15/2018)
• Create a checklist to use for project planning (due 02/01/2018)
• Document all new hire resources into one list with the HR team (due 03/01/2018)
Signatures and Dates

FIGURE 17-1:
A sample review form.

Things to avoid:

>> Debating/arguing over feedback

>> Focusing on "who" gave what feedback over the content of the information

>> Skimming over the difficult stuff

>> Unclear language and ambiguous terms (more, better, faster)

>> Cellphones, laptops, and other distractions

Following up for the win

Conducting a well-rounded, well-researched, well-prepared performance review leaves employees feeling much more positively about their performance and their relationship with their manager and the company. The energy that a modern review can provide to your culture is almost palpable. Imagine a whole team of people walking away from a review understanding the impact they have on the organization and with a clear idea of what to do next to continue to develop and grow.

Before you skip off into performance paradise, there's one more thing to keep in mind. You could even argue it's the most important part to keep in mind: follow-up.

It's critical that the manager and employee continue to talk about the goals set and areas to work on for the next six months. The surest way to halt all progress is to only talk about performance every six months — which is how most outdated models are based. Instead, use the dates and accomplishments outlined in the review to establish milestones and touch points. If you're using the one-on-one models and goals framework from Chapters 18 and 19, then you can transfer the information from the review sheet right into your system for those.

Here are some tips to help keep performance in focus after the review:

>> **Action item review:** Use the dates and action items outlined in Figure 17-1 to create calendar reminders to review. In fact, simply schedule a "performance check-in" at the end of the performance review. During this session, review progress that was made.

>> **Development planning:** If the improvements outlined require training, reading, or other skill development, take time to schedule and process that at the end of the review. If someone needs to attend a course or read a book, help the employee transfer that to his or her calendar and then schedule follow-up time with the manager.

Increasing Transparency in the Performance Improvement Process

Having a clearly defined performance improvement process is an important step in creating a transparent and just culture that allows for accountability. Every organization should have a documented process for handling the conversations, process, and outcomes when someone's performance is not up to standard or when an infraction may lead to termination.

Taking the time to document and share a process around performance improvement sends a clear message that employees will always know where they stand, even if that's on shaky ground. It provides managers with an outline to follow when things start to fall apart around their employee's performance.

Culture is about communication and relationships. Defining how performance infractions and improvement communication will be handled in your organization will help improve the relationships your employees and managers have around handling these circumstances. In far too many organizations, there's a lack of definition and understanding about what to do and how to handle the difficult process of communicating that performance is not satisfactory.

A progressive discipline policy allows you to create a structure that ensures employees have been given fair warning and a chance to improve performance while also creating a strong sense of accountability.

Understanding the four goals of the progressive discipline policy

The progressive discipline policy follows a three-step process (see Figure 17-2) that is aimed at helping improve performance and in most cases never gets beyond the first two steps to a final warning. In this process, there are four goals:

1. **Identifying the current performance issue:** The employee should be made aware in clear and specific language what is happening that needs improvement. The more observable, measurable, and specific the description of this can be, the better the employee will be able to attempt to change performance.

2. **Clarifying the performance expectation:** The employee should have a very clear idea about what great performance looks like when it's being done well. It's also important to clarify a timeline for improvement — is it expected immediately or is there time to show steps toward improving? This part of the process should be as clear and specific as the first part. By defining exactly what successful performance includes, you will help your employee better deliver the desired outcomes.

3. **Outlining the required steps to improve:** This section outlines what the employee should or can do to take action. It may include additional training if necessary or changes to workflow/schedule. The employee should leave the conversation understanding what he or she can do to improve, not just the end goal.

4. **Discussing the consequences of continued performance issues:** This section should define what happens if the employee doesn't make improvement or doesn't make improvement in the time frame provided. If the employee's job is in jeopardy, the employee has the right to know that.

Drafting your performance improvement process

All this work spent defining and thinking about your process for performance improvement conversations should be shared. Take the time to document your approach to performance improvement in your employee handbook and review it during new manager training to make sure everyone has the same understanding.

A typical policy will look something like Figure 17-2.

TIP

There are many templates available online that can be accessed with a simple search for "performance improvement plan document." Simply pick one, make edits so that it sounds like your organization, and save as a template to use in these cases.

Step 1: Counseling and verbal warning

Step 1 creates an opportunity for the manager to schedule a meeting with an employee to bring attention to the existing performance, conduct, or attendance issue. The supervisor should discuss with the employee the nature of the problem or the violation of company policies and procedures. The supervisor is expected to clearly describe expectations and steps the employee must take to improve performance or resolve the problem. This should include the consequences of not improving performance or behavior.

Step 2: Written warning

This involves more formal documentation of the performance, conduct, or attendance issues and consequences.

The manager and either the manager's manager or an HR representative meets with the employee to review additional incidents or information about the performance, conduct, or issues as well as the previous actions taken. The manager outlines the consequences for the employee of his or her continued failure to meet performance expectations.

A formal letter of warning requiring the employee's immediate and sustained improvement should be signed by the employee, manager, and witness. A warning outlining that the employee may be subject to additional discipline up to and including termination if immediate and sustained corrective action is not taken may also be included in the written warning.

You can create a standardized form to use as a template for this conversation to ensure the information is captured, documented, and stored.

Step 3: Performance Improvement Plan and final written warning

The third step in the progressive discipline procedure is the Performance Improvement Plan and Final Written Warning.

In this phase, the manager works in conjunction with an HR representative to prepare a detailed account of previous attempts at improving performance including coaching, training, and documentation, will outline what expectations need to be met and what qualifies as meeting them, and the consequences of not meeting them and time frame (if applicable).

FIGURE 17-2:
A typical performance improvement policy.

Chapter **18**

Perfecting the One-on-One for Culture Connections

When it comes to communication, almost everything you do affects your company's culture. From meetings to town halls, from performance reviews to new hire onboarding — the way your team communicates sets the tone for your culture and subsequently for your brand. But there's one powerful place that can really help drive culture, and that's the communication between an employee and his or her manager during effective and impactful one-on-one conversations. There's no better opportunity to connect and listen to your employees then during a regularly scheduled one-on-one meeting. If culture is largely about the way we communicate and the relationships we have at work, then the time that employee and manager set aside together is one of the critical opportunities for the manager to listen and be helpful. If done right, these conversations can uncover deep truths, reveal previously unspoken concerns, and highlight future growth opportunities for both the employee and the manager, as well as the organization as a whole.

In fact, the one-on-one is so paramount to the successful building of culture that it's one of the first recommendations I typically make to organizations seeking to improve their culture. No amount of visioning, values creation, or hiring delivers the same level of result as a really effective platform for one-on-ones. But don't use that as a reason to slow down your efforts in those areas; you really supercharge your culture when you take it all into account and make improvements across the board.

In this chapter, you discover why the one-on-one conversation has such a strong impact on culture, what's wrong with the way many organizations do it, and how to improve the one-on-one culture at your company.

Getting Started with One-on-Ones

If you aren't typically doing one-on-ones with your team, you should communicate the reason behind the new approach. In most cases, if you communicate the intended results instead of just the extra burden of an additional meeting, your team will be receptive and open to it. If you follow the guidelines in this chapter, you'll be off to a positive start that will keep them coming back for more.

If you've been doing one-on-ones but recognize that they suffer from a bunch of the ailments outlined previously, then you need to reset expectations with your team. Send a simple email or go over in your weekly staff meeting that you want to improve the quality of your one-on-ones. Note how you hope to change them and what employees should do to prepare for the next conversation.

TIP

In general, you should aim to do one-on-ones at least every other week to make sure you are able to stay connected and focused on helping your employees achieve the things they are aiming for. Weekly is even better if possible.

Setting up a framework

By establishing a consistent and simple outline for your meetings, you can help create a cadence and framework that's easy to replicate week after week. When your employees don't have to worry about what is going to happen in the meeting, it gives them more opportunity to focus on setting the agenda and thinking about desired outcomes.

See Table 18-1 for an outline of a 45-minute one-on-one conversation.

TABLE 18-1   **Outline of a One-on-One Meeting**

Time	Action
10 minutes	Use this opening time to review any action items from last time and to catch up on personal life.
20 minutes	This is the employee's time to set the agenda. The employee should come with items to review, explore, and problem-solve together. Use the questions in the "Asking Better Questions" section below to dive deeper into specific areas.
10 minutes	This time is for the manager to review any important updates or changes. Avoid the tendency to use this time to provide performance coaching or corrective coaching. Both of these are best done outside of the one-on-one and as close to the issue as possible. Instead, share important company news, recognition for great work, or other departmental updates that impact the work of this employee.
5 minutes	Use the final five minutes to review commitments, accountabilities, and action items due between this session and the next one. The person who controls the agenda — generally, the employee — should make notes of the agreements. The easiest way to do this is to simply store the notes in the meeting invite in your calendar or with a shared document that you both have access to and refer to frequently.

Respecting the time

Let's deal with the elephant in the room. You might be worrying about making time for all these one-on-ones. Managers in modern businesses have a lot on their plate between managing employees, meeting deadlines, serving customers, analyzing reports, and all the other things that go along with the role. I'm sorry to say that I don't have a magical answer to give you more time in your day or to remove the list of action items in your inbox. But I do know that focusing on these important one-on-ones will improve your culture exponentially. In the long run, they will save you time (and money) by improving your relationships with your employees and their relationships with the company. This means less time consumed because of tenure, termination, disengagement, and finding out about issues too late. All of this adds up to a lot more time to get back to that inbox.

The most difficult thing about growing your business and ensuring your culture grows in a positive way is the realization that your two most important assets— relationships and time — just don't scale well. You can't force relationships and you can't create more time. When it comes to developing the kind of one-on-one process that drives results and improves the culture, you simply have to invest the time in the relationship.

REMEMBER

You can't cancel your one-on-ones. These are a means to building the most important relationships in your career. Honestly. The people that report to you determine the results your team achieves and the success of your organization. You have to treat the one-on-ones as sacred times.

In a perfect world, you wouldn't have more than 10 direct reports, which means you'd spend about two hours a day in weekly one-on-ones. But the world you live in may be far from perfect, and you may have 12, 15, or 20 direct reports. In that case, I've seen positive results with every-other-week meetings and even shorter 30-minute sessions. Whichever you choose, respect the time you've dedicated to the relationship and show up consistently.

Envisioning the Ultimate One-on-One for the Employee

As you start to imagine what the ultimate one-on-one with your employees can look like, you should remind yourself of the main goals for these sessions. This is your chance to listen, clarify, and explore from your employees' perspectives. These conversations should be about your employees' challenges, their opportunities, their futures, and their careers. This isn't the time to focus on project status updates and the issues you want to address with them. Those should be handled in project meetings/status email reports and during in-the-moment coaching conversations.

Listening

During your one-on-one conversations, your main purpose is to understand what's going on from your employees' perspectives. You already have a handle on your perspective on things at work, your coworkers, and the work to be done. This is your chance to uncover what all that looks like from their point of view.

TIP

Here's a list of useful open-ended questions you can use in order to listen more during your one-on-ones:

>> How did you discover that?

>> What would that look like?

>> Tell me more about that.

>> Why is that?

>> How do you feel about that?

>> What would that take?

>> Why is that important to you?

>> What do you hope to achieve?

>> What would success look like?

>> What role would you like to play in that?

>> What needs to happen next?

REMEMBER

The mindset of the manager going into the one-on-one will set the tone. If you approach it less like a meeting you have to attend and more like a chance to catch up with someone you want to learn more about, you have a better chance of connecting and learning. By focusing on listening and uncovering more information about the employee and his or her perspective, you start to uncover new possibilities — not only in his or her performance, but for your business, customers, and improving your culture.

TIP

You may want to give yourself a little reminder before every scheduled one-on-one that says something along these lines:

> "During my one-on-ones today, I want to understand what's most important to my employees. I'm going to give them space to open up and communicate what their experience is like right now without judgment or pretense. I want to be helpful and ask questions that guide and enlighten versus providing answers and solutions right away.
>
> My job is to ask them leading questions, to brainstorm with them, to be in their corner, not to chastise them for their problems or to dismiss their difficulties by jumping to solutions before they feel heard."

It may seem a little hokey, but it can be a gentle nudge to turn your judgment off for a bit while you explore their perceptions, hopes, and plans.

PRACTICING EMPATHY

It's helpful to keep empathy in mind as you head into the meeting. You may hear someone struggling with something that's second nature to you or find out that they're having difficulty with one of your favorite people on the team. In either case, it's not helpful or useful to approach those situations from your point of view. You have to leave room for their interpretations so you can focus on how to be helpful in assisting them move through whatever challenge is ahead of them.

Clarifying

The one-on-one offers the chance to clarify expectations, motivations, and road maps. You'll often be halfway there simply by asking probing questions that elicit a response from your employee. But you can also use this as a time to document the accountabilities you've each accepted as well as the next steps involved in those areas.

While you shouldn't use too much of the one-on-one time to share your ideas and goals, you may find that you sometimes need to clarify parts of big projects or initiatives. This will usually come up if the employee is concerned about some action the company is taking. It's okay to spend some time connecting around these topics, because it's what's on your employee's mind.

Some of the key areas that can be improved through more clarification include:

>> Vision for a successful project completion

>> Employees' goals for career development and professional growth

>> Concerns about projects, coworkers, or the company culture

>> Employees' needs from the manager

Being helpful

A big sign of a productive and impactful one-on-one culture is the manager helping employees move forward and solve problems. This isn't about you having the answers and telling them what to do; rather it's about helping them uncover solutions, identify resources, and develop a game plan for achieving the important things they'd like to accomplish.

Being helpful can take many forms:

>> Providing resources and extra support

>> Asking probing, open-ended questions to help the employees begin to uncover solutions for themselves so they leave the conversation feeling proud and better able to handle situations like the one being discussed in the future

>> Identifying key stakeholders and partners and helping to establish a communication path

>> Recommending books, training, or other learning opportunities

>> Working on a project road map and action plan together

>> Researching options and creating a pros/cons list for each approach

Asking Better Questions

If the goals of your one-on-ones are to listen, clarify, and be helpful, then you need to arm yourself with great questions to open up the conversation and focus on the topics that matter most.

As you spend time together, you'll likely jump around to different areas. One week the employee may want to focus on long-term goals, and another time he or she may bring up team communication issues. Use the blocks of questions and prompts that follow to guide your conversation.

TIP

When you first get started, you may find it useful to send questions ahead of your meeting to give your team some ideas about the kinds of things to discuss each week. As time goes on, they'll become less dependent on you to guide the conversation, and you can use these questions as backup to use for taking a deeper dive.

Read on to collect subject ideas and sample questions:

> **» Identifying short-term goals:**
>
> - How is XYZ project going? What's next?
> - Is there any part of your project/goal that is unclear?
> - What's blocking you from making progress? Are you experiencing friction? How can I be helpful?
> - Is there anything you see happening at work that you wish you were able to be part of? How?
> - What can I do to make things easier?
> - How do you feel about the priorities of the team right now?
>
> **» Seeking long-term goals:**
>
> - What do you want to do next after this position? Why is that important? What do you need to achieve that? How can I help?
> - When you think about the future, what do you imagine yourself doing?
> - Do you feel like we're helping you advance your experience and career? How so? What more could we do in that area?
> - What are you currently doing that you feel is in line with your future goals?
>
> **» Improving the company culture:**
>
> - What do you think makes our company culture great? What do you think stops us from being better?

- If you were in charge, what would you do to improve the culture here?

- What information do you think we should share more openly? How would you do it to improve transparency?

- From your perspective, what's the biggest problem at our company? What should we do to fix it?

» **Improving yourself:**

- Are you learning new things? What's the last skill you picked up here?

- How do you like to receive feedback?

- What feedback have you recently received? How did you respond? What are you doing with that feedback now?

- What's a recent situation you wish you handled differently? What would you do if it happened again now?

- What areas of the company do you want to learn more about? Why? How could you start?

- What do you see as the key skills for your role? How would you rate yourself? Why? What would you like to improve? How can I help? What will you do?

» **Gathering manager feedback:**

- What do you like best about my management style? Why that?

- How could I improve my management style to make it more effective for you? What would that look like?

- Do you want more or less direction from me in your work?

- Is there anything you wish you knew about me?

- When have I best supported you? How can I best support you now?

- What do you think my biggest opportunity for improvement is? How would that help? What should I do?

- If you were me, what would you spend less time on, more time on, or differently spend time?

» **Striving for meaningful work:**

- What makes you happiest about coming to work?

- Is this job more than you expected when you accepted it? How so? What would you change about it?

- What worries you at work?

- Is there a part of your job you wish you didn't have to do?
- What would make you leave us for another opportunity?

>> **Building relationships:**

- How are things going outside of work?
- Are you able to balance your work and personal life?
- What's one thing we could do at work to improve your personal life?
- Do you have any trips planned? Why there? What are you most looking forward to?
- How are the kids, spouses, grandparents, cats?
- What did you do in the past in your free time that you are too busy for lately? How could I help you find more time for that?

>> **Building teams:**

- Who on the team do you most enjoy working with? Why?
- Who do you not enjoy working with? How could that improve? What can you do about it?
- How could we improve the way the team works together?
- Who has done something great that has gone unnoticed? How should we recognize them?
- How would you like to be more helpful to others on the team? What can I do to help you do that?
- What do you like best about our team? What could we do to make it even better?

>> **Improving the work:**

- What are the three biggest things you feel you waste your time on each week? What could we do instead?
- Why are you excited about that project? How can we make other projects exciting as well?
- What's working best in your work routine? What's the least effective part of it?
- Are there any meetings you feel are unnecessary? What would you do instead?
- What's an inexpensive thing we could do to make you improve your workday?

>> **Connecting your one-on-ones:**

- During our last one-on-one, you were frustrated/excited/optimistic about XYZ. How has that been going?

- What have you done about XYZ since our last session?

- During our last one-on-one, you agreed to XYZ? How is that going?

>> **Creating clear agreements:**

- What can I hold you accountable for the next time we meet?

- What can I be accountable to you for the next time we meet?

Debugging Your One-on-Ones

One-on-ones have the potential to be such a positive force in your company culture arsenal, so why aren't more people getting the results they want? Most managers I know start with good intentions around one-on-ones with their team, but things start to fall off track during their routines. Maybe the one-on-ones start to lose their focus and frequency. Perhaps the impact of the one-on-one starts to diminish to the point that they feel more like drudgery and yet another status update between managers and employees. One-on-ones are like any other solid communication in a relationship between two people — it takes work, it takes commitment, and it takes intention. And just like those other relationships, the one-on-ones can sometimes get buggy and bogged down. The following sections cover a few quick fixes for some of the common one-on-one bugs.

Losing the frequency

WARNING

It may be a last-minute emergency meeting, an unavoidable client call, or a string of doctor's appointments during your one-on-one time slot. Whatever the case, if you notice that the only thing consistently happening with your employee's one-on-ones is that the employee somehow ends up canceling them, you know you have an issue to solve.

People show up for things that matter. They don't make excuses or allow for distractions if the meeting is helpful, useful, and something to look forward to each week. So if you're seeing this habit, take a look inward to figure out what's going wrong.

Could the problem be that you're simply using the meeting to get project updates? Is it that you don't really help employees solve their biggest problems and find answers to the questions slowing them down? Are you focusing on giving them the performance coaching feedback you really should be delivering in the moment?

Whatever the reason, you have to take responsibility for shifting the focus back to listening, clarifying, and being helpful. It won't take many meetings with you focused on those things to make the one-on-one sessions something your employees look forward to each week.

TIP

If you notice one-on-ones being skipped, use this statement to bring the employee back around: "I've noticed we have started to miss our scheduled one-on-ones more frequently and I want to apologize for not making them more valuable for you. I'd like to fix that." Then try the following questions to get back on track:

>> What have you most enjoyed about work in the last month? Why that?

>> What's been the most exciting part of your role to you in the last six months? How can you and I work together to make the next six months include more of that for you?

Updating on status

If you notice that your one-on-ones are starting to sound like a project status update or metric review session, then it's time to make a change. If your employee simply could have sent a short email update or submitted a "report card" of metrics instead of meeting with you, then have the person do that. But then refocus your meeting on listening, clarifying, and helping.

These conversations should be about the obstacles, the opportunities, and the learning behind the updates and metrics. Encourage your employee to use the time more effectively. Focus on asking better open-ended questions that give employees a chance to elaborate and explore.

TIP

When your one-on-one's could have easily been sent in an email update, try the following statement to move them from "status update" to "performance enhancing conversation": "I realize our last few meetings have started to look like status updates and I want to make sure I'm providing you value in them. Let's start our next meeting talking about the following questions:

>> How are you feeling about the depth of conversation we are having in our meetings? Is there something we could change to make them more impactful?

>> How can I help improve our conversation during our one-on-one? What would make this more useful for you?

Talking too much

This one is about you, not them. If you find you're doing more than 20 percent of the talking, then it's time to reevaluate your sessions. Focus on open-ended questions that force employees to do more of the speaking.

Open-ended questions typically begin with a "w" or "h," as in who, what, where, why, and how. For example, "How did you uncover that potential roadblock on this project?" or "What do you plan to communicate about the new initiative this week?" Closed-ended questions typically start with a "d" or "a," as in "Do you know what to do next?" or "Are you ready to move forward with that project?" Focus on the "w" or "h" questions to encourage more communication from your employee during your conversations.

Avoiding the difficult conversations

If it starts to sound like your employee is just giving you the positive notes each time and not diving into anything challenging or criticizing, then it's a sign that your trust level isn't high enough to encourage this type of candor. This is a critical issue. If your team can't be honest with you during your one-on-ones, there's no chance they're going to speak up during staff meetings, project reviews, and other critical opportunities.

You must ask specifically about what's not working, what could be better, where things have failed and what was learned from the failure, and even what you could be doing as a manager to help them be more productive. This level of transparency and willingness to work through the failures, negative stuff, and challenges together starts to shift the culture from one that fears the opportunity that can be found in failure and turns it into one that celebrates the chance to grow, learn, and create something better together that happens when things don't work out as originally planned.

If all else fails, just call it out by saying, "I've noticed you seem to only be sharing the good news and you avoid giving me any critical feedback. I'd like to hear the criticism too so we can work through those challenges together."

Skipping the prep

When your employee starts showing up without an agenda or anything to talk about, it's a sign that you need to calibrate expectations for the meeting. Employees may assume that you're the one who will show up with a list of concerns, update requests, and project notes. If they've worked at a company with a different one-on-one approach, then that's probably the only thing they've ever experienced.

Take time to reset expectations and to help them understand the types of things you'd like to talk about each week. Address the subject directly and specifically to get things back on track.

Supercharging Your One-on-One Platform

One-on-ones are helpful in boosting company culture by improving the quality of conversation between employee and manager. But can they be helpful in other areas of your organization?

The answer is a resounding "yes." You can use the questions listed in the preceding section, "Asking Better Questions," to improve the quality of the conversation and relationship in other areas that also have a culture-enhancing impact. The types of content and perspectives uncovered by the questions suggested throughout this chapter are useful in other areas of the company where the business and culture would be served by bringing more ideas to the table or improving the amount of meaningful conversation happening between people in the organization. Here are some of those opportunities:

>> **Interdepartmental:** Schedule managers and leaders from other departments to occasionally meet with each other and with people from each other's team. The questions you select can focus on learning more about how to work together more effectively, encouraging a deeper understanding of each other's work, and collaborating on new ideas for improving the organization. Improving the relationships between departments is an impactful way to drive engagement and boost your culture.

>> **Executive to front-line:** If you've ever seen an episode of *Undercover Boss,* then you can understand the positive impact of having the most senior leaders in your company spend time with your front-line teams. While it may take time for the trust to develop for them to be completely honest and open, I've found that most employees are interested in having a connection with the executives and happy to share their ideas for improvement.

» **Customers and partners:** In most cases, you're probably reading this book because you want to use culture as a way to improve your customer offerings — whether service, products, or technology. Some of the most loved companies have a culture focused on customer service, so why not approach the customer relationship with the same one-on-one approach as you use to improve your employee relationships? Reaching out to clients to listen, clarifying their goals and reasons for using your service, and finding ways to be helpful can really boost relationships. Make this a core piece of most of the positions in your organization to spend time listening to and learning from your customers and partners.

Chapter **19**

Setting Clear Objectives to Boost a Productive Culture

umans love solving problems, making things more efficient, and finding ways to accomplish things that haven't been done before. We are at our best when we have challenges to overcome. A simple look back in history proves this point. Innovation, from fire to wheels from electricity to electric cars, has come from humans having a challenge and goal. Stay warm. Move heavy things. Powering up our products. Reducing fossil fuel usage. All of these big objectives were accomplished because we love conquering challenges. The same is true of the people on your team. Strong cultures are driven by engagement — and having clearly defined objectives increases that engagement. When your employees have a challenge with a big goal expressed in clear language and measured consistently, the culture is full of fired up people working together to achieve the next big thing.

Many organizations spend their time focused on telling team members *how* to work instead of clarifying what results matter most. In this chapter, I explore the link between objectives and culture, laying out a framework for creating a goal-setting system that both guides your team and improves your company culture.

Understanding the Link between Objectives and Culture

Keeping up with employee engagement is vital to keeping your organization in tip-top condition. If entire groups of people are not engaged at work, then what does that do to company culture?

WARNING

A company full of people that aren't that fired up is a pretty drab place to be — meetings without energy, projects without any focus, conversations that don't go anywhere, and constant searches for greener grass somewhere else. It's partly why companies compete for talent by offering dog parks, nap rooms, and free espresso. After spending time in offices around the world, I can tell you that all the puppy chat times, mood music, and latte hours don't do a whole lot to improve the conditions in organizations full of disengaged people.

So where does the heart of engagement live? You guessed it: setting inspiring objectives, sharing progress along the way, seeking input, and then letting people design their own work to deliver on those results.

One of the things people want most out of their work experience is to feel like they're making progress and feeling a sense of purpose. They are driven by a sense of belonging by understanding how they contribute to the bigger picture. The millennials aren't the first generation who wanted those things; they were just the first generation that could easily find other places to work with the Internet or easily start their own online business. The sense of purpose doesn't need to come from saving the world one child at a time or improving conditions for animals in zoos. A sense of purpose comes from having some clarity around where things are headed, how each person's work impacts the company's success, and making sure that there's meaning in all activities. This can only happen if success is defined, if progress is shared, and if your team is given some space to create their own path to achieving results.

To help your team begin to understand how they contribute to the overall company objectives and to help highlight the progress being made, you have to get clear on sharing progress. Use the desired objectives to create a common purpose, make sure to define the impact employees make toward those objectives, share frequent updates, and get their help in readjusting when progress isn't happening.

Creating a common purpose

All great teams need clarity around what they are trying to achieve together and a way to track progress toward that objective. This is where the scoreboard comes in. By creating a shared place for your team to see the big objective and how they are going toward achieving it, you start to align their efforts and give them a common purpose to work toward. This shared initiative will start to pull everyone together into one cohesive team rowing in the same direction. Ask:

>> Do the employees in your company understand how the business works? In other words, do you teach them how the business works?

>> Do they know how you make money?

>> Do they know how you spend money?

>> Do they know what metrics and numbers your executives and stakeholders use to measure success?

>> How well can they speak to it?

>> Is this part of your orientation and ongoing training?

It's amazing the number of employees who have no clue how any of that works and how few companies spend any time teaching it. This is the first place to start. You can include this in your orientation, your manager training, or as part of ongoing learning. Be sure to create follow-up so that it's repeated frequently.

Defining the impact

It's common for leaders to begin sharing the details about how the company is doing in a way that has no context for the employee. The goal in sharing the information is to help provide employees with information they need to better perform their jobs, provide innovative ideas to help achieve desired objectives, and create engagement around the core results for the company. But if they have no idea what you are you talking about when you say EBIDTA or what goes into the cost of goods, then you are wasting everyone's time. Each employee should understand how he or she impacts your business.

Here are some of the questions you should ask to ensure you're helping employees define the impact they are making on the overall company objectives:

>> How well do employees know how the work they do impacts the main business results (such as, profit, sales, cost of goods, marketing spend)?

>> What kind of training can be done to help employees understand the main objectives and associated results for the company? For example, can you teach everyone how the business works, makes money, and spends money during orientation and onboarding?

>> Can employees speak to their part in achieving the overall objectives?

>> How much can employees define what other people do and how that drives results?

Sure, this gets tough when we try to understand how certain departments impact the bottom line when they aren't directly responsible for sales, marketing, or operational costs. Departments like IT, HR, and Accounting are sometimes left out of this type of work because it is harder to measure their impact. Instead, I recommend rethinking how you measure success in those roles. While those positions aren't in traditional customer service roles, they are serving your internal customers. Make sure that you are also finding ways to connect the work they are doing to the final outcomes. For example, you can measure the cost per hire for the HR team and then link that to overall company profitability. You can tie employee satisfaction scores from IT support ticket requests to overall efficiency and employee turnover. These critical roles provide the foundation for the front-line team, who then bring the customer into the sales and service end zone.

Sharing updates

There's a reason that sports, video games, and the stock market have scoreboards that highlight the current score and results. They drive engagement, level the playing field by putting the results front and center, and make it easy for everyone to understand where things stand at any given time. They help define strategy. They provide a way to track progress. They make it easy to teach the rules — what earns points, what loses points, how you get ahead, and what the overall goal is to help move things forward.

Keeping the team informed about the results they are helping to achieve and the progress toward achieving the big organizational objectives is one of the critical components for engagement. In organizations where the culture and team help to support and improve the objectives, it is because the results are being shared frequently in a way that everyone can understand. They can see how the work they do impacts the achievement of those objectives.

Here are some ways to improve the way you share results with your team:

>> What's the frequency in which the company shares real results (such as, sales numbers, cost numbers, profit statements) with employees?

>> Do employees get a real view into the sales, expenses, profits, and progress on a regular basis?

>> Is that information presented in a way that everyone can understand and process?

>> Does it make it easy to understand progress or is it shared in a way that requires a PhD in mathematics?

REMEMBER

It is critical that your team understands what the numbers and results mean at a front-line level. Make sure you are breaking down the information in a way that impacts how they can do their job in order to help maintain or improve those results.

Including their feedback

>> How does the update being shared impact employee work?

>> Is the update used to adjust individual and departmental objectives?

>> Are employees being asked and included in developing strategies to improve metrics and achieve desired results? Or are they simply there to take orders?

Figuring Out Why Things Don't Get Done

You want to get things done. Your manager wants to get things done. Your employee wants to get things done. Your customer wants you to get things done. So why the heck do we all struggle to get things done? How is it possible to fill an organization with smart, capable, productive people and then still accomplish so little?

When the right results aren't being done at work, it's usually not because your employees don't care or aren't smart enough to get it done — it's because they are unclear on what matters most. They aren't able to accurately prioritize their attention because the objectives they are aiming for and the results they should be achieving haven't been defined.

Lack of clarity and prioritization

Most modern organizations have many moving parts happening every single day. People are working to keep things moving. People are working to get things started. People are working to get things fixed. People are working to get things transformed. The reality is that there's a lot to focus on, and with all that focus it's easy to lose sight of what matters most.

Your team is pulled in a bunch of directions and helping shift their attention and focus to the right things is critical for success. Part of the role of leadership is to maintain an unwavering focus on those priorities and to ensure employees have clarity about what matters most now. This level of clarity and prioritization serves your customers, your business results, and improves your culture by helping your team achieve more of the right things together. Check out the "Updating and resetting priorities" section later in this chapter for ideas on how to prioritize.

Hit me baby one more time

If your objectives start to feel more like New Year's resolutions, then you may have a problem. You know the resolutions we all forget about by the third week of January? They start with good intentions and some initial energy, but then when life gets in the way, we all completely forget about calling Mom, losing weight, and meditating.

The same thing happens with our company objectives and results. Management thinks employees get it, so they stop talking. You think everyone sees the same information you do, so the progress updates start happening less frequently. You worry about beating a dead horse, so you move on to new topics and think the employees will stay focused with just a midyear update. The reality is that we need to see the information frequently in different mediums for it to stay top of mind and in focus. Meetings should include updates on these objectives and results. You can send out monthly written updates via email. Try recording a video update talking about the latest results each month.

REMEMBER

The job of the leadership team is to constantly be reminding, repeating, and refreshing — in weekly meetings, in status updates, on TV screens, on company forums, on the company intranet. Keep the objectives (and progress) in front of your people.

Setting Up the Scoreboard

If you're going to ask your employees for engagement and make them responsible for achieving results in your business, then you need to start with defining success early and often. This is best achieved by a top-down and bottom-up approach. Your goal is to create a place where they can see the objectives and key results along with a current update on how things are going. This can be as simple as a spreadsheet, a whiteboard dedicated to this work, or TV screen in your office that highlights the current results. (Check out Chapter 12 for some scoreboard examples.)

TIP

If the larger organization isn't ready to adopt using and sharing the kind of data in a scoreboard, you can still create something for your division, location, department, or team. If you're reading this section by yourself, you can even just start using this in your work and life. The biggest culture impact happens when the entire organization is aligned, but any progress in setting up the goal system will help achieve better results.

Clarifying the core objectives

Core objectives should be inspirational and exciting. If you've done a good job at using your culture and vision to hire and onboard, then your employees will likely be pretty pumped up about the big things you have in store.

Here are two examples of a core objective:

> Bad example: Increase our sales by 10 percent in the next quarter.

> Great example: Close our biggest quarter-to-date by bringing in our biggest client yet and beating previous records by at least 10 percent while improving our skills and developing professionally.

You want there to be enough clarity that even an outsider would understand what your team is trying to achieve. This also helps unify the culture and create a sense of community so that everyone feels like they're rowing in the same direction (and actually helps ensure that they are). You'll find that employees start to talk about the objectives and results. They will start to discuss new ways to achieve the results because they are no longer just simply doing what their boss said but are striving to solve a problem. You've given them their big heavy thing to move and they will find a way to build their wheels — improving your culture, product offerings, and brand in the process.

Employing scorecards to track progress

Find simple ways to share the information with your team. Create one hub where they can access all the information to understand how things are going, where things stand, and how much more is needed to achieve the organizational objectives. This can be stored in a shared electronic drive on a spreadsheet or using technology like Domo (www.domo.com).

Some of the things that you should consider including in your scoreboard include:

» Organizational-level goals and progress toward achievement (for example, sales, new markets, new customers, customer lifetime value, and so on)

» Critical operational numbers (such as, cost of goods, profit per employee, marketing spend, customer acquisition cost)

» Employee-related results (employee Net Promoter Score, culture survey results, and so forth)

Improving frequency for sharing

TIP

The more frequently you can update the scoreboard and provide feedback to your team, the better. You can use screens around your office to share updates. You can use shared spreadsheets to provide weekly recaps. You can host monthly town halls where you share this information and review current results compared to the target results. For more information about creating scoreboards, see Chapter 12.

Regardless of how you get the information in front of your employees, it's important that they get the information in order to adjust their efforts and work toward achieving the overarching goal.

Using Objectives and Key Results to Drive Culture

Setting up your scoreboard is just the beginning of establishing a culture-boosting goal platform. The next step is trickling that high-level scoreboard into an easy-to-use model. While goal systems have been around forever with lots of different names, the overall point is to create clarity and set direction for the team.

The easiest and most practical method to use is the OKR framework. OKR stands for *objectives and key results.* Your organization will typically define one to three core objectives and then assign the objective(s) some key results that are used to measure progress. The key results tell you whether the objective has actually been met.

Once you've done this process for the organization as a whole, you'll typically repeat it by trickling down to the department and individual level. The next sections help to identify objectives and establish results.

Crafting inspiring objectives

In your company, aim to have one to three objectives for the year. These are the main priorities and focus. The objectives should be inspirational, qualitative, and time-specific. Think deeply about the big wins for the company. What would be a huge success? What is required to move into new markets? Where do you need more growth to compete and thrive?

Here are some good examples:

>> Double our same-store volume this year

>> Sales numbers are double compared to last year

>> Change the way people eat on the go

>> Improve the fitness of office workers in West Hollywood

>> Launch a bestselling new product

Each of these seems achievable yet daring and bold. They're inspirational and actionable. They set the intention for the team but don't quite define how we know if we achieved the objective — which is why we need key results to help measure success.

Defining clear key results

The shift from focusing on activities to focusing on results drives engagement and encourages employees to express discretionary effort. You've hired smart people to help get things done — why tell them exactly how to do it? Employees today want some autonomy and freedom to get things done in the way that's most productive and effective for them. If you've focused on being really clear on your vision (see Chapter 6), have done a good job at defining values and behaviors (see Chapter 7), and used both of those to hire and onboard better (see Chapters 9 and 10), then you should be in great hands when you allow your employees to work toward results.

WARNING

Imagine if your employee were to focus on the activities a manager has defined and doesn't achieve a specific outcome. Is it okay simply because the person did the activities? Or do you really still just want the outcome? Of course, it's the results. Disengagement and resentment are bred in environments that focus on activities and then hold people accountable for results. It's confusing, inconsistent, and unfair.

Good examples of key results include:

>> Thirty percent of customers return weekly

>> Achieve a referral rate of 40 percent

>> Maintain a 90 percent uptime

>> Average customer purchase increased 10 percent

Each of these is measurable and helps define how you'd measure success of a specific objective. For each objective, you want to define three to five key results. Really work hard to make sure this doesn't just sound like a to-do list but rather gets really specific about how you'll know if you've achieved the objective.

Once you've established OKRs for the organization and your department, each employee will work with you to define his or her own OKRs for the quarter. The same rules should apply to individual OKRs as the organizational and departmental versions.

Checking on progress

There's nothing that waters down an engaged team more than lack of follow-up and support. Once your employees have bought into the goal process, you have to create a system to check on progress. In most organizations, a mix of regularly scheduled one-on-ones (see Chapter 18) and mid-quarter check-ins is a solid enough approach. In other organizations, you may want to adopt monthly goal check-ins. Anything more than every six weeks makes it difficult for your managers and employees to track progress, share feedback, and make adjustments based on results and desired results. If you aren't sure where to start, go with the monthly check-ins. If that works, keep it going. If you find that it's not enough time to make progress, then slide the dial back to every five or six weeks.

During the check-ins, you want to consider these questions:

>> How are your priorities going?

>> What can I do to help?

>> What's the progress of key results since the last check-in? What's been accomplished? Where do things stand today?

>> Based on the current status and progress, how confident are you about achieving each key result/outcome? Why? Why not?

>> What's impacting the progress? Has anything come up to change priorities?

>> What needs to happen next to improve results? How can the manager help?

REMEMBER

Keep the conversation from becoming a simple status update. Check-ins should be focused on creating a conversation about progress, issues, next steps, and planning for goal achievement. Use these conversations to follow up on milestones along the way to achieving the bigger result. This can be a helpful way for the manager to assist the employee with exploring other ways to achieve the objectives if progress isn't made versus waiting until the end to realize a new method could have helped get the desired result. Status updates can be handled via email. Use the check-in to move things forward and unlock performance.

Updating and resetting priorities

At the end of each quarter, you and your employees will close out the quarter's objectives. You can do this by scoring them based on what percentage of the goal was achieved. For example, if one of the objectives was to hire 100 people and you hired 80 people, then you'd score that an 80 percent. A solid review looks similar to the check-in discussed in the preceding section but includes some extra time to reflect on learning and future actions from that learning.

You also use this time to reset objectives and results for the upcoming quarter. If the organizational and departmental objectives were set for the year, then your employees will take stock of current progress toward those objectives and establish new objectives and results for themselves. If there are updated organizational or departmental objectives, then those should be reviewed together before setting individual objectives.

Avoiding the Common Mistakes of Organizational Goal Setting

As I've worked with teams using objectives to improve culture, there are a few common things that get in the way of a successful goal platform. Success isn't always measured by achieving all the objectives — in fact, I'd suggest that that's not a successful platform because if everything is being achieved, then you aren't setting aspirational enough objectives. Creating easily achieved objectives is just sandbagging the system. You might as well not set them at all. A successful goal platform is one that helps ensure the right work is getting done, your employees are clear on what matters most, and you're achieving something like 70 to 80 percent of the things you aim to achieve.

It's also important to be upfront about that with your employees so that people don't feel like they've lost if they don't achieve 100 percent of the goal. It's about setting an audacious goal that gets people excited, engaged, and challenged to go bigger with their performance. Throw the ball over the tall fence — and then figure out how to go get it.

Unclear organization priorities

There's something really exciting about startups. Whether restaurants, tech companies, or service firms, I've always been attracted to the early days. Helping a company begin to take shape when everything is at stake is exhilarating. The clear purpose is to get a product off the ground, hit some crucial break point that ignites growth, or land a few key clients. During those days, the objectives are easy to see and easy to track.

As teams and organizations grow, the priorities start to get confusing. Companies try to be all things to all people and end up watering down their culture. In companies big and small, use the goal process to set some defining results for your team. Share the progress frequently to keep engagement up.

Setting too many objectives

If you notice that your organization is starting to suffer from goal creep with more than three high-level objectives, stop and focus. You want to create clarity about what matters most and give your employees a central call-to-action, not define every single one that may be beneficial.

In an effort to make it easy for people to see how they can contribute to the objectives, many leaders end up creating too many objectives. Instead, create just a few and then help your employees see how they can contribute to achieving them. Start with the most important company objectives — the two or three really big things that matter most. Then ask a series of "How does that happen?" and "How does *that* happen?" questions to keep refining how each employee helps to achieve those top-level objectives. For example, if one of the main goals is "increase live accounts 50 percent this year," then you can ask "How does that happen?" This may end up with adding 10 new sales representatives by a certain date. When you ask "How does *that* happen?" you may find some objectives for your human resources team. In this way, all the individual objectives should roll up into the few most important objectives for the company.

Creating very short-term objectives

It's really common when getting started with objectives for your employees to create really short-term objectives that are easily accomplished in a few weeks. Overall you're looking for the kinds of results that will take up more of the quarter. Often these types of short-term objectives are also written in a way that's more of a to-do list than an actual outcome (see the next section).

Allowing results to become to-do lists

"Be more present."

"Improve my leadership skills."

"Review new program materials and prepare for launch."

Each of these are actual objectives and results I've seen documented in organizations I've consulted with on company culture improvements. These are not objectives or results. These are simply to-do list items that will help create some specific result.

Double-check all your objectives to make sure they are actual results and not simply someone's to-do list. If it can be accomplished this week, it's probably just a task list item.

Using the objectives to punish or reward people

If you use your goal system to make compensation, promotion, or termination decisions, then you're putting the entire process at risk of becoming one big sandbagging session where employees and managers alike are scared to go for anything big and meaningful because of the fear of losing out or failing.

REMEMBER

The decision to promote someone, fire someone, give someone a raise, or not give someone a raise should be a byproduct of the improvement you've seen through the goal setting, the one-on-ones, the performance reviews, and other coaching opportunities — not just because of the successful completion of a goal cycle.

Communicating vaguely

Few things are more frustrating at work than feeling like you were making progress only to find out that the project you've been working on isn't important or aligned with current organization objectives. I've seen this happen even when an organization has done some of the work toward setting organizational objectives for the year. The culprit is almost always vague language and objectives/results that are not specific and measureable. Double-check your objectives to make sure they don't have words like *better, more, less, quality,* and so on. You should see specific results that are measurable. The power in communicating objectives and results is in the ability to measure the success. If two people are trying to determine whether a goal was met, there should be one correct, objective answer, not two subjective ones.

Chapter **20**

Using Recognition to Reinforce Company Culture

"**I**f you see something, say something."

I remember seeing that sign every day I'd ride the train back and forth to work. It was a reminder to notify the station attendant of suspicious activities or packages on the train, but it always reminded me about recognition at work. If you see great behavior, you should say something. You'll likely get more positive behavior in return and encourage a culture full of the kinds of actions that drive your business forward.

In this chapter, I explain how to create a recognition program that promotes the positive cultural values and behaviors you want to see more of and how to develop programs that drive results. Throughout the chapter, I give dozens of ideas that can be used to improve your culture through leveraging strategic rewards and recognition. Identifying a few to try is a good way to get started in your company.

Benefiting from Recognition

Regardless of the kind of culture your organization has today or wants to have in the future, I can't think of a negative impact of improving the amount of recognition within your organization. Once you've developed an intentional approach to values and culture, you can establish recognition programs that reward people for doing the things associated with those areas.

Recognition has this interesting way of encouraging more of the same behavior. From a young age, we're tuned into getting approval and praise from teachers, parents, and leaders. We repeat the behaviors that got us attention, candy, good grades, love, approval, snacks, and gold stars. I'm not sure why people think that suddenly stops when we become adults. When we receive recognition or rewards, our brain releases dopamine into the orbitofrontal lobe of the brain. Dopamine gives us a quick fit of positive feelings that become addictive — so we want some more of it. This can start to encourage the behavior you want to see at work.

We all need recognition and approval. It helps motivate us to do it all again. It keeps us focused on the good things we're doing to have a positive impact on those around us. At the cultural level, it starts to codify the behaviors and actions that are "on brand." This means that they are the behaviors that are in line with the expectation of the brand. The ones you want to celebrate and encourage to happen more often. By focusing on recognizing them, you send a strong message to the company about what matters, what's valued, and what's celebrated.

TIP

Throughout this chapter, you will find a bunch of ideas for programs for your company. Don't worry — you don't need to try them all at once. Get started with a couple that you can execute consistently — and then grow from there as you start to see positive results.

Understanding Real Recognition

When it comes to recognition, most programs make the mistake of focusing only on money. From bonus programs to incentive awards, the common thinking is that cash is king. This may be true in organizations that live in the kingdom of winning at all costs, but even there, this type of extrinsic motivation often rewards people for the wrong things. Even though such things are the easiest to measure — improving a sales number, landing a big client, finding cost efficiencies — rewarding them is not the same as rewarding the values, behaviors, and culture of the organization. It can be the culture of the organization that creates the conditions that allowed for improved sales, landing bigger clients, and finding ways to save money. The positive relationships, feeling of safety, and community created by culture can encourage employees to produce those results on a more consistent basis.

REMEMBER

In the land of culture, recognition is about taking the time to notice the small things that make a difference to the environment you work in. It's about gratitude and celebrating the smaller wins that make your company a great place to work. Making the commitment to recognizing and rewarding people in your organization for meeting expectations should be a core part of your organization's culture — whether formal, informal, conservative, casual, friendly, or reserved.

Don't get me wrong — money can be a positive reward for employees, but it isn't often the motivating factor in whether an employee does the kinds of things that boost your culture and improve your team. Of course, money will always be a motivator and can drive specific behaviors, but there is a whole world of recognition that enhances culture, engages employees, and improves business results that should be explored as well.

Creating a Culture of Appreciation

If you want to have a culture where people value each other, boost each other up, and have high levels of psychological safety, then it's critical to establish a culture of appreciation. In a culture of appreciation, people go out of their way to recognize each other's contributions. They take time to celebrate milestones, achievements, and progress toward goals. While employees will often run with this on their own once it is started, you'll need to take the leap at putting some systems of appreciation in place to get the ball rolling.

Saying thanks

One of the fastest ways to get the recognition train moving is to have management model the behavior you want to see in the organization. Make it an expectation for your leadership team and include it in your management review process and employee feedback. Simply ask, "Does your manager take time to appreciate the positive things happening on your team?" or "Does your manager offer enough positive appreciation to you?"

When I've talked with employees around the world, I've consistently heard that some of the most meaningful recognition has been a handwritten note from their manager thanking them for something specific. Make a plan to write a thank-you note at least weekly. You can create a recurring task in your to-do list system or schedule a recurring calendar invite to take 10 minutes a week to write a thank-you card. In a world of #selfies and management-by-instant-message, there's something really authentic about getting a handwritten note from your manager.

If you decide to do a weekly thank-you card writing session, why not extend it a little further and write one for someone in your personal life as well? If cultural leadership starts with managing yourself (see Chapter 4), then improving your relationships outside of work is destined to have a great impact on your approach to appreciation at work too.

Ending your meetings

Incorporate more appreciation and recognition into your organization by anchoring the act of recognizing others into current systems you already have in place. Because I've not met an organization that doesn't have some steady flow of meetings, I suggest starting there. I learned this little trick from the people at Zingerman's (the Michigan-based deli famous for its revolutionary business practices and history of positive business growth) a long time ago and have incorporated it into every place I can.

At the end of meetings, leave some time for the people in the meeting to recognize someone else. It doesn't need to be about the meeting or even about someone else in the room. Just leave a few minutes at the end (and marked on the agenda) to give recognition and thanks to others. This doesn't have to be part of every meeting, but your results will be better if it does happen consistently. You also don't need to force each person to say something — or even force anyone to say something if there isn't anything to highlight.

Doing this will start to change the overall vibe of your meetings, and then your organizational culture will start to see some positive light. Again, this works for any kind of culture, regardless of how formal or informal. Taking time to be appreciative fits inside of all organizations.

One of the benefits you'll start to see is that employees will become more aware of the work of others, even if they don't work with them. If Lisa in Accounting keeps getting brought up in meetings she isn't even in, then other people in those meetings who may not work closely with her will start to become more aware of her work and positive contributions.

Assign someone from each meeting to take notes on the appreciations. Then find a way to share those across the organization — whether it's posted on a wall, compiled in a shared document, or available some other place where everyone can see (see the next section for ideas). You'd be surprised how often people will read these appreciations and learn about each other.

One of the requests I hear a lot from employees is that they want other people to understand what they do better. Using this technique is a surefire way to start to bubble up awareness and empathy.

Creating public appreciation

An easy way to get recognition and positive appreciation out in your organization is to make it public. Here are some ideas:

>> **Digital wall:** If you have a TV screen that shares company updates, share celebrations, milestones, and other recognition moments for employees. List their name, photo, and the achievement.

>> **Intranet page:** An intranet page that refreshes daily with the same type of information from the digital wall idea can help keep the ideas front of mind in a company that works digitally.

>> **Technology tool:** Look to tools like Facebook at Work, 15Five, or Reflektive to create public spaces for team members to give each other positive feedback.

>> **Shared document:** A simple shared document updated daily can be an easy way to keep recognized employees in view.

>> **Corkboard and pushpins:** You can do it the old-fashioned way with a corkboard and pushpins. Put these in public areas and allow employees to list the things they'd like to recognize others for. You can even raise the stakes a little by giving away monthly prizes to one of the people recognized and even one of the people who took time to recognize someone else. If you are trying to encourage more recognition in your culture, this is a fun way to get it.

>> **Culture kudos cards:** A really fun way to get employees to recognize each other and to celebrate your culture is to create "culture kudos cards." These are cards that list all of your values and associated behaviors on them. It also has a space to list an employee's name and a few lines to write about some positive thing the employee did in association with the value checked off. You can make these available in public areas (or even online) so that employees can easily complete them for each other. Share them during meetings, all-hands, and other team gatherings.

TIP

Create branded thank-you cards and stock each employee with 13 cards every quarter with the expectation that they give out at least one per week. Send a weekly nudge email to encourage them to send them out.

Leading the way

Most managers want to do great work. They want to engage and motivate the team while delivering results and service for the organization. The same is true when it comes to hitting the mark on providing recognition to the team. Create a clear example of what recognition looks like at your company. The leadership team has to be the example that role-models how people in the organization should recognize each other for their accomplishments.

Take some time in your next leadership team meeting to think about ways that managers can include recognition into their daily habits. Here are some questions to get ideas flowing:

>> **How much recognition is enough?** The answer to this is typically "a lot more than we are currently doing." Most often I hear from employees that they aren't hearing enough about what's working and what their manager wants more of, but they definitely hear when they mess up. If you need an absolute number, then aim for a ratio of 5 to 1 positive to negative.

>> **What types of things can you easily recognize?** These can be things associated with your values, desired more in your culture, celebrated by your customers, or contributing to positive business results. It should be a mix of things that you can easily spot daily.

>> **How do you know if you've done enough?** You won't. Just keep doing it anyway. Aim for more than you think you need without giving away false praise for things that don't really matter. This isn't about giving people a phony nicety to make them feel happy at work. This is about recognizing all the little things that go unnoticed every day yet contribute to a positive outcome.

REMEMBER

I know someone out there is thinking, "Really, Mike?! I have to reward people doing their dang job?" My response to that is yes, and doing so is your dang job as a manager, so stop reading, get up, and go recognize someone for doing great work! Money is just one of many reasons that people stay (or leave) a job. Sometimes it's not even one of the top reasons either. The money part of the employment equation is the one thing your competitors can easily match or beat to get your employees — so finding other ways to make them feel valued and building your culture can become your true differentiating factor.

Showing your work

Remember show-and-tell during grade school? You'd get to bring something in from your home and tell your classmates about it as a little way of sharing something you were proud of. Sometimes it would be a parent who had a cool job, and other times a rock you brought back from your trip to Florida. This joy of sharing the things we're proud of doesn't go away simply because we pull into the office parking lot.

Giving people the opportunity to highlight the work they're doing and are proud of producing is a great way to provide recognition for their contributions. You can coordinate a weekly, monthly, or quarterly session where people on the team do a show-and-tell type event. Depending on your organization and the size, you can sort out the right cadence, size, and number of presenters. These don't have to be mandatory, but you'll probably find over time that people really like going to them.

TIP

Here are some ways to incorporate this show-and-tell type method into your world:

>> **Lunch-and-learn style:** Provide a group lunch while a few people present some of their latest work, research, or results.

>> **Webinars:** Have someone lead a 30-minute webinar about their latest work, highlighting their process, their research, and the results. Record this for playback. You can even create a playlist with all the sessions stored for future viewing. This can be curated into videos to be shared online, with new hires, during all-hands meetings, and at end-of-the-year parties.

>> **Teaching sessions:** Have employees from different departments share their skills. Engineers can teach some basic coding, designers can showcase how to make better social media graphics for sharing, recruiters can teach how to boost your LinkedIn profile, and so on. This should be done thoughtfully to make sure that it is something employees want to learn and will opt in to attend. If you have a training department, you could even have them help the presenter put together their session for maximum impact and success.

Baking it in early

You can get your people thinking about recognizing each other and sharing successes from their very first day. If you'd like to increase the amount of recognition and rewarding going on around your culture, there's no better place to start than with your newest people. Here are some ways to encourage them:

>> Encourage your orientation leaders to incorporate moments of appreciation into their training so that new hires are seeing the behavior being modeled right away.

>> Ask your new hires to send a thank-you card each day during their initial training to someone who displayed one of your values or highlighted something in your culture.

>> Include stories about cultural champions and examples of your values in action throughout your orientation. Update your examples and stories frequently to include current employees and recognize new wins. People love being part of that company story.

>> Create a project that new hires complete together over their first 90 days where they have to gather and organize examples of your values and culture in action. Then ask them to present the project at a town hall, company gathering, or to the executive team.

Recognizing Milestones

Finding ways to celebrate the milestones and wins for each person on your team goes a long way toward creating a sense of oneness and boosting your culture. Take time to think about how you can approach milestone celebrations consistently.

Personal wins

Create a consistent way for your team to celebrate the personal wins in each other's life. Depending on the size of your organization, this can be centralized or done within each department. Decide what works for you from a budget perspective and then get everyone on the same page about celebrating the milestones, including:

>> Babies

>> Birthdays

>> Home buying

>> Graduations

>> Divorce (Yep! One company I worked with even gave a gift card if someone was going through a divorce as a little way to say, "We get it. It's tough. We are here for you.")

Some organizations tend to shy away from recognizing that the humans who show up at work each day are actual people outside of work as well. To create a culture, it's worthwhile to think about how you can celebrate the entire person who is part of your team.

WARNING

It's important to make sure the employee getting this type of personal recognition is into it being celebrated at work. This is where good managers come in with knowing their team and recommending what's best. For some it may be a card left on their desk, while others want fireworks from the roof. It's okay to not treat people equally as long as you treat them fairly.

Cheering for work anniversaries

Even if your organization decides to stay away from doing the personal milestones (which I highly recommend for all organizations), you should establish a consistent way to celebrate work anniversaries. These are the milestones you should celebrate for everyone in your organization:

>> **Monthly or quarterly celebrations:** Pick a day at the beginning of each month or quarter to recognize all the people celebrating anniversaries that month or quarter. Depending on the size of the organization, you can even have someone talk about how that person has positively impacted the team and culture. You'd be surprised at how sincere people are and how touching the tribute is.

>> **Annual recognition:** If you have an annual company event, take time to recognize all the anniversaries from the previous year. Depending on the size and tenure of your team, you may do some as a big cohort (all your 1-year anniversaries) and others as individual recognition (a 5- or 10-year anniversary).

TIP

This is great for social media sharing as well to celebrate your culture (see Chapter 8).

6

The Part of Tens

Chapter **21**

Ten Free Ways to Boost Your Culture

C ulture is a mix of relationships, behaviors, norms, attitudes, beliefs, and actions. Finding ways to enhance and intertwine all these components may mean taking a look outside the box.

Sometimes you may be looking for a quick idea to give your culture a little lift, something light and easy to put into place. For those times, here are ten ideas you can use in any type of organization to see an immediate culture boost for the people involved. Have fun!

Starting a Book Club

When Oprah Winfrey started a movement by launching a book club on her eponymous juggernaut talk show, she was doing more than simply using her massive platform to propel an unknown author into stratospheric fame. She was bringing people together in a way that fostered community, drove engagement, and heightened relationships. People from around the world joined each other to share perspectives and experiences. Whether through a virtual event, an in-person meeting, or an author's appearance on the talk show, people had a chance to connect with each other in a way that doesn't often happen anymore. While Oprah accomplished a great many things through this book club, one thing is for certain: Reading, sharing, and connecting around a book are positive ways to improve culture.

Starting a book club at work is something anyone can do and is relatively easy to maintain. It's as easy as picking a book, sending a notification/posting in a shared area, scheduling some time, and then facilitating a conversation around the reading. Commit to doing it four times this year, with a different book each quarter.

Here are some tips to help you execute your new book club:

>> **Enlisting help:** As you get started leading a book club, have someone help organize, lead, and get other people to join. This is a great way for you to develop a relationship with someone from another team with whom you don't normally work. Find someone who has a different network of coworkers so that you can both leverage your relationships to bring a mix of people into the group.

>> **Getting leadership support:** A book club is a prime opportunity for leaders to learn more about employees, share their ideas about things they normally don't discuss, and build trust and relationships. Review your idea with the leadership team, ask them to join, and ask for their help in announcing the meetings.

TIP

You may even be able to swing some budget for the company to pick up copies of the book for everyone or reimburse some of the purchase price. I know, I know — I promised the ideas in this chapter were free, but just putting it out there!

>> **Picking books:** There really isn't a "right" book to get started. Look for books that have widespread appeal or that may help with a specific issue you're having in the organization. Choosing a fiction book can be a fun way to kick off the summer. Diving into a book that helps with professional development can help everyone feel like they're getting some free coaching.

TIP

In some cases, you may be able to choose a book to go along with a theme. Maybe the public library is having a community reading, or perhaps an author is doing a speech/book tour and you can all attend that as well. As your group develops, you can even send out a simple survey giving people an opportunity to vote on which book they want to read next!

>> **Leading meetings:** Your goal eventually is that the book club sessions will run themselves, but it often takes a little nudge to get it going. Speak about the intention of the book club to kick things off — share why you started it, what you hope happens, and that you hope everyone contributes. Emphasize that your role as a leader will be to guide the conversation by preparing thoughtful questions for review.

>> **Preparing ahead of time:** In advance of the meetups, divide up the reading over the course of how many meetings you'll have. For example, if you're meeting once a month for three months and have a 21-chapter book, then review 7 chapters in each session. Prepare by sending some questions to think about ahead of time. You can often find these online by searching the book title and "book discussion questions."

Adopting a Freaky Friday Day

Remember the movie *Freaky Friday,* in which the mom and the daughter swapped roles but stayed in the same body? While entertaining and goofy, the moral of the story is that it taught them to have a little more respect, understanding, and empathy for each other. Sounds like a pretty good match for your company culture, right? And don't worry — you don't need to visit a mystic or be put under a spell to experience it.

When I was leading businesses in the hospitality industry, I witnessed how easy it is for people in the office to lose touch with what's going on out in the field. To solve that, we had all the "corporate" staff spend one day per quarter working in one of the restaurant, retail, or hotel locations to experience what was happening on the front lines. The store–level employees loved showing off what they did and working alongside someone from the office, and the office employees got more connected to the brand and culture. Often, they would come back to the office with new ideas about how they could improve some process that they were involved in, whether it was accounting, design, or marketing.

This is relatively simple to replicate by taking some time to match people up. You could easily have someone from your Customer Support department spend a day in the field with a salesperson, or have your HR Manager help the Client Services department for a day. A great way to maximize the impact is to have the employees do a short write-up or video review of their day, highlighting what they've learned and what a day at work is like for the person they followed.

It can be really impactful to have the executive leadership team committed to the program and leading the charge as well. Create your very own version of the hit TV show *Undercover Boss* without the costumes or free cars.

REMEMBER

The goal of this type of program is for leadership to learn more about what the people on the team do every day. This should be about getting your hands dirty and doing the work alongside of them. Be thoughtful about not creating an environment where the employees feel like they need to "perform" for the leadership team coming in. Review this goal with the leadership team before kicking off a program like this in your company.

Bringing the Services to Them

In today's never-enough-time mindset, it can be hard to squeeze in the important appointments and need-to-do items into nights and weekends for your employees. Things like haircuts, fitness classes, meal prep, and even routine doctor's visits can be difficult to fit in. Why not bring the services to them instead? It shows a commitment to your employees to find ways to simplify their lives — and more and more pro-culture companies are finding ways to do exactly that.

This doesn't mean you have to pay for these services — but you can be the one organizing and taking sign-ups even if the employees are paying for it themselves. Reach out to local businesses to see what's available or do a quick search for the service areas and "office visit" to learn more about what's available in your area. Everything from yoga class to chair massages and barbers to car washers can be brought to the office.

Codifying Your Culture

You greatly improve your chances of getting what you want from other people if you take the time to get clear enough that you can share with them your expectations and desires. Your company culture is no different. It deserves to have a codified version of "how things work around here" via a culture code document. In the world of computer programming, the code is what makes the programs run. Your company has a code as well — a culture code.

Netflix. Zappos. HubSpot. The Motley Fool. Disney. They've all taken the time to get clear on their desired culture. In some cases, it's as simple as sitting down and typing out what matters most. In other cases, you can enlist a whole group of people to help co-create your culture doc. This doesn't need to be an exercise in HR/marketing wordsmithing, but it should be a from-the-heart attempt to get down the things that you really care about. Think about bringing to light the way your company operates, why you believe what you believe, and how you feel people should act at your company. This document should help codify the way things happen in your company.

TIP

If you want to see samples of some companies' attempts at making their desired culture clear, then just search "company culture deck" or visit www.culturedocs.com to get some inspiration.

Teaching What You Know

One of the most wanted things I see in surveys, from conversations, and in the media is that employees today want more professional development and career growth. Sure, sometimes this means "promotion," but often it means "progression." They want to learn, share, and grow together. All of this is a huge opportunity for your culture and brand.

Let your employees teach each other by creating a lunch-and-learn type program where they can learn different skills from each other. Not only does this help the people being taught learn something new, but it also puts the teachers into professional growth mode by having them develop public speaking, presentation, and training design skills. This also helps to bring people together in ways that they normally wouldn't connect and begins to develop the kinds of relationships that bust silos and boost culture.

The skills being taught and learned are usually work-related, but they don't have to be. I've seen classes on everything from learning how to give better feedback to public speaking, from beatboxing to design thinking. Let your imagination flow!

Walking and Talking

People in great cultures are connected to each other even when they don't work on the same projects or teams. These relationships can permeate the culture to help boost empathy and engagement. One of your primary goals as a culture leader should be to create more opportunities for the people on your team to connect with each other.

A walk-and-talk program is where you match employees with one another (or even in small groups of three or four) to "walk and talk" each month. When I've rolled programs like this out at organizations, they end up being an employee favorite. You can get this started relatively simply.

To start a walk-and-talk program:

>> Make an announcement detailing the program and include details about the goals of the program, the frequency (monthly matches work well), and set up some guidelines to help people make the most of their time together.

>> Make the matches for the month and send out notifications sharing who is matched with whom.

>> Send a survey at the end of the month to get feedback. You can also schedule a group meeting where people can highlight their experiences meeting people from the organization and sharing what they learned in their walk-and-talk.

Celebrating Failure

One of the things that can really diminish a culture is if people are scared to share their failures. We know that learning from failures is a positive way to move forward, accept reality, and create something better (see Chapter 13). But, it's really scary to do in actuality. People are worried about being seen as weak, worried about getting in trouble, and fear the possibility of losing status with their peers. Finding ways to celebrate failure as an organization can help normalize failure so that your team can move on quicker. If you are asking people to come to work, aim high, and take risks — then you have to make failure a part of the norm for your team.

One of the easiest ways to get started is to create a specific day of each month as the day you celebrate failure. Maybe "First Failure Fridays" where you have people share a big fail from the last month and the learnings from that failure. If you are using a messaging service or other email communication tool like Slack, you can create a channel where people post their fails and learnings for others to celebrate along with them.

Applauding Diverse Leaders

In addition to all of the ideas in Chapter 16 for using diversity and inclusivity to improve your culture, you can also celebrate leaders from a diverse range of areas. This helps to improve culture by bringing more awareness to diverse groups that may exist within your company and also open the understanding of others on your team.

An easy way to get started is to look up the different months that are designated for different groups (for example, February is Black History Month, March is Women's History Month, September is Hispanic Heritage Month, and so on) and then celebrate leaders from those groups. You can do this by creating a company blog that is updated weekly with a highlight of a new person or do the same thing via email. To create even more engagement from your team, you can focus on leaders from those groups that are related to the type of business you are in. For example, if you are a technology company celebrating Women's History Month, highlight stories about women in technology in your weekly update. You can even watch a movie around the theme as a movie night and then lead a discussion around it afterwards.

Telling Stories Together

We all love to hear stories. We like telling our stories. They increase engagement and can foster empathy. We love them in books, in commercials, in movies, and in our lives. But so few companies create opportunities for employees to share their stories and hear each other's stories. Connecting with each other in this way can really boost culture by bringing people closer, creating more awareness of each other, and increasing empathy between employees.

Hosting storytelling events at your company can be an easy way to get started. Choose a theme (such as favorite childhood memories, first jobs, or vacations) and announce that you will be hosting a storytelling event. During the event, employees can sign up or enter their names into a drawing and will then need to come up with and give a 7- to 10-minute story around the theme. Plan for a 60-minute event your first time out.

TIP

If you have an employee who is particularly versed in storytelling (an actor, writer, improv performer, or marketer), ask if he or she would volunteer to lead a mini-workshop helping the participants prepare an upcoming story.

WARNING

This is an activity done best by employees who volunteer, as the point is not to make people feel uncomfortable. So don't force anyone or volunteer someone else to tell a story. If you think you have an employee with something unique to offer, speak to them individually expressing how you'd love for them to share at the upcoming event.

Making the Suggestion Box Clear

If you aren't actively seeking input from your employees about how things are going, then get started with that first. You can simply send a survey once a month that asks, "We want to be a great place to work. How are we doing? What's working? What could use some work?" Make it easy for people to respond and send feedback.

Then share the feedback you received and assign someone specifically to work on areas that could use improvement. This is making the suggestion box clear. You should redact specific names and identifying characteristics, but otherwise share the information. You can post it on a wall, share it on an internal forum, or just email it out. The goal is that you show people that you're listening and then make concerted steps toward improving things.

Now I know you may be thinking, "What if they all ask for 50 percent increases in salary?" or "How am I supposed to put a pool on the roof?" But in my experience, employees are typically pretty reasonable. And if they do want a pool on the roof or 50 percent increases, those desires don't go away by simply pretending they don't exist. Collecting their ideas and then sharing back with them (even when you can't do something) at least gives them the same information you're using to make decisions.

Chapter **22**

Ten Ways That Job Applicants Can Read Company Culture

You may have picked up this book to learn more about improving your current organization's culture. But you also may have picked up this book thinking that it might help you identify a better culture to join. If so, this chapter is for you. It gives you ten (or more) ways you can assess your potential future employer to see if the company is a good fit for you.

TIP

Don't dismiss this chapter if you're not looking for a job but instead you're looking to improve your culture. You can reverse engineer these steps to make sure your organization is delivering on the culture promise during your interviewing. Use the following sections as a road map or checklist of areas that need improvement for your culture to rock.

Before you start thinking about what job you want or where you want to start looking, you need to get really clear on the type of experience you're aiming to have in your next position. It will do you no good to dig into understanding a company's culture if you aren't clear on what type of culture is a good fit for you.

Even organizations with famed cultures (Disney, Apple, Google, Zappos, Southwest Airlines, Wegmans) have very different cultures — some are fun and irreverent, others are more conservative, some are focused on doing big world-changing things, and others are aimed at delivering amazing customer experiences.

To get started on your vision:

1. **Grab some paper and something to write with.**

2. **Imagine yourself two years from now and write that date on the top of the paper.**

3. **Think about that date and write down a few bullet points about what you'd like to be able to say you've accomplished or done by that date.**

   This can even be the type of work you're doing, the type of people you're working with, or the kinds of things you're producing. Give yourself about eight to ten things on your list that you'd be happy with if you could make them happen by that date.

4. **Now imagine you took a time machine to that future date and were watching a day in your future life.**

   Start writing about what you see in your future on that date. Really describe the environment, the people you work with, and the style of work. Are you in lots of meetings making decisions as a group? Are you working alone to produce deep, concentrated projects? Are you talking to clients and customers each day? Are you managing others? What's that look like? How do you do it? How are you being managed? What's your relationship like with your manager? Spend about 20 minutes just writing down everything you "see" in that future vision of success.

5. **Take a day or two away from the vision before coming back to clean it up and add any more details that help to further define what you want to create for yourself.**

   Start to think about what kinds of things you would need to see in a workplace to know that it would help you create that life for yourself. What type of office? What types of projects? What type of leadership? You'll want to have this information to start to review the kinds of cultures you want to seek out.

REMEMBER

I'm not suggesting that you hold out forever for the perfect job if you need to pay the rent. Sometimes you have to do something now to be able to get where you want to go later. I am suggesting that having a better idea about what you're really looking for is useful as you look at options. If you're going to make concessions about taking a less-than-perfect job, then at least you'll be clear on that from the start instead of being surprised later that you're unhappy. There will be a long list of things that matter as you look for a new position: the leadership, the impact the organization makes, the location of the office, the money and compensation, the knowledge and experience you'll gain, and the overall cache of the brand you are joining. Each person prioritizes that list differently based on his or her goals, career vision, and current status in life. It's important to do this *before* you start looking for the job so you can focus on the things that matter most to *you*.

Once you have a clear vision in place, you can connect the following 10 ideas to turn that vision into your next job.

Researching Online

Before the mid 2000s, employer branding was mostly about company websites, glossy stock photos, and benefits brochures. Like consumer brands before it, the employer brand was completely controlled by the employer. If you wanted people to think you were kind and philanthropic, you'd share images of your team volunteering while highlighting all the groups you support. If you wanted to boost your brand as a creative place to work, you'd use bright images and teams working in "open spaces."

Then social media and review sites shifted things (just like they did with consumer branding). The media was now controlled by the people, and the organization's job was simply to produce the kinds of experiences that got people talking. With sites like Glassdoor, LinkedIn, Facebook, Twitter, and even Google reviews, employees took over the wheel of building (and sometimes destroying) employer brands.

As a job applicant, using the online resources can help you understand what a company is like beyond the happy stock photos and lists of perks. Once you've gotten clear on the type of culture you want, examine past and present employee reviews on these sites, specifically for:

>> **Themes and patterns:** What themes and patterns do you notice? Do things seem to be getting better or worse? As you read the reviews, do you see people frequently listing the same types of pros and cons? Do you notice trends within certain departments or even certain managers?

>> **Words and phrases:** Are there specific words and phrases that stand out? Do the reviews mention the kinds of things that matter most to you like training, development, or certain kinds of perks? If you have moved to a new city and are looking for a company culture where you might make friends, do you see people making comments about the team fostering that type of thing? All of this will impact your experience as an employee and should be involved in your consideration.

>> **Inclusivity:** Does the company seem to promote an inclusive place where new ideas and new people are welcome or does it sound like everyone has a similar background/experience?

>> **Team:** Does it look like employees work there for awhile or does it look like people leave quickly after starting? This could mean that there are culture issues for new hires and you'll want to dive deeper in your interviews to learn more. Does it look like people have had great career opportunities and promotions within the company?

Compare these reviews to information you see on the company website. Does it look and sound like the same place? Or does the company's website seem like an entirely different experience? You will start to get a more holistic view of the company culture when you compare all this information together. Use this to start to form your own opinions. If you are early in the interview process, use this information to help focus some of the questions you ask during the interview. You might want to ask about career development in more detail if you see lots of online comments about career stagnation or even rapid professional growth.

Recruiting Responses

You've been there. The job posting promises a great place to work — an environment full of respect, positive relationships, and strong collaboration. As you read about the culture and the commitment to employee success, you start to think, "Wow, is this place real?" Then you submit your resume or fill out the 125 questions that the application system requires, and then you wait. Sometimes you get an automated response from a recruiting robot; other times, you get nothing. Was your submission successful? Did it disappear into a pile of craftily wordsmithed documents? Is anyone out there? Hello?!?

REMEMBER

The response you get during the recruiting process can give you a clue into the company's culture. The more time and energy an organization puts into designing a positive applicant experience, the more likely that company is to have a positive employee experience. If the application process feels more like a cattle call, then make sure you investigate deeper if you do end up in an interview.

Here are some ideas:

>> Did you receive a response from your submission? Was it personalized? Was it written in the same voice as the rest of the company's career page/job posting?

- ❯❯ Was the job posting clear and specific, like the company really understands what it wants and what success looks like? Or was it a copy-and-paste of every other posting of the same job title?

- ❯❯ When you spoke to someone on the phone, was the person friendly? Excited to talk to you? Curious about what you were looking to do next in your career?

- ❯❯ Did the scheduled phone screens and interview calls start and end on time?

- ❯❯ Were you able to speak to the manager you'd be reporting to on the phone? Did that person seem invested in finding a great new employee?

Once you've thought about the answers to these questions, start to think about what that tells you about the culture of the company. What do they value? How do they treat people? Are those things in line with your desired work culture?

Marking First Impressions

Congrats! You've made it to an in-person interview. You'll be visiting the office and meeting some of the employees. For a lot of job applicants, this stage causes anxiety and nervousness, which makes them focus on their own energy — sometimes so much that they miss some valuable feedback.

When you arrive for your interview, start to look around to see what you can learn. You can often tell a lot about a culture by watching how people interact and how the office is designed. Culture is something you can feel. Make sure to give yourself enough time that you can observe for a few minutes before your interview starts. Look for some of the following:

- ❯❯ Were the instructions easy to follow to get to the office?

- ❯❯ Were you greeted and welcomed by someone who seemed happy to see you?

- ❯❯ Do the people in the office look excited and active? Are they laughing and talking to each other? Is it more conservative and quiet? Neither of those is better than the other, but one of them is probably a better fit for you.

- ❯❯ Do you see people collaborating? Are they working alone? Again, neither is better, but one is probably better for you.

- ❯❯ Can you tell that the company has invested in the building? Is the office cozy and warm? Modern and sleek? Trendy and hip? Conservative and clean? Again, none of these is better than the other, but they do contribute to a totally different type of culture. So be clear about where you want to be and where you can do your best work.

Use the observations to start to paint a picture of the company culture. Can you see yourself thriving there? Do you think it's the kind of place that you'd enjoy contributing to each day? Use your career vision from the "Getting Clear on Your Career Vision" section earlier in this chapter to start to match your first impressions to your desired outcome.

Noting Interview Questions

An effective interview should be focused on learning more about each other — the company learning about you and you learning more about the company (and your future boss). The questions and style of interview should create the opportunity to do exactly that. If you notice that lots of the questions are aggressive in tone or accusatory, then maybe that environment and that style of communication aren't right for you. If the questions are all over the place and unrelated to work, then maybe the position isn't as clearly defined as you want — or maybe you're okay with that. Either way, pay attention to the interview questions and style. They can be indicative of how things may play out later.

Finding the Right Time and Place

Here's the deal: People take jobs for all types of reasons. Maybe it's the chance to work on a specific type of product. Or perhaps they're following a specific leader they really want to work with (or liked working with in the past). Maybe they're working through some things personally and need a place to lie low for a while, so they take a job that's less demanding. Or perhaps the job has some great benefits that can help them finish college with their employer's help. All those are perfectly fine reasons to take a job. You're always looking to improve your status in life, and this doesn't always mean you're trying to climb the corporate ladder. Improving your status in life isn't necessarily about improving some materialistic part of your life — it is about taking stock of your current needs and then making choices that serve your current situation best. You have a big life, with lots of moving parts, and, at different times, your career will take more or less of the spotlight.

Make sure you have a clear career vision so you know what you're trying to do next and what you need from your employer to get there. Find a job and an employer that gets that. Using the career vision you crafted, use the following questions to start to match companies with your career vision to make the best choice for you:

>> Is having programs for people just starting their professional careers important to you?

>> Is working on lots of different types of projects in line with your current desire to build some projects into your resume?

>> Are you interested in moving into leadership roles? Dig deeper into how the company prepares people to take those roles and if it has a commitment to promoting from within. You can seek out examples of both.

Investigating the Manager Relationship

During the interview process, you'll likely get to spend time with the person who will be managing you (often called the "hiring manager" in corporate recruiting speak). Take this time to really explore how working together will be. When you talk to disengaged and unhappy employees, the root cause often comes down to their relationship with their manager. Find out how the manager likes to communicate. Dig deeper into the size of the team you'll be on and how that group is managed. Are there team meetings? What is discussed? How are decisions made?

Learn more about what your manager is looking for from you. What would make this hire a win for the person? What type of employee does the manager most enjoy supervising? How are one-on-ones and professional development conversations handled? How does the manager deliver feedback?

Talking to Other Employees

You really can't get a better view into a company's culture than by spending a little time with other employees. You can get a glimpse into this using the online tools recommended in the "Researching Online" section earlier in this chapter. You can also get a snapshot of this by watching people interact when you're onsite for your interview. But nothing beats being able to chat directly with a few people who currently work there.

Ask the recruiter (or hiring manager) if you can talk to other people at the company during your onsite interview. But don't waste your question with, "How is the culture around here?" People will often just fill the space with niceties that don't help you learn more.

Instead, try to dig deeper into the areas that matter most to you. Ask for specific examples they've seen or been part of, such as:

>> What type of development experiences have they had?

>> How often does the team hang out together? Was it easy to make friends?

>> What types of assignments and projects are they working on?

>> When was the last time something didn't turn out as expected, and what happened?

Learning about Career Growth

If you're looking for opportunities for promotion, professional growth, or gaining new skills, then be specific in seeking that information. It's pretty common these days for career websites and job postings to talk about potential and growth opportunities, so use that as your chance to get more details.

TIP

Here are some ideas for gaining insight into what potential there is for growth:

>> Instead of "Is there room for career advancement?" ask "Can you give me an example of someone who started here within the last year and how that person's career trajectory has been?"

>> Instead of "What does the career path look like for someone in this role?" ask "Can you tell me about someone who accepted this role in the last year or two and what that person is doing in the organization today?"

>> Instead of accepting the job description at face value, ask "What does success look like in 6 or 12 months from now if I accept this position? How would you measure whether it was a good decision to hire me?"

Talking about Teamwork

You'll be spending your day working with other people in some capacity (most likely). Take some time to learn more about how that happens at the company with which you're interviewing. You want to find out how teams work, how they collaborate, how they're assigned, and what you should expect from being part of the team. All of these things point to the culture of an organization and should start to shape your ideas around how working here will feel for you. Culture is about the condition inside the organization. It's about the way things are handled and how it feels to be part of the team. This is your chance to uncover more about those critical areas. Here are some questions to ask:

>> Do people often work alone? Or is everything brought to a group level conversation?

>> Are decisions made by consensus? By consultation? By directive?

>> Tell me a little about how the team works together. Do you have any examples from the team I'd be joining of working with people in other departments to get something done?

Uncovering Potential Challenges

Making a decision requires that you understand both the potential upside and downside of a role so you aren't surprised later. You can do this by conducting your own reference check on the company and your potential boss. Ask specific questions during the interview process and meet with current employees. The more you can uncover about a company, its culture, and how it deals with trying times before accepting a position, the better chance you have of finding the job that fits you. Find out what challenges may occur and how they're handled by asking:

>> When current employees come up against challenging roadblocks in this role, what are those typically? How do they resolve them?

>> What would you expect to be the biggest challenge I will experience in the next 90 days, 6 months, or 12 months in this role?

>> What kinds of roadblocks/frustrations have people in this role experienced? How did they overcome them?

Index

A

ability, measuring, 203–204
abuse of power, 92
acknowledging emotions, 62
action, based on emotions, 62
action plan, based on culture survey, 39–40
action-focused feedback, 91
active listening, 58–59
activities, training, 207
Ad Game activity, 241–242
advanced level promotions, 272
advice from team, in offer letter, 171
affinity groups, 277
agenda of meeting, sharing, 280
airlines, impact of culture on, 18
all-hands meetings, 226–227
alumni networks, 145, 152
always open positions, 148–149
ambiguity, as cause for improvisation, 236
announcements, in onboarding experience, 181
annual recognition celebrations, 339
A-players, hiring, 172–173
applicants, assessment of culture by. *See also* candidates; hiring; recruiting
  career growth, 358
  career vision, 356–357
  employees, talking to, 357–358
  first impressions, marking, 355–356
  interview questions, noting, 356
  manager relationship, investigating, 356–357
  online research, 353–354
  overview, 351
  personal vision, clarifying, 351–353
  potential challenges, uncovering, 359
  recruiting responses, 354–355
  teams, investigating, 358–359

application process, 148–149
appreciation. *See also* recognition program
  role in leadership, 90
  in staff meetings, 225–226
armchair psychologist, playing at interviews, 173
attention, role in communication, 216
attitudes, managing, 124
attracting talent. *See* recruiting
awareness, self, 51–52, 53. *See also* self-management

B

baseline metric, 30
behavior design
  bias impact, reducing, 268–269
  in hiring practices, 269–270
  overview, 268
  in performance management, 270–272
  promotions, influencing, 272
behaviors. *See also* values and behavior statement
  aligning values with, 123–125
  in company culture, 8, 115
  defining values with, 124
  in individual values assessment, 121
  performance reviews of, 292
  relation to values, 67–68
  setting for ideal candidates, 159–160
  supporting new beliefs, 77
beliefs, personal
  awareness of, 72–73
  behind book, exploring, 77–78
  changing, 75–77
  in company culture, 8
  investigating, 73–74
  overview, 72
beliefs boxes, 73–74, 75–76

benchmarking company culture. *See also* culture survey
  culture dashboard, 41–45
  employee opinion survey, 45–48
  overview, 29
benefits
  in competitive analysis for recruitment, 150
  in offer letter, 170
  pitfalls related to, 13–14
  of training, explaining, 205–206
bias
  behavior design to reduce impact of, 268–272
  culture fit idea as expressing, 155–156
  recognizing, 266–268
blind resumes, 269
blocking time, 80–81
blogs
  communication through, 229–230
  employer-generated, for recruiting, 142
  using new hires to recruit via, 192
bonus programs, 332–333
book clubs, 229, 277, 343–345
bosses. *See* leadership; management; self-management
brand
  employer, 137–139, 145–146
  expressing diversity through, 275
  in offer letter, 170
  organizational values as creating, 119
  relation to values blueprint format, 128–129
brand affinity, 23–24
breathing exercise, 56
brutal honesty, as form of feedback, 247
buddy system
  clarifying buddy expectations, 188
  overview, 187
  selecting buddy, 187–188
  structuring program, 189
budget, role of culture pockets in getting, 256
business. *See also specific related topics*
  changes in, updating training for, 211
  improvisation in, 236–242
  training regarding running of, 210–211

business metrics affected by culture. *See also* benchmarking company culture
  brand affinity, 23–24
  customer service, 22–23
  overview, 18
  productivity, 23
  profits, 20
  recruitment, 22
  sales, 19–20
  talent retention, 20–22

C

cable service operators, culture of, 27
call for change, communicating, 219–220
call-to-actions, recruiting through, 137, 149
calm, as benefit of mindfulness, 55
campaigns, around values, 130
cancellation of one-on-one meetings, 312–313
candidates. *See also* applicants, assessment of culture by; hiring; interviews; recruiting
  experience of, crafting, 162–163
  ideal, defining, 156–160
  selling job to in job description, 160–161
  tip for choosing best, 174
candor, 15
care, self, 60–61
career vision, matching company culture to, 356–357
careers page, on website, 136, 146–149
cell phone providers, culture of, 27
chain restaurants, impact of culture on, 18
change
  benefits of mindfulness for response to, 55
  clear next steps, establishing, 221
  guiding with communication, 220–221
  mission statement as rudder for, 99
  motivating, role in training, 204–205
  need for training to produce, 212
  strong call for, communicating, 219–220
check-ins
  goal, 326–327
  with new hires, 186–187
clarity in goals, 322–323, 328, 329–330
clients, one-on-one meetings with, 316

closed-ended questions, 314

clothing, ordering, 276

coaching for performance, 90–91

coaching time, scheduling, 81

co-creation, in improvisation, 241–242

coffee chat programs, 227–228

collaboration, 15

command-and-control style leadership, 84–85

common purpose, creating, 318–319

communication. *See also* one-on-one meetings

  book clubs, 229

  call for change, 219–220

  with candidates, 163

  categories of, at work, 218–219

  clear next steps, establishing, 221

  coffee chat programs, 227–228

  common pitfalls, 230–231

  in company culture, 8

  email and text, overuse of, 230–231

  emotion in, 230

  guiding change with, 220–221

  improving, 218–221

  information versus, 217

  listening, 231

  opportunities for, creating, 227–230

  overview, 215–216

  role in company culture, 216

  #showyourwork sessions, 228

  signs of toxic culture, 15

  in staff meetings, 221–227

  through video, technology, and blogs, 229–230

communication plan, for culture survey, 34–35, 36

company awareness

  in onboarding, 185

  training regarding, 210–211

company culture. *See also* benchmarking company culture; *specific aspects of culture*

  at-risk, recognizing, 14–15

  bad, effects of, 24–27

  components of good, 12–13

  conditions, controlling, 10–11

  defined, 8–9

  importance of, 9–10, 17

  manifesto on, writing, 63–64

  molding, 10

  as operating system, 9–12

  overview, 1–4, 7

  as perfect result, 11–12

  perks, pitfalls related to, 13–14

  translating personal values to, 66–68

Company Culture Code, 77–78

company mission (mission statement)

  clear and inspirational, 101–107

  constructing, 105–106

  examples of, 106

  good versus bad, 99–100

  launching, 107–109

  objectives, clarifying, 103–105

  in onboarding experience, 185

  overview, 97

  purpose of, 98–100

  stories, starting with, 101–103

  testing, 107

  versus vision statement, 98

company values

  aligning with desired behavior, 123–125

  behavior, defining with, 124

  common themes, identifying, 123

  in company culture, 8, 115–117

  as creating brand, 119

  in culture pockets, 258–259

  defining, 120–123

  group values session, 122–123

  for ideal candidates, 159–160

  importance of, 116–117

  leadership as defined by, 118

  management, role of, 121–122

  objectives related to, defining, 104

  in onboarding, 179, 185

  overview, 115–116

  as reducing risk, 119

  training regarding, 209–210

  values and behavior statement, 126–131

  values interviews, 120–121

company vision (vision statement)

  drafting, 110–113

  editing, 112–113

  finalizing, 113

D

daily staff meetings, 223

dashboard, culture

  employee referral program, measuring, 45

  exit interviews, learning from, 42–43

  online review systems, 43–44

  overview, 41–42

  turnover, learning from, 44

dashboard, for staff meetings, 223–224

debriefing, after interviews, 168–169

decision-making

  behavior design, 268–272

  diversity, effect on, 266

  inclusivity in, 278–280

  influence on personal values, 65

  mission statement as framework for, 99

  regarding emotions, 62

  role of values in, 130

  vision statement use for, 114

"Delivering Happiness" approach, Zappos, 23

departing employees, eNPS for, 42–43

descriptive knowledge, 202–203

detractors, in eNPS, 33

development opportunities. *See also* training

  in employee opinion survey, 46

  as goal of employees, 193–194

  role in talent retention, 21

  tying to values, 131

development planning, 300

digital wall, 335

discipline policy, progressive, 300–302

discretionary efforts, by employees, 20

diversity

  behavior design, 268–272

  benefits of, 265–266

  bias, recognizing, 266–268

  celebrating leaders, 349

  importance of, 264–265

  inclusivity, improving, 274–278

  inclusivity as part of, 264

  inclusivity in decisions, 278–280

  overview, 263

  transparency of efforts, 272–274

E

eating intentionally exercise, 57–58

education, defined, 200–201. *See also* learning; training

effort, feedback focused on, 250

email

  culture survey follow-up, 38

  launching culture survey through, 35, 36

  onboarding drip campaigns, 149

  overuse of, avoiding, 230–231

  signature section, leveraging, 144

emotions

  in communication, 230

  in feedback-rich culture, crafting, 249

  recognizing, 61–62

  in values and behavior statement, 126

empathy, practicing, 307

employee Net Promoter Score (eNPS). *See also* culture survey

  calculating, 33

  defined, 31

  for departing employees, 42–43

employee opinion survey

  versus culture survey, 31

  following up on, 47

  launching, 47

  overview, 45

  questions for, designing, 45–47

  workshop based on, 47–48

employee referral program, 45, 152

employee takeover events, 141

employee-generated content, recruiting through, 136, 140–142

employees. *See also* hiring; recruiting; *specific related topics*

  assessment of culture based on, 357–358

  buddy system, 187–189

  in competitive analysis for recruitment, 151

  complaints of, solving, 88

  as core customer, 87–88

  culture survey, connecting with after, 38

  culture survey results, sharing with, 35, 40

  departing, eNPS for, 42–43

  distribution of culture content by, 144–145

in training, 207–208

on values and behavior statement, 128–129

on vision statement, requesting, 113

financial targets, 18. *See also* business metrics affected by culture

first day, formula for perfect, 183, 184

first impressions of culture, on applicants, 355–356

first week details, in offer letter, 170

first week orientation checklist, 183–185

fit, culture, hiring for, 155–156

flexible work hours, 275

focus, mindfulness and, 55, 57

follow-up

culture survey, 35–40

performance reviews, 299–300

staff meeting, 225

former employees, as recruiters, 152

Foursquare activity, 240–241

Freaky Friday Day, 345–346

front-line time, scheduling, 80

future story

crafting personal, 68–70

related to energy, 71

vision statements as, 109–110

G

gender issues

gender-balanced job postings, 270

non-inclusive behavior, calling out, 278

non-negotiable compensation, 270

pay equity, 274

uniforms, ordering, 276

get-togethers, team, 261–262

Glassdoor, 44, 151. *See also* online review systems

goals. *See also* business metrics affected by culture

in best company cultures, 12–13

checking on progress, 326–327

clarifying for mission statement, 103–105

common mistakes, 327–330

common purpose, creating, 318–319

communicating, 329–330

culture, driving with, 324–327

and culture, link between, 318–321

for diversity, 273

employee opinion survey workshop, 48

employees, impact on, 319–320

failure to achieve, reasons for, 321–322

future story, crafting, 68–70

group values session, 122

for ideal candidates, clarifying, 158–159

inclusivity, improving with, 279

key results, defining, 325–326

number of, 328

OKR framework, 324–327

one-on-one meetings, discussing in, 309

overview, 317

performance reviews, basing on, 292

punishment or rewards based on, 329

reminders of, 322

resetting, 327

reviewing at all-hands meetings, 227

scoreboard, setting up, 322–324

sharing updates, 320–321

short-term, 329

toxic culture, signs of, 15

of training, defining, 206–207

for weekly staff meetings, 222

Google Alerts, 151

Google Forms, 30

gossip, as sign of toxic culture, 14, 93

government agencies, culture of, 27

gratitude, role in leadership, 90. *See also* recognition program

great leaders, characteristics of, 85–87

grocery markets, impact of culture on, 18

group values sessions, 122–123

groupthink, reducing risk of, 265

growth, professional. *See also* training

in employee opinion survey, 46

as goal of employees, 193–194

role in talent retention, 21

tying to values, 131

H

happiness at work, 90

health insurance companies, culture of, 27

new employees, recognition of, 337–338

new hires. *See also* onboarding; training
  onboarding experience of, 178–179
  orientation day for, 181
  recruiting, using for, 191–192

nice lies, as form of feedback, 246

90-day check-in, 186–187

non-negotiable compensation, 270

NPS (Net Promoter Score) system, 32

nutrition, in self-care, 60

O

objective data, performance reviews based on, 271

objectives. *See* goals

observable behavior, aligning values with, 124–125

offer letter, 169–171

offices
  first day tour of, 184
  inclusivity in, 275–276
  information about, in offer letter, 170
  services, providing in, 346

OKR framework, 324

onboarding. *See also* training
  asking for reviews during, 145
  buddy system, 187–189
  combining vision and current practices, 182–187
  evaluating current process, 180–181
  feedback regarding, requesting, 190–191
  first week orientation checklist, 183–185
  importance of experience during, 176
  key areas of, 176–177
  90-day check-in, 186–187
  organizing with technology, 190
  overview, 175
  perfect first day formula, 183
  pre-hire checklist, 182
  recruiting during, 191–192
  30-day check-in, 186
  values, role of, 130
  vision for, crafting, 178–180

onboarding drip campaigns, 149

one-on-one meetings
  asking questions, 309–312

being helpful, 308

cancellations, dealing with, 312–313

clarifying during, 308

framework for, 304–305

general discussion, 304

honesty during, 314

investing time in, 305–306

listening during, 306–307

in other areas of organization, 314–315

overview, 303–304

preparing for, 314–315

status updates, avoiding, 313

talking too much during, 314

One-word-at-a-time story, 239

online research, by applicants, 353–354

online review systems
  culture dashboard, 43–44
  recruitment, enhancing, 22
  reviewing employer brand on, 138

open floor sessions, at all-hands meetings, 226

open positions. *See also* job descriptions
  always open, 148–149
  clear purpose for, creating, 157–158
  in competitive analysis for recruitment, 150

open-ended questions
  in culture survey, 31, 33
  in one-on-one meetings, 306, 314

operating system, company culture as, 9–12

opinion survey, employee
  versus culture survey, 31
  following up on, 47
  launching, 47
  overview, 45
  questions for, designing, 45–47
  workshop based on, 47–48

organizational chart, in offer letter, 171

organizational culture. *See also* benchmarking
    company culture; *specific aspects of culture*
  at-risk, recognizing, 14–15
  bad, effects of, 24–27
  components of good, 12–13
  conditions, controlling, 10–11
  defined, 8–9
  importance of, 9–10, 17

performative knowledge, 203

perks, pitfalls related to, 13–14

permission, in feedback-rich culture, 249

person, feedback focused on, 250

personal beliefs

  awareness of, 72–73

  behind book, exploring, 77–78

  changing, 75–77

  in company culture, 8

  investigating, 73–74

  overview, 72

personal manifesto, 63–64

personal values

  of management, 121–122

  origins of, 65–66

  overview, 65

  translating to company culture, 66–68

personal vision of culture, clarifying, 351–353

personal wins, celebrating, 338–339

PFD (perfect first day) formula, 183, 184

physical exercise, in self-care, 61

Pinterest, 142–143

planning, vision statement use for, 114

pockets, culture. *See* culture pockets

position profile review, 181

positive feedback, 249–250

power, abuse of, 92

pre-hire checklist, 182

pre-orientation. *See* onboarding

prescreening, in hiring process, 164–165

presentations

  at all-hands meetings, 226

  employer-generated, for recruiting, 142

  in training process, 202, 212

press, in competitive analysis for recruitment, 150

primacy, in performance reviews, 285

prioritization, 322–323, 327

product training, 184–185, 209

productivity, effect of company culture on, 23

professional growth. *See also* training

  in employee opinion survey, 46

  as goal of employees, 193–194

  role in talent retention, 21

  tying to values, 131

profitability

  company culture, effect on, 20

  diversity, effect on, 264–265

  performance reviews, effect on, 290

progressive discipline policy, 300–302

promoters, in eNPS, 33

promotions

  behavior design, using to influence, 272

  role of training in, 194–195

prompts

  for group values session, 122–123

  for story-gathering workshops, 102

prospective employees. *See* candidates; hiring; interviews; recruiting

psychological safety, 249, 260

psychologist, playing at interviews, 173

public appreciation, 335

publishing results of diversity efforts, 273

purchase size, relation to culture, 19

purpose

  in employee engagement, 318

  mission statement as providing, 100

  for open positions, 157–158, 159

  role in talent retention, 22

Q

Q&A sessions, at all-hands meetings, 226

quarterly recognition celebrations, 339

Quora platform, 143

R

raises, creating system for, 274

ranking, based on performance reviews, 285

reactive work, scheduling, 80, 81

recency, in performance reviews, 285

recent hires. *See also* onboarding; training

  onboarding experience of, 178–179

  orientation day for, 181

  recruiting, using for, 191–192

recognition program

  benefits of, 332

  ending meetings, 334–335

Notes

Notes

Notes

Notes